Natural Allies

Natural Allies

Hope and Possibility in
Teacher-Family Partnerships

■

SOO HONG

Harvard Education Press

Cambridge, Massachusetts

Paperback ISBN 978-1-68253-424-3
Library Edition ISBN 978-1-68253-425-0

Library of Congress Cataloging-in-Publication data is on file.

Published by Harvard Education Press,
an imprint of the Harvard Education Publishing Group

Harvard Education Press
8 Story Street
Cambridge, MA 02138

Cover Design: Ciano Design
Cover Photo: RyanJLane/iStock/Getty Images

The typefaces used in this book are Aldine 401 for text and Humanist 777
for display.

For Lauren and Christopher—
you are the ones who show me what it means
to be a good parent and teacher

CONTENTS

Introduction   1

1 ILENE CARVER: Taking the First Step   25

2 MEGAN LUCAS: Transforming Practice   47

3 CINTHIA COLÓN: Remembering Roots   77

4 ANNIE SHAH: Engaging Community   101

5 JULIA FINKELSTEIN: Sustaining Culture   125

6 New Hopes and Possibilities Through
  Culturally Sustaining Family Engagement   155

  Notes   195

  Acknowledgments   209

  About the Author   213

  Index   215

INTRODUCTION

Marie is the mother of two children, one of whom is school-aged. Her son Jackson, now in fourth grade, was diagnosed with a learning disability the prior year by a teacher who, according to Marie, "was the first teacher to really see him for who he was." In years prior, Jackson had struggled to read; with these mighty struggles, he became frustrated and disappointed in himself, especially as he witnessed the seeming leaps and bounds made by his classmates. His greatest challenge was second grade, a year that both mother and son like to put behind them.

A socially introverted young boy fascinated by Marvel comic books and building—out of LEGO blocks, recyclable materials, toothpicks, popsicle sticks, dominoes, and playing cards—Jackson became withdrawn at school during that year. He felt ashamed by his inability to read like his classmates. When it was time to read, he sought the solace of science books and magazines. The illustrations always communicated a story and the text on the pages was not overwhelming.

At school, his second-grade teacher, in an attempt to encourage him to read books that were appropriate to his reading level, began to forbid him from reading the books he loved. He could no longer take the *DK Knowledge Encyclopedia* to his reading nook. Instead, he was sent along with *Elephant and Piggy* or *I Can Read!* books featuring Pete the Cat, Paddington, or Amelia Bedelia. Angry and frustrated about his struggle to read and the punitive use of his beloved books, Jackson became defiant. Refusing to read the books from his teacher, he instead began to tear out their pages, slowly and silently, hiding them inside the book's back cover.

It wasn't long before his teacher discovered his acts of defiance, and a couple days later, Marie was called in to discuss the situation. Jackson's teacher was visibly frustrated with Jackson's "antics," which she believed were getting in the way of her ability to support him academically. She assumed Marie didn't know what happened in the classroom, but she did. To the teacher's surprise, Jackson had told his mother about the incident the day he was reprimanded by his teacher. When Marie asked him why he would do such a thing "when you love books so much," Jackson's eyes welled up with tears. In the only explanation he could muster, he sobbed and asked, "Why does she have to punish me because I can't read like the other kids?"

What this teacher didn't understand or care to comprehend was that Jackson's anxieties about reading were spilling over into all aspects of his classroom experience. Marie explained that his struggles were affecting his friendships; he was no longer willing to break out of his shy personality and "into friendships with kids who could give him a break from the troubles he was enduring every day in the classroom." He did not look forward to school; every upset stomach led to a long and protracted battle about whether he could stay home.

As Marie tried to broach these topics with Jackson's teacher, she was met with sharp rebuke. In a tone of unwavering confidence, the teacher reported that for as long as she had known him—which had only been a month and a half—she had noticed that he was a "loner," a child who preferred to play by himself rather than with others. She believed the reading issues were a separate matter and one that she was addressing in her work with him at school. Marie responded with her own explanations: "Yes, he likes to do things on his own, but he has always enjoyed friendships until this year," and "When you have a boy like Jackson who wants to read so badly but is having trouble learning how, can't it create some hardship in other parts of his life in school?" Each of Marie's explanations, however, was dismissed. Hesitant to blame or challenge the teacher in that moment, Marie recalls this conversation with deep shame and regret that she "did not stand up for Jackson more than I did."

As the conversation came to a close, Jackson's teacher recommended, "If you send him to school well fed, with a lunch to eat and a good night's sleep, then you can let us take care of the rest. Let's focus on what we each do best."

■ ■ ■

2

Who knows what is best for the child? Is it Jackson's teacher, who has training and expertise in child literacy? Or is it Marie, who has the long view on her son's development and can zero in on Jackson's response to the social, emotional, and academic demands that are placed on him? Is Marie's view tainted because she is singularly focused on Jackson, or is the teacher's judgment clouded by her responsibility to twenty-six other students? Why are Marie and Jackson's teacher so naturally inclined to be in confrontation with each other? If their views are conflicting, who knows what is best for young Jackson? Who has the authority to act on that knowledge?

These questions lie at the heart of every debate about school transformation: Who knows how best to improve our schools and classrooms? What are some of the common refrains in this debate? Schools need instructional leaders who commit to carrying out a vision of school improvement and stick around long enough to see it through. Teachers must design classroom learning environments to be student-centered and engaging. For teachers to carry out their plans successfully, they need guidance and professional support from the moment they begin their teacher education programs, through their early years as a novice teacher, and well into their careers as school communities, programs, and policies evolve. All the while, we must think about the diversity of school communities and not lose sight of the ways race, class, and opportunity impact the dynamics of student-teacher interaction, the curriculum that influences how they see the world, and the policies that seek to build equity across schools. Most of us would acknowledge that children—their academic, social, and emotional development—are, or at least should be, at the core of every conversation about school transformation.

But what about their families? What about parents like Marie? Are they to step aside and allow educators to do what they believe is best for the academic, social, and emotional development of their children? Even with the best ideas and intentions about school reform, there is a curious silence about the role of families.

SCHOOLS, FAMILIES, AND POWER

The dissonance between Marie and Jackson's teacher, and often between families and schools, represents a power struggle. Jackson's teacher and mother are at odds about the child's challenges and how best to address them, but as this situation illustrates, and is often the case, schools and teachers are in a position of power over parents when it comes to the education of children. How is this realized?

Sociologist Willard Waller identified this conflict between parents and teachers, noting that the adversarial nature of their relationship made them "natural enemies."[1] He argued that parents and teachers were inevitably and naturally in conflict due to their competing goals and intentions. Parents seek to advantage their child in the school system and promote that child's well-being and success, but teachers seek to promote the learning and well-being of all children. These fundamentally disparate orientations to schooling and its purposes set parents and teachers on a collision course where small differences can be seen as egregious errors in judgment and intention. Most importantly, if parents' interests are viewed as private and teachers' interests are a public good, then setting a common vision for educational transformation will be impossible.

This characterization of parents and teachers as natural enemies is incomplete, however. Differences in social class, language, and culture can create distinctions between home and school as well. These contrasting settings may lead children and their families to see the home and school as worlds apart.[2] This can be particularly true for immigrant students, students living in poverty, and students of color. Immigrant parents may view the school as a place that will integrate their children into the larger society, providing opportunities that were not available to them when they themselves were children.[3] School can become a place where children are taught to be "American," and being American usually means white and middle class.[4] Historically, schools have been sites of cultural assimilation—be it the Indian boarding schools at the turn of the twentieth century, which sought to eradicate tribal language and culture; the earliest kindergartens, where white middle-school teachers sought to teach parents and children habits of hygiene, cleanliness, and order; or even present-day schools, with their focus on monolingual instruction.[5] Consequently, the education of immigrant youth and children of immigrants continues to be shaped by policies and practices that devalue students' funds of knowledge, placing them at the margins and perpetuating inequality of educational experience.[6] This marginalization results from ideologies of cultural deficit as well as the dominance and superiority of the English language in schools.[7]

If schools seek to assimilate children into the larger society, then the gulf between home and school persists. If educators believe the school's dominant culture is preferable, they learn to view students' families through perceived deficits. Void of any connection or mutual understanding, parents might perceive teachers as uncaring and teachers might assume parents are uninterested in the educational process.[8] This can only widen the gulf between home and school and reinforce the tendency to blame each other for any struggles that arise.

One of the clearest windows into a school's relationship with students' families is its family engagement practices. It is striking how strangely universal the methods for parent involvement have become. Bake sales, PTAs, parent-teacher conferences, and back-to-school nights are just a few of the common rituals of parent engagement in schools.[9] These practices may be, in many schools, well received by parents who view these rare glimpses into schools as precious and meaningful, but the sheer uniformity in how schools design parent participation also assumes there is *one* way to involve families.

By relying on these parent involvement traditions, schools have designed a suite of engagement practices that are school-centered rather than family-centered in their approach.[10] These rituals of involvement focus on activities for parents rather than their engagement or connection to a school community. With a focus on presentations, such as those given by teachers at a parent open house, and highly structured conversations about student progress, such as those of a parent-teacher conference, these family engagement strategies operate on the assumption that schools know what is best for children, and parents must listen and follow.[11] Additionally, schools often place a higher premium on planning the event and miss the importance of creating thoughtful and meaningful invitations to participate.[12]

These interactions show us that not all players in public schools are equal. Schemes to encourage parent participation in schools will fail to transform education if they operate with the "presumption of equality between parents and schools, and the refusal to address power struggles."[13] While a parent's lack of knowledge or formal expertise in educational matters may signal incompetence to educators, the imbalance in power between educators and families can discourage parent participation in schools.[14] When schools do attempt to include parents in school decision-making, they may not provide the necessary knowledge to fully inform and engage parents; intentional or not, this invites passive rather than full participation.[15] And certainly, in an era when families encounter challenges with immigration status and the specter of harsh and punitive consequences looms large among mixed-status families, a family's engagement and interaction with the school may be riddled with serious issues of trust and insecurity. Without prying and causing families to feel anxious, schools can consider the myriad ways that a family's participation in school is influenced—beyond the typical assumptions of parent care or interest. And while it may feel that the work is done when the programs for parents are scheduled and the school doors are opened, a school's stance toward families—perceptions about their knowledge, about what they can offer to schools and their children, and about their involvement and participation—is continually communicated through the everyday interactions between educators and families. It is a reflection of who has power in schools.

Demanding Power from Schools: Parents' Rights

Schools are under increased pressure to deliver successful outcomes for students, and this can be a source of stress and demoralization for teachers.[16] Heightened expectations for success and the high-stakes nature of standardized assessments may lead teachers to turn to formal expertise or follow school or district directives. Within this context, parents may feel that they lack the information to be adequately informed and cannot ask the right questions to engage in conversation with teachers or support their child's progress and development. In turn, educators may blame parents for the challenges students face in the classroom.

When parents sense that the system works against them and serves to disempower them, they may design strategies to demand power from schools. Often in the spotlight of the media, this strand of policy and practice focuses on parents' "rights" to challenge schools, districts, and educational policies and often pits parents and educators against each other. Increasingly, these efforts use the courts as a mechanism for effecting education reform; while parents are the public faces of these cases, educational interest groups and neoliberal reformers often drive and fund the efforts.[17]

One such case is the *Vergara v. California* decision on seniority rights and tenure. Nine public school plaintiffs filed a lawsuit in 2012 to challenge the tenure process of teachers. The student plaintiffs argued that they were taught by inferior teachers who were protected by tenure provisions and were thus denied equal protection of the law. A Los Angeles County Superior Court judge ruled that the statutes of tenure were unconstitutional in 2014; two years later, the Court of Appeal's three-judge panel unanimously reversed the trial court's decision.[18]

The lawsuit was followed by a series of similar legal efforts to weaken teacher job protections through the courts.[19] Six parents from Newark Public Schools filed a suit to prove that seniority-based layoffs were detrimental to their children's educational experience.[20] In Minnesota, the parents of five children filed a lawsuit arguing that teacher protections contribute to the achievement gap between white students and students of color. They argued that policies favored ineffective veteran teachers over effective teachers who lack seniority.[21] A similar case in New York pitted a parent group, the New York City Parents Union, against the very policies that seek to protect teacher tenure.[22]

It is important to note that these high-profile cases have the backing and private funding of education reform groups.[23] The *Vergara v. California* case was funded by Silicon Valley technology entrepreneur David Welch and his organization Students Matter. In New York, Welch's involvement provided an infusion of funding and legal expertise for the suit. Subsequent *Vergara*-style lawsuits were supported by Partnership for Educational Justice, a national education reform group founded by former CNN anchor Campbell Brown that seeks to challenge teacher job protections across the country.[24]

Parent trigger laws have also framed the interactions between families and schools as fraught with conflict and adversarial in nature. The policy allows parents to intervene in the operation of schools by petition when school performance is deemed "failing" due to low test scores over a period of two or three years. Parents of children in these schools, with successful petitions, can close the school, reconstitute the school by replacing faculty and staff, convert the school to a charter school, or make use of private school vouchers. While only two California communities have actually exercised the parent trigger option thus far, seven states (California, Indiana, Louisiana, Mississippi, Ohio, Connecticut, and Texas) have enacted parent trigger laws of varying types and twenty-five states have considered the legislation.[25]

Efforts to enact parent triggers can thrive in a system where parents feel they lack voice, choice, and agency, leading to questions about who has the power to determine the fate and future of schools.[26] Similar to the claims of plaintiffs in the cases to upend teacher protections, parents report a sense of desperation in reforming a broken public school system. The claims in parent trigger cases highlight schools' lack of responsiveness to parental concern; parents make the case that this is a consequence of the actions of educators who choose to protect their own interests rather than those of children.[27]

Parent trigger legislation efforts and challenges to teacher tenure follow a common pattern of blaming poor educational outcomes on teachers, school district officials, teacher unions, and administrators. With the spotlight of the media, parents are the face of these campaigns to reform schools and hold teachers accountable. Like the private funding that generated momentum for the suits to challenge teacher protections, parent trigger efforts have been fueled by the support of foundations such as the Walton Family Foundation, the Eli and Edythe Broad Foundation, and the Bill & Melinda Gates Foundation—three organizations that support Parent Revolution, a group that initiated the first parent trigger legislation and continues to support efforts nation-wide.[28] The movement has built support from a variety of conservative political institutions such as the American Legislative Exchange Council (ALEC) and the Heartland Institute.

These are just some of the ways parents' "rights" become highlighted in the mainstream media's coverage of educational reform. These efforts, funded largely by conservative foundations that represent a preference for neoliberal policies, attempt to paint parents and teachers as foes in a broken public school system that can be fixed only through the injection of choice and competition into the public sector. The Walton Family Foundation alone has donated $335 million to charter schools and spent more than $164 million in 2013 to support institutions and organizations that promote and advocate for charter schools.[29] We see a protracted struggle between schools and the families they are called to serve. When families in a school community exercise the parent trigger or when parent plaintiffs reverse the layoff of a young untenured teacher, there is a sense that we are democratizing public education: parents are exercising a choice that should be theirs and having their say.

But these efforts do not transform the culture of schools, nor do they repair the relationship between families and schools. What they do is signify that a battle is being waged for the hearts and minds of parents. Corporate reformers and neoliberal organizations seek to challenge the historical arrangement of public schools and transform the options that are available to families. The very shape and function of parent engagement and democracy are being re-created.

Organizing for Power Within Schools: Parent-Teacher Solidarity

Can parents and educators enjoy common fates and shared interests in improving public education? There is a newly emergent strand of parent organizing that proves it is possible. In this forceful yet far less well-funded framework, parents and teachers are not adversaries or foes; instead, they are allies working toward common goals.

These acts of solidarity are crafted with care and trust and sustained with devotion and dignity. They emerge, sometimes, through a process of healing broken relationships between educators and parents, and between schools and communities, but in their protracted struggles to demand educational equity in schools, parents and educators have begun to understand that their hopes and aspirations for change are intertwined.[30]

Under the leadership of then president Karen Lewis, the Chicago Teachers Union (CTU) created the GEM Alliance (Grassroots Education Movement; https://gemchicago.org/) in 2008 to integrate parents and community organizations as key partners in the union's work to transform schools. In an effort to move away from the service model of unionism—where a teacher brings an individual issue to the union for support in its resolution—and the public perception that unions are purely in the business of contract negotiations, CTU brokered partnerships with parents and community organizations to focus on the need to organize in their buildings against violations of students' rights as well.[31] When parents and community partners pushed CTU to be more confrontational in their challenge to Mayor Rahm Emanuel's school privatization plans, the union listened. Together with parents and community partners, GEM marched to the mayor's home to protest.[32]

CTU's creation of the GEM Alliance is also an acknowledgment that historically, teacher unions have had a tenuous relationship with communities of color. For too long, unions have stood in the way of community demands for educational equity and school improvement. Issues of deep-seated mistrust, manipulation, antagonism, and power must be addressed. However, the growth of teacher activism, and its synergy with community-based education organizing efforts, highlights a future path for change in public schools where unions and communities have shared interests in demanding equitable change.[33]

In 2012, when CTU went on strike to challenge the mayor's proposal to create high-stakes evaluations for teachers, cut teacher benefits, and remove the cap on class sizes, parents stood alongside teachers on the picket lines. Polls showed that the majority of parents supported their efforts from the start, despite the hardships that a labor dispute can place on families.[34] The success of the strike was built, in part, by the union's alliance with parents and community groups and establishment of shared interests. As one parent put it, "We want a fair contract for the teachers because their working conditions are our kids' learning conditions."[35]

Three years later, parents stood alongside community members in Chicago's South Side neighborhood of Bronzeville to protest the closure of Walter H. Dyett High School.[36] The school's closure solidified for parents the school district's disinvestment in the majority-black community in favor of the new young professionals and families that were gentrifying the neighborhood. On August 17, 2015, twelve parents and community members of the recently formed Coalition to Revitalize Dyett launched a hunger strike to protest the school's closure as well as the school district's lack of transparency and responsiveness to parent demands to save the school. With concrete plans to reopen Dyett High School as an open enrollment high school focused on global leadership and green technology, the Coalition demanded a response from CPS. For thirty-four days, parents and supporters showed their steadfast devotion to a community and the school that was at its center. They participated in the strike for their children but also for the teachers—many of whom were black women—who would stand to lose their ties to the community and their livelihood as teachers.[37]

When CPS announced that Dyett would be reopened as an open enrollment arts high school and not the green technology and global leadership academy they envisioned, parents and community organizers continued the strike. When asked why, parents explained that it was never just about Dyett. As sociologist and Chicago native Eve Ewing explains in her account of the Dyett action, "A fight for a school is never just about a school. A school means the potential for stability in an unstable world, the potential for agency in the face of powerlessness, the enactment of one's own dreams and visions for one's own children. Because whether you're in Detroit or Austin or Louisiana or Chicago, you want to feel that your school is *your* school. That you have some say in the matter, that your voice can make a difference."[38]

Beyond Chicago, parents and community members have rallied to save public schools from disinvestment, closure, and harm. In Shreveport, Louisiana, parents hosted meetings and shared a petition to save a local elementary school from closure. Detroit parents and community members marched in front of state offices to protest the school closings. In Austin and in Philadelphia, parents have staged massive protests and community meetings to fight the onslaught of school closings. In every instance, parents demand that they be heard, that they have a say in the future of their schools. They fight a sense of powerlessness that the school generates.

In New York, the NYC Coalition for Educational Justice (www.nyccej .org/) brought educators, parents, and community members together to launch the creation of 130 community schools across New York City. Threatened by the proposed slate of school closings, parents, educators, and community organizers collaborated to propose the establishment of community schools instead. For schools that were experiencing declining enrollment and disinvestment from the district, their re-establishment as community schools would serve to recast schools as hubs for deep and meaningful collaboration among parents, educators, and the community. Parents and teachers saw their fates as intertwined; they wanted to save the schools that they had invested in and to create an enhanced environment for student learning and development. Community schools would seek to support the whole child and foster parent engagement by providing health, nutrition, and social services to families.[39]

Parent-teacher coalitions have grown out of this solidarity movement. The Coalition for Educational Justice (CEJ), Journey for Justice Alliance (J4J), the Dignity in Schools Campaign (DSC), and the Alliance to Reclaim Our Schools (AROS) are just a few of the coalitions that have brought together educators, parents, and community members who see their interests in educational equity as a common fate that necessitates partnership, alliances, and solidarity. Working to combat issues like school pushout, zero-tolerance policies, and privatization, these coalitions bring together grassroots organizing and advocacy groups of educators, parents, and community members to ensure the right of every young person to a quality education.

BUILDING SOLIDARITY THROUGH PARENT-TEACHER RELATIONSHIPS

These public actions for parent-teacher solidarity represent what is possible when educators and families view each other as allies in an educational justice movement. Relationships and alliances are cultivated in the space of local communities, often with the support of community organizers and community-based organizations. In these spaces, parents share their stories of a child's struggles in school, their sense of being unheard, and their questions about what can be done. They sit alongside teachers who talk about their own challenges in the classroom and their own sense of powerlessness and frustration. As plans to strike, converse, meet, and problem-solve develop, there is space for parents and teachers to find common ground and build a greater understanding of each other.

But these public collaborations are not enough. While they do underscore the important coalitions that must be built between parents and teachers and can reshape the public discourse on parent-teacher relationships, we need strategies that seek to build cultural change *within* schools as well. When CEJ jump-starts the creation of 130 community schools in New York City, the school must open with teachers who see children holistically and seek to cultivate relationships with their families. When Dyett High School reopens as an open enrollment arts high school, the educators in the building must know and appreciate the hard-fought parent and community action that gave new life to the school. The alliance with the community cannot end when the campaign is over.

Instead, the alliance between parents and teachers must continue and be imbued in the life and culture of the school. How and under what conditions can parents and teachers collaborate to support the education and development of children? What kind of cultural change will this require and how can that be enacted in schools?

Family and Community Engagement: Benefits and Challenges

Studies of family and community engagement in schools have illuminated the benefits of teachers collaborating with families to support student success.[40] When schools engage families effectively, students make academic gains, school attendance is improved, graduation rates and college enrollment increase, and students' social and emotional well-being is enhanced.[41] Students whose parents are involved in the school are more likely to say that their teachers care about them and report satisfying relationships with their teachers and the principal.[42] When teachers and parents work together, students benefit.

Parents benefit from this collaboration, too. High levels of engagement in a child's school encourage parents to be optimistic about their child's achievement and more likely to expect an upward trajectory of improvement in school.[43] Parents report a greater sense of belonging in a school community when they are engaged in the school, connected to their child's teacher as well as to other parents.[44] School engagement leads parents to sense that they are working together with a child's teacher to support their success.[45]

There are benefits for teachers as well. While teacher job satisfaction has declined significantly, teachers who engage parents report greater job satisfaction.[46] Despite the constant whir of activity in a classroom, teaching can be a solitary practice. Teachers, especially those who are new to the profession, can feel its isolation. Teachers yearn for connections that help them sort out the issues of the day or talk through a challenging situation. Additionally, these connections to parents promote optimism about student achievement and reflect positive relationships between families and schools that are cultivated by plans for parent and community engagement.[47]

Would it be beneficial for teachers to view students' families as a network of support that enables them to address questions and challenges, share moments of success, and, consequently, view their practice as collaborative in nature and in pursuit of continuous improvement and change? If so, what would it take?

Any exploration of this question requires consideration of the context within which these parent-teacher relationships are embedded. Without meaningful connections to families, teachers are often guided by assumptions about families or parent roles in supporting their children, particularly when it comes to students living in poverty or students of color.[48] Without understanding the challenges parents face in attending school events, teachers may assume a lack of caring.[49] When teachers struggle to communicate with parents, they can assume that parents are hard to reach, when in fact schools are often very effective in reaching white middle-class families. When challenges arise with a student, teachers can be quick to blame families rather than assuming that parents are doing their best and willing to partner with teachers. As mentioned previously, there is a history of distrust and antagonism among educators and families in low-income communities and communities of color that is often unaddressed.[50] This can prompt parents to develop a sense of independence or distance from school staff that keeps them uninvolved in the life of the school.[51]

Studies of school culture have emphasized the problems that weaken the relationships between schools and families, particularly within communities of color or low-income communities.[52] Researchers have also highlighted examples of successful school-community partnerships that integrate community resources, and seek to improve family engagement through effective school programming or district-community collaboration.[53] These analyses provide us with a helpful overview of the stakeholders involved and some clear direction on how schools and districts can design policy and practice to integrate family and community engagement while considering the inherent challenges in the work.

But old habits die hard. In a 2014 study of collaborative district-level organizing efforts to enhance parent-school relations, Ann Ishimaru found that even as new organizing approaches sought to cultivate relationships between educators and parents, the dominant *institutional scripts* in schools—norms about the role of parents, professional authority, control, and power—got in the way.[54] These scripts, rooted in a long history and unchallenged beliefs about parents, "were simultaneously rewritten and reinforced" even as these new efforts sought to institute change.[55] These situations can produce mixed messages to families, when, for example, schools invite parental involvement but implicitly communicate that what they desire is deferential, supportive, positive, and compliant behavior from parents.[56]

Ishimaru's work is a beacon of light, because it is centered in the change processes that schools and districts enact to improve parent-school relations.[57] Most of the studies of school culture tend to focus on the seemingly static issues surrounding parent-school relationships—the problems, the limitations, the misunderstandings, the brokenness. It remains less clear how schools and families have reformed, reimagined, and transformed their relationship and collaboration.

As the institutional scripts of Ishimaru's study show, there is a need to explore the deep cultural shifts that these new partnerships and relationships require. They demand authentic, long-term commitments that are not often captured in one-time events or periodic programming.

Deep cultural shifts require explicit examinations of the values and beliefs that undergird a community. Deficit orientations toward students' families and communities are profound and prevalent in schools that serve communities of color or other marginalized communities, such as poor, immigrant, and undocumented families. Instead, educators must view families for the community cultural wealth they possess, "the array of cultural knowledge, skills, abilities, and contacts possessed by socially marginalized groups that go unrecognized and unacknowledged."[58] This includes a family's aspirational, familial, social, navigational, resistant, and linguistic capital. As Tara Yosso explains, this presentation of community cultural wealth—a family's hopes and dreams for a child's future, the communicative and social skills promoted by use of a native language, the sense of kinship and community history nurtured in the home, as well as the oppositional behavior that challenges inequality and unfair treatment—provides strength and opportunity for children and must be acknowledged and incorporated in schools and classrooms.

The Parent-Teacher Relationship Examined

The most common interaction between families and schools is the parent-teacher relationship, yet with all the attention and scholarship on family engagement, that relationship has received scant attention. Sociologists have often explored this relationship through its conflict-ridden nature, as well as the social class and cultural forces that shape it.[59] Studies of parents' experiences have focused on perceptions of and interactions with school staff. Studies of teachers, even when focused on culturally responsive teaching or culturally sustaining pedagogies, are often silent on the issue of parent engagement. In fact, there is little attention to a teacher's engagement with families beyond a specialized focus on understanding and improving the parent-teacher conference.[60]

Interactions such as the parent-teacher conversation seem like high-stakes exchanges, where parents and teachers alike have much to prove, both in their knowledge and expertise about children.[61] These isolated and formal interactions, however, do little to develop or build trust between parents and teachers. The casual, day-to-day social exchanges between teachers and parents—during arrival and dismissal, while passing in the hallway, or on a phone call—are the places where trust can be built. Building a sense of trust between families and schools is a key part of school improvement, the "connective tissue that binds individuals together to advance the education and welfare of students."[62]

How can we capture and understand the relational trust that can be built—over these day-to-day social exchanges in schools—between teachers and parents? How are these relationships built and sustained, and why do teachers and parents choose to engage with each other in these ways? At the site of parent-teacher solidarity that seems so critical to school transformation, how and under what conditions can parents and teachers function as "natural allies" rather than "natural enemies"?

Karen Mapp and Paul Kuttner, in the development of the Dual Capacity Framework for Family-School Partnerships, lay out the goals and conditions that are critical to the development of effective family engagement efforts in schools.[63] They explain that part of the challenge stems from the fact that none of the stakeholders tasked with building effective family engagement practices (teachers, administrators, school staff, parents, and community members) have had sufficient guidance in doing so. In particular, while school districts have begun to step up their efforts to engage parents in districtwide and school-based parent universities and parent academies, there is minimal support for school staff.

In order to promote a sense of partnership between teachers and families, Mapp and Kuttner identify a set of *opportunity* conditions that underlie effective partnerships. These conditions are linked to learning; are rooted in relationships of trust and respect; nurture the intellectual, social, and leadership development of educators; enhance collaboration; and promote engagement and interaction. Mapp and Kuttner also describe *organizational* conditions, which are the infrastructure needed to provide and sustain partnerships. These organizational conditions should be systemic—integrated into systems of training and professional development—and should provide the resources to be sustainable.

Whether or not school districts have prioritized the support and development of effective family-school partnerships, scholars and practitioners increasingly are creating and developing practitioner-oriented resources to guide willing teachers, administrators, and parents as they seek to develop more meaningful partnerships in schools.[64] In-depth case studies of parent-teacher-community collaborations are also an essential part of understanding both the complexity of parent-teacher interactions and the contextual factors of race, ethnicity, language, and immigration that shape them.[65]

These resources and research accounts highlight the need to create cultural shifts in how schools perceive, interact with, and engage families and communities. To support these shifts, researchers must make long-term, in-depth commitments to studying the relationships of teachers and parents at work—the challenges, the moments of possibility, the dynamism, and the evolution.

WHAT IS GOOD HERE? EXPLORING HOPE AND POSSIBILITY IN PARENT-TEACHER RELATIONSHIPS

While the "problem" of parent-teacher relationships is clearly evident, there must also be significant exploration of their goodness and humanizing role in education.[66] We must be committed not only to documenting the challenges educators face but also to exploring more deeply why they occur. If, for example, parents are not overtly involved in schools, could there be intention behind their nonparticipation? Rather than being an indictment on parents' caring (or lack thereof), are the boundaries between home and school consciously set by parents to protect their children?[67] These explanations move us away from the negative assessments of parents that emerge through deficit frameworks and toward uncovering the acts of care and core beliefs that motivate parents.

We also need to critically understand the ways that teachers successfully engage with families to meet the needs of diverse students. The organizing efforts at Dyett High School and CEJ are a reminder, however, that these parent-teacher collaborations do not occur in a vacuum. Relationships between educators and families are created, challenged, and shaped by the ever-present political and policy context. School closures build a sense of distrust and abandonment among the families whose school communities are sanctioned and shut down. The revolving door of young, novice teachers in urban schools with little to no training can affect how fully and well a family can be known among educators in a school. Regressive and punitive immigration policies shape the everyday realities of how families move about their communities, where they go for connection, and whom they trust with their challenges. A student's undocumented or DACA status influences where they may attend college. Despite the well-meaning outreach of a school counselor or teacher, these family experiences, harbored and protected by families, can be deeply influential to a family's decision-making process yet inaccessible to educators.

The successful campaigns for Dyett High School and community schools in New York City reveal that teachers and families can work together to push for change in school districts, but what about inside the school? These education organizing efforts focus on the engagement and relationship-building that is inherent in those collaborations, unlike the more static representations of parent-teacher relationships in schools. How do parents and teachers understand each other? How do they build relationships of mutual respect and collaboration? These school-based teacher-family relationships are not clearly understood, yet they have the potential to shed light on school transformation efforts. We need deep and thorough explorations of these relationships— their creation, sustenance, and evolution.

This book seeks to fill this void and illustrate the ways that families and educators can work collaboratively. In the same way that scholars have deeply examined portraits of success and goodness, this study seeks to provide in-depth portraits of teachers who have created authentic spaces for collaboration and caring with families.[68] I use the methodology of portraiture, developed by Sara Lawrence-Lightfoot, to capture the goodness and humanity in these teachers' relationships with families, not in an effort to deem them perfect, but to emphasize that in searching for goodness, we discover empathic and holistic ways of seeing what's possible.[69] To challenge the deficit-framed obsession with failure and pathology, in portraiture, "the researcher who asks first 'What is good here?' is likely to absorb a very different reality than the one who is on a mission to discover the sources of failure."[70] The powerful rhetoric of uncaring and uninvolved parents, teacher-parent antagonism, and parent contestations of educators' rights and protections requires that we take a step back and disengage from pathologizing parents, teachers, and their relationship.

In this spirit, the following chapters sketch the portraits of five teachers—Ilene Carver, Megan Lucas, Cinthia Colón, Annie Shah, and Julia Finkelstein—who are committed to the deep appreciation of, partnership with, and cultural sustenance of students' families. Some questions that guided the study were: What do these relationships look like and how do they progress over the school year? Why are teachers motivated to build these relationships? How do teachers and parents describe their interactions and relationship?

I spent two years meeting with teachers, administrators, community members, and public school parents to identify potential participants for the study. The referrals led to phone conversations and then in-person meetings at the school to get a sense of each teacher's story as well as her school environment. I selected five teachers for the study who, in diverse and varied ways, were committed to families and fostered their own unique approaches to cultivating those relationships. They all imbued a sense of hope and optimism in their work with families while being honest and thoughtful about the challenges they faced. The five teachers in the study reflect: 1) a long-term commitment and proven track record of success in engaging families and communities, 2) engagement with diverse urban communities that may superficially be viewed as "hard to reach," and 3) diversity of age, years of teaching experience, and race/ethnicity.[71] These teachers present a range of pathways to the profession (graduate teacher training, teacher residency, Teach For America, etc.). They teach in elementary and middle school classrooms, working with both native speakers and emergent bilinguals. Four of them teach in the Boston Public Schools and one teaches in the District of Columbia Public Schools.

The project, in its entirety, spanned three years. During the first year of the project, I met informally with the individual participants to get a sense of them as teachers. I visited their classrooms and learned about their journey as educators and their commitments to families. These conversations allowed me to get a clearer sense of their family engagement practices, which in turn allowed me to plan the data collection in the second year in a way that was uniquely designed to their practices. The majority of our work together was completed during the second year of the project: I conducted interviews with each teacher throughout the academic year, using an interpretive approach to the interview process.[72] With interviews interspersed throughout the year, I could both follow up on observations made and also plan subsequent visits to their classroom or the school to support emerging questions. I could also explore if and how their perceptions of their relationships with families were changing or evolving.

In addition to the in-depth interviews, I also observed teachers in their classrooms to get a sense of how they interacted with students and how family and community were integrated into classroom experiences. To understand the variety of ways teachers engaged with parents and caregivers formally, I also attended every formal event they had with families, such as school open houses, parent-teacher conferences, family presentations, and schoolwide family events. These events allowed me to connect with parents, family members, and caregivers.

Over the course of the year, as I became familiar with the students in the classroom and their families, I began to work with each teacher to select a few parents that I could get to know more closely. This allowed me to hone in on particular students, connect with a group of parents consistently throughout the year at the school, and interview them about their engagement at the school and with the teacher. These interviews with parents provided me with insight into how parents' relationships with teachers evolved and developed.

All of the teachers in this study work in schools that provide resources and support to engage families and communities. So it became important to talk to the colleagues in their building that they partnered with, the family coordinator who helped them connect with parents who were difficult to reach, teacher colleagues who planned family events collaboratively, and the administrators whose support and expectations for family engagement were influential.

At the time of the study, three of the five teachers in the book—Cinthia Colón, Annie Shah, and Julia Finkelstein—worked at the Young Achievers Science and Mathematics Pilot School in Boston, Massachusetts. Through their narratives, I seek to explore how the school and community context shape these teachers' interactions with families. What are the resources and supports that are in place to support teachers as they seek to engage families? Each teacher's portrait explores the interplay among teacher practice, institutional support, and school culture, but in the final chapter, I discuss some of the ways Young Achievers specifically has built a vision of family engagement into the culture and everyday experience of the school.

The book strikes a balance between the personal narratives of teachers and their evolving interactions with families during the 2013–14 academic year. The personal narratives, gleaned primarily through in-depth interviews over a three-year span, reflect teachers' motivations, experiences, and attitudes toward family and community engagement. The interactions reflect a wide range of practices that teachers use to build relationships with families. Some of these practices may feel familiar, others dramatically new, but they are all shaped and crafted by each teacher's vision for family engagement. Ultimately, it is my hope that these teacher narratives honor the practice of teaching, sketch the tender relations between parents and teachers, and present us with a new framework for understanding family-school partnerships.

An Overview of the Book

The book opens in chapter 1 with a portrait of Ilene Carver, a veteran teacher at the Dudley Street Neighborhood Charter School, an in-district charter school in Boston. Ilene's commitment to families originates from her experiences as a community organizer and public school parent. She describes the importance of a teacher's mind-set and beliefs about families, and illustrates how those beliefs have shaped and influenced every aspect of her engagement with students' families. As a teacher leader whose family engagement practices are well known and highly regarded, Ilene discusses the role she plays in supporting her colleagues in formal and informal ways.

Chapter 2 introduces us to Megan Lucas, who teaches at Stanton Elementary School in Washington, DC. With the support of an outside organization, the Flamboyan Foundation, Megan and her colleagues addressed the climate of animosity and distrust between parents and teachers that escalated after a school turnaround. When Stanton educators engaged in a schoolwide effort to improve family engagement, Megan began to see her relationship with families as a critical part of her practice as a teacher. Her story reflects the importance of systemic change in schools and the key support that can be gleaned from outside organizations.

Chapters 3, 4, and 5 feature three teachers from the Young Achievers Science and Mathematics Pilot School in Boston. Chapter 3 introduces Cinthia Colón, whose pedagogy of caring is a reflection of her own knowledge of and relationships with students' families. She explores how her experience as an immigrant from the Dominican Republic shapes her commitment to serving as a mentor to students of color and immigrant students, as well as her vision for engaging families.

While many of the teachers in the book focus on their relationships with families, Annie Shah, profiled in chapter 4, views the local community of Mattapan, the city of Boston, and beyond as an extension of her classroom. While learning about Boston neighborhoods by visiting various branch libraries across the city, Annie and her students discover that one community, Chinatown, does not have a branch library—the only neighborhood in Boston without one. After learning the story of the city's unkept promise to rebuild a branch library in Chinatown, her students embark on an ambitious community action project to hold the city accountable. Using their new knowledge, Annie's second graders shape community action.

These four teachers have charted a path for engaging families that has evolved over their teaching careers, but chapter 5 introduces us to a second-year teacher, Julia Finkelstein, who works with emergent bilinguals at Young Achievers. She explores both the rewards and challenges in engaging families from the perspective of a novice teacher who works exclusively with immigrant, Latinx families. The sole middle school teacher among the five teachers, Julia explores the role of and strategies for family engagement in middle schools.

The final chapter brings these narratives together to discuss how we can reimagine family engagement in schools. The chapter examines how tradition, values, and beliefs about families' roles inhibit innovations in engaging families and communities. The discussion considers the ways in which schools have traditionally marginalized and excluded families and proposes a new framework for schools as *grounded* institutions—schools that are rooted in and reflect the full cultural lives and experiences of students' families and communities. To cultivate schools as grounded institutions, educators must dramatically redesign their family engagement practices in ways that are *culturally sustaining*. Thus, the book concludes with three framing suggestions to advance a model of culturally sustaining family engagement: repair relationships through the development of relational trust and healing, renew perspectives by bringing new voices into the conversation, and reinvent the school with a vision for family and community engagement.[73] Only by doing so can schools build a true alliance with families based on their shared goal and commitment to support the growth and development of the child.

1

ILENE CARVER
Taking the First Step

On a brisk December morning in Roxbury, I park my car and cross the street toward the front entrance of the Dudley Street Neighborhood Charter School. The school is an in-district charter school that is part of the Boston Public Schools and has been open for two years. On this morning, the schoolyard is quiet and still as stray leaves blow across the blacktop and a lonely winter cap hangs on one of the jungle gym poles. The building is small but imposing—a compact brick building nestled on a narrow residential street that opens into a wide and busy main road in Roxbury. I walk up the school's front steps for a second-grade family literacy event, eager to see what the children have prepared for their guests.

As I enter the building, a gracious man welcomes me and asks if I am here to attend the second-grade event. He directs me up a flight of stairs and I immediately enter a hallway flooded with adults, babes in arms, and young children. There is a buzz of conversation, and then I realize the crowd results from a bottleneck outside the George Mason second-grade classroom. Second-grade teacher Ilene Carver stands by the door. She is a petite white woman in her sixties with dark-framed glasses, trim wisps of light brown hair around her face, and a magnetic smile. Ilene greets each family member by name and with a warm embrace. Some parents arrive with young children and extended family who are each introduced to Ilene as they arrive. A veteran teacher of twenty years, Ilene exudes ease and confidence as she greets the families. She is present, engaging, and utterly welcoming.

Once we enter the room, we settle into undersize student chairs, stand along the back wall, or huddle into the small gaps and spaces in the crowded room. I stand up to give my seat to a student's grandmother. From my corner of the room, I count more than seventy adults with a dozen babies and younger siblings in tow. As I look around, I notice the man who greeted me at the entrance and realize he is a parent. He waves to his son standing at the front of the room.

Children are the presenters today. They sit front and center, with Ilene off to the side. They welcome the group and prompt the adults to introduce themselves. The room is filled with parents, grandparents, aunts, uncles, godmothers, sisters, brothers, stepdads—an extended family of loved ones. They stand alongside students' reading buddies, community volunteers, a literacy coach, the principal, and an assortment of teachers. The introductions in the room are heartfelt, often followed by proclamations of love and pride: "I love you, baby," or "I'm so proud of my grandson today." Amidst the flashing smartphone cameras, students share their agenda for the morning and move swiftly and confidently into the program—reciting poems, explaining why they chose to share them, and encouraging us to read along. All the while, Ilene stands off to the side, turning pages on the easel, nodding with an encouraging smile as students move through the program on their own.

After the class presentation, the second graders turn our attention to the "special part of the day" when they will share their newly published stories with us. Each child holds up a hand, waving a storybook with a colorful cover and newly bound pages. Soon after, we are on the rug or gathered together at small tables, listening to stories about playground outings with Dad, Thanksgiving dinner at Grandma's, a lunch date with Mom, and feelings about a new baby sibling in the house. In the loud and busy room, adults lean in close to hear every word. Readings are followed by lively discussion about author choices, feelings provoked in the story, and vivid illustrations.

As we wrap up the last round of stories and Ilene encourages us to share our final comments and questions, a grandparent in my group remarks on the full and wide presence of adults in the room. She wonders aloud, "I just hope there's someone here for all of [the kids]." I myself wondered at the start of the presentation how, on a weekday morning, the room can be filled with family members, many of whom must be working parents and caregivers. The family members I talked to described the necessity of being there. From parents who had adjusted their work hours that day to attend, to grandparents standing in for parents who could not attend, to older adult siblings who attended with their own children, students' families made a commitment to being present. Akari, a bright and cheerful young girl who has just read us a story about a weekend visit with her father, overhears the question from the grandparent in her group and proclaims, "We all have someone special here today; Ms. Carver makes sure of that. This is a *family* celebration."

BEGINNINGS

As I leave Ilene's classroom, I notice the wall by my side is splashed with a beautiful collage of family photos and handwritten love letters from parents to children. One reads:

Dear Nikki,

From the day you were born, you have been a blessing and I am so proud to be your mom! You are a daughter, a sister and great friend to others. Everything you have done so far amazes me and I can only hope you continue to be as lovely as you are. Not only are you kind, but you are smart, talented and beautiful. As your mom, I hope you continue to excel in school by practicing each subject. In addition to working hard, I will be here to guide you and help you with anything you need.

—Love, Mom

Attached to the letter is a photo of Nikki and her mom. Sitting at Nikki's classroom desk with their arms wrapped around each other, the pair smiles warmly into the camera. Theirs is part of the mosaic of heartfelt notes and family photos that adorn the well-traveled hallway. It is the place where the lined-up George Mason second graders linger before entering the classroom; it is the place where parents and caregivers stand and wait when picking up their children; it is a place that lets every visitor know that these children are wrapped in a web of families with hopes and dreams for them.

Realizing Hopes and Dreams

These messages—of families' hopes and dreams for their children—were written two months prior in September, when Ilene begins to forge relationships with students' families every year. During that first gathering, Ilene stressed the importance of communication to the room full of family members. She told families that "her door is open" and that she wants to know about their concerns as well as those things they believe are going well. She explained that these open lines of communication allow her to work more effectively with their children: "The children know we will be in close contact, and that helps us work better in the classroom because they know that you and I are working together." At this, adults nodded and raised their eyebrows at their grinning children.

Many teachers, like Ilene, may be interested in parent participation, but how does she fill the room with family members so early in the year? While it may be the first time the families have entered the classroom space together as a community, it is certainly not the first touch point they have had with Ilene. Many have been in communication with her since the end of the summer. She explains, "to wait until the school year starts and I haven't been in touch with the family, that limits my ability to know and understand that child." For this reason, every summer, as soon as the new classroom rosters have been formed, Ilene sends a postcard to each new child to welcome them and a letter to families to introduce herself and let them know that she will be in touch over the summer. Before the school year starts, she calls each family to begin what she hopes is a "year of open communication in support of their child":

> I want families to know that I'm delighted to be their child's teacher and that I work at a school that really believes in the power of family partnerships. I know that we all want their child to have the best year

possible and that, in my view, means we have to set up communication as early as possible. That's a really important time . . . to say, "Is there anything you want to tell me about your child that I need to know before we start school?"

During those early conversations with parents and caregivers, Ilene learns what those families believe to be important narratives about their child. Sometimes, they are light-hearted stories that give her insight into a child's personality or preferences. She recalls, "I've learned about likes and don't likes . . . sometimes I laugh when families will say to me, 'Oh, my child gave such-and-such teacher a really hard time last year . . . so you need to be really firm and really—don't give an inch!'" Families may also share personal matters that shape a child's fears or anxieties about school or ask for help when children struggle. The purpose of the call is "to take that first step in establishing trust. It is not automatic that parents of color will trust a white teacher," Ilene explains, "given the pervasiveness of racism in our society and the 'them' and 'us' paradigm that continues to be dominant in many schools." She ends every call by sharing her phone number with parents to encourage communication and assuring them that they will hear from her again soon. Knowing that families' communication styles and methods may vary—some prefer text or email instead of phone calls, or have certain times of the day that are better than others—she gets the best contact information for each family before this call is over. To Ilene, "it is all about what's best for families."

So, when families walk into the George Mason classroom in September, it may be the first time that they've met Ilene face-to-face, but it is never their first conversation. In fact, many parents and caregivers attend the school event during that early, busy time of year for the same reason one mother shared: "I was sincerely excited to meet Ms. Carver today after the calls we have had together. I just knew she was someone I wanted to get to know." At the start of that evening, there were hearty greetings between Ilene and family members. I overheard one mother exclaim, "It is so nice to meet you finally! I feel like I know you already; this is such a blessing to meet you."

In that moment, I recalled my own experiences as a first-year teacher and the intense nervousness I felt when parents began arriving for the school's fall open house. I knew little about the families at that point, and I remember feeling awkward as parents came into the room and slid quietly into seats. I tried my best to exude confidence and knowledge but sensed I was failing. In particular, I remember that one of my students accompanied her mother to the open house and sat through the entire presentation seemingly inattentive to what was happening. The next morning, when she entered my classroom, she told me how strange it was to be at the open house, because she had never seen me "so serious and official." I had to agree with her, but I didn't know another way.

Toward the end of the September evening in Ilene's classroom, after parents and children had enjoyed their time together, parents sat huddled over child-sized desks writing messages of hope and describing their dreams for their children. In the quiet room, Ilene moved from table to table sharing a warm word and often a full embrace. She thanked each person for coming, squatted down to put her hand on the child's shoulder, and expressed pride and adoration for that student. She then asked the family to huddle in close and snapped the photo of the family that would soon adorn and brighten the walls of the hallway. In that quiet moment, I was struck by the sense of connection and humanity. Looking on as Ilene connected with each family, I wished in all earnestness that my twenty-three-year-old self had known this way of being with families was possible.

Taking the First Step and Creating Authentic Invitations

This first step is fundamental to Ilene and, in her mind, "shapes the atmosphere and climate for the year." While she does emphasize to parents that communication must be two-way, she believes that it is a teacher's responsibility to act first and "initiate the relationship-building with family members." From her own experience as a mother in the Boston Public Schools and as a long-time urban school teacher, she knows that schools and families can suffer from strained relationships and a deep sense of mistrust: "So often, families, especially families of color, have—not just had, but have—horrible, disrespectful experiences with teachers and school institutions when it comes to how they are treated. And so I feel like, each year, we're beginning a journey together—children, teacher, and family members—and that it's really important for me to do what I can and to do it with all the respect in the world."

For Ilene, though, knowing and recognizing this is not enough. "I have to understand that doing something—doing one thing at the beginning of the year—doesn't eliminate a history of negative and often racist experiences that families have endured," she explains. Given the serious misgivings that parents and caregivers may have about teachers or the institution of school, Ilene believes it is "important to initiate as soon as possible a relationship of respect" and recognition for the unmatchable expertise parents bring.

Knowing that these families may have their misgivings, she tries to communicate in earnest to let them know: "I am aware that you are your child's first teacher and most important adult and I know that for your child to have the best experience this year, I need to learn everything I can from you, anything you want to let me know that's going to help your child." Ilene believes that all families want to support and celebrate their children's achievements. She shares that, within urban schools, there has historically been a sense among some teachers that parents are disinterested or uninvolved in their child's education when they do not turn out in large numbers for school events, but she argues, "this couldn't be farther from the truth and that only reflects an incomplete understanding of our students' families."

Among her colleagues, Ilene is admired and respected for the massive turnouts at family events and student presentations. I have never seen anything quite like it. When I ask Ilene about the overwhelming response she receives from her families, she recalls her early experiences in the community with her daughter Rachel. From the age of three, Rachel danced with a studio in Boston that organized a yearly recital held at the historic Strand Theatre. At every recital, Ilene recalls:

> The moms and dads would be cheering the kids on, doing the dances with them, just making clear how proud and supportive and how great these kids are. And I always keep that in my mind, as kind

of the excitement about your child doing something that matters. It makes the kids feel so great and makes the families feel so incredibly proud to show their love and support like that. And I do what I can to try to replicate that in my classroom and create this sense that through our classroom community—which includes the teachers, it includes the children, it includes the family members—that together, we are so proud of you for your academic growth and achievement. Just like families cheer their kids on—on the sports fields, in the concert halls, in the theaters, and those other contexts—we're coming together for you to applaud the learning and the progress and what you can do now that you couldn't do two months ago.

In many suburban communities, parental presence and community celebration may be taken for granted. Parents come out for student exhibitions, parent-teacher conferences, and open houses. That these turnouts are dissimilar in urban communities of color is not an indication that the parents are different or feel less committed to celebrating their children. It is, in fact, according to Ilene, "a message that the school has not adequately tapped into this boundless supply of love and admiration for their children." For Ilene and her colleagues who are committed to building these relationships with families, there is a central belief "that parents and family members in our urban schools care just as much about supporting their children as anyone else does." To be successful in gaining parent support, schools must create "conditions where family members feel welcome and respected and know that the school believes that—sees and appreciates the importance of their role in supporting their child's learning."

Anticipating and Understanding Challenges: The Importance of Persistence

Throughout her years as a teacher, Ilene has been committed to making home visits, when it made sense, to meet and get to know parents, grandparents, and caregivers. She recalls the stories that parents shared with her during those visits: "There are many families in the Boston Public Schools who have experienced disrespect when they were students themselves, growing up in Boston or in some other urban school system. Parents and family members have experienced disrespect from school professionals, teachers, and other school staff."

Ilene knows that many families have neither trust nor feelings of generosity toward educators, and these sentiments stem from negative experiences with schools. Consequently, Ilene's expectations about the first, second, or subsequent interactions she has with families are realistic: "I don't expect in all cases to be welcomed with open arms."

During her first year as a teacher, Ilene encountered a parent who was particularly resistant to her outreach. Countless times, she had left messages for Mrs. Wilson, an African American mother whose daughter Rochelle was in her class. Ilene continued to call, particularly later in the fall, to invite Mrs. Wilson to a family presentation. It was important to Ilene that every child have a family member in the room, so she left specific messages asking Mrs. Wilson to join them for the family presentation. Mrs. Wilson did indeed show up and was able to see her daughter take the stage (or the classroom rug) and share a poem for the visitors.

Many months later, after they had established a sense of trust and openness, Mrs. Wilson finally shared with Ilene the great hesitation she felt when first interacting with her:

> [Mrs. Wilson] said to me at the end of the year when we had our family conference, "When you first started calling me to invite me to come up to school, I was not interested. I did not want to answer the phone, I did not want to talk to you." She said, "I have four kids in the Boston schools and no teacher had ever called me except to tell me that one of my kids was messing up, and I got those calls every day on a regular basis and sometimes from all four of my children's teachers on the same day."

Over the years, teachers had called Mrs. Wilson repeatedly to complain about her children's behavior, demand her support, and in the process, judge her for what they perceived to be inadequate parenting. Every call featured another negative story and added another scene to a drama that was unfolding in each child's classroom. Teachers were exasperated and confrontational. Mrs. Wilson had learned to expect these calls and was not interested in starting this conversation again with yet another teacher. But then there was a turning point, according to Ilene:

> [Mrs. Wilson] said to me, "When you first started calling, I did not want to talk to you." But, she said, "When you kept on calling and when you invited me up for the first family presentation—where my daughter got up . . . and she spoke in front of a whole room full of people and I was so proud of her—after that, I changed my mind and I was glad to talk to you because I knew that you really cared about my daughter and you were . . . helping her to become the best student that she could be."

Ilene believes it would be naive to expect that a parent like Mrs. Wilson, who has felt marginalized by teachers, would embrace Ilene "with open arms the very first time you make a call." But Ilene's experience with parents like Mrs. Wilson reveals that these relationships are not only possible but can even flourish with persistence and an understanding that there is a story behind every unreturned call. As Ilene explains, in her "100 percent experience, if you are respectful and if you are persistent," then it becomes "possible to build a relationship with every family." For many teachers, whose work may feel solitary, these relationships can be a lifeline as well, because "families are really clear about how much they value those kinds of partnerships."

"WE ARE A TEAM": THE FAMILY CONFERENCE

The parent-teacher conference does not always elicit warm and pleasant memories. As a child, I remember being fearful of what my teachers would reveal to my parents during that one and only time they would meet. As a teacher, I was racked with nervousness. Particularly as a young teacher, I felt the need to prove myself and often worried that parents would see me for the young, inexperienced teacher that I was. I often spent the days leading up to conference time preparing my room, organizing student assessments and work materials, and compiling notes to guide me through the conversation. As a parent, I always surprised myself with the tense defensive posture I felt during meetings with my child's teacher. In a school full of teachers who generally seemed to know and understand my children, why was I, a former teacher and now education professor, so ready to be defensive and read between the lines of our conversation? Surely, my privilege and credentials would protect me from the anxiety that I knew many other families experienced during these encounters.

Ilene understands the challenges inherent in parent-teacher interactions, but she remains steadfast in the belief that parents offer invaluable feedback. The conference represents one of the first opportunities for her to sit down and talk with the family about the child's experiences. Early in the year, when the first conference takes place, she feels that parents have much to add to her somewhat limited perspective:

> The conference also is a time for me to share with families the kind of snapshot that I have of their child at that point, which is very preliminary—I've known their child for six weeks. But also to personally invite families, which I've already done over the phone and may already have done face-to-face in a more quick meeting, but to say, "Your knowledge about your child is always going to be so much deeper and more thorough than what I know" and that "I depend on you to tell me whatever you think is important for me to be the best teacher of your child."

This stands in contrast to the goals of traditional parent-teacher conferences, in which teachers report on what they have learned and understood about the child. Teachers share student work that illustrates their academic and social assessments about the children, and the conference is based on teacher talk and knowledge. This is not the kind of conference Ilene has in mind:

> Certainly the conference is not, in my view, one where the teacher and the parent come and the teacher reports what he or she has seen and then everybody goes home. That's not what the conference is. It is very much a three-way sharing of how things are going and what we want to work on together to ensure that children will experience pleasure in learning and learn the things that they and we think will allow them to have self-determination over their lives.

Unlike traditional parent-teacher conferences, Ilene's conferences begin with an invitation for family members to share their reflections on their child's experience in the classroom and for the student to share his or her own likes and dislikes. The child is present for the entire conference and participates throughout. When asked why she chooses to include the student in what she calls a "family conference," she explains, "It's not something we're doing to the child, it's something that, together, we're agreeing we need this to happen. I wouldn't think that at a conference you would do goal setting without the person . . . upon whom you were setting the goals, right?"

I had an opportunity to see Ilene in action one afternoon in October when I was invited to join a student, Alicia, and her parents for their family conference. I had gotten to know Alicia during my visits to Ilene's classroom and found her to be a social and gregarious second grader. During informal times when children worked together in the classroom, Alicia was always a popular partner. With her bold and spunky personality, she was not shy around her peers.

On this October evening, the five of us—Alicia, her parents, Ilene, and I—walk into the classroom together, and Alicia leads us to her desk. We pull up our pint-sized chairs and gather around her desk. The conversation starts with a short welcome from Ilene, who emphasizes that "we are here to celebrate *you*, Alicia." Ilene asks Alicia to tell us how the year is going so far for her and what she enjoys about it. Alicia is uncomfortable as she shifts in her seat. Although she has seen me in the classroom before, I wonder if my presence makes her uneasy. I recall Ilene's comment to me earlier that day. "It is a special conversation, but it sometimes takes a little getting used to for the child in that space. They are not used to being included in those kinds of conversations."

Noticing her uneasiness, Alicia's parents, Isabel and Marc, begin to talk about the strides she has made in the classroom since she started last year. They are positive and encouraging; Alicia begins to smile and soaks in the compliments as her mother talks about her love of writing at home and her father shares his pride in the big efforts she has made to become a better friend in school. She is still calm and quiet but as each adult lifts her up, she shyly looks up at them to smile. It is an unusual moment for a child—to listen quietly while the adults who are important to you speak thoughtfully, attentively, and exclusively about you.

Alicia's parents are focused on the good strides she is making this year. Her father is impressed by her newfound independence in completing her homework. "She just knows now when she comes home that she's got the homework and so without us hovering over her, she is getting it done and she's really independent. That is such a big difference from last year." At home, Alicia spends more time reading and now, she and Isabel have a routine of reading together. Isabel asks if this time together is still something worthwhile for a child Alicia's age. "I know you want the kids to read at home, and she is getting really good at that, but is it also good for her to listen when I'm reading to her too?" Ilene explains that children develop a love of reading when finding different ways to read and being able to read different kinds of books. She fondly remembers reading with her own son, Andrew, well into his teen years because it was something they loved doing together. To Isabel, she suggests, "do it as long as you possibly can and for as long as she enjoys it."

This leads to a conversation about books at home. A developing reader, Alicia quickly goes through the books they have at home and is often looking for new and different choices. When Ilene begins to explain that students can borrow books from the classroom library to take home, Alicia immediately nudges Marc aside to pull a plastic Ziploc bag from a shelf behind him. She pulls out the books that are inside and explains, one by one, what she is reading. Marc is noticeably surprised by the book selection because they seem "too simple" and "basic" compared to the books they have at home. This observation leads to a discussion about assessing the appropriateness of a book. Ilene explains that books with pictures are not necessarily simple or beginner-level books but often encourage children to process meaning in different ways. The themes covered in these books are also age-appropriate.

Alicia is a key participant in this conversation. She reads a short section of a book aloud to her parents to illustrate that its pace and difficulty level seem "just right." She flips through the pages of the book while the adults are talking, but she is just keeping her fingers busy; she is quiet and attentive. Alicia seems to enjoy the celebration of her work and the love and care that blanket the interaction.

Alicia's parents also have concerns. Isabel shares her disappointment with the PE class and the lunch period, times of the day that are more disorderly and disruptive. She also feels the PE teacher treats Alicia harshly and can be unforgiving. When Alicia comes to his class late for legitimate reasons, she is chastised for her tardiness and not allowed to participate in the class. There are also times when Alicia stands in the midst of conflict between classmates and is unjustly accused of being part of the interaction. These incidents are troubling to Marc and Isabel, who feel that Alicia no longer looks forward to those times in the day. Ilene listens carefully, neither judging nor taking sides. She asks questions that allow her to understand the situation more fully and resolves to talk to the PE teacher about their concerns and loop back with them. Marc clarifies, "This is not a criticism of you; it's not even your class, but I feel like you can understand and help us improve the situation." To this, Ilene responds, "We are a team. We have to work together to support her."

In a conversation with Marc a few months later, he and I return to the discussion at the family conference. He recalls that they eventually resolved the issues with the PE teacher, but it was helpful to have Ilene's support throughout the process. As a parent, he explains, "I have my daughter's interests in mind and when something is going on, we feel that we have to bring that up as her advocates. But schools can be defensive and teachers can disagree or justify a situation. But my involvement in Alicia's education is non-negotiable . . . when parents are involved in their child's education, that only supports them academically." He goes on to explain that in other experiences with schools, "any presentation of a problem can be seen as a confrontation." He and his wife's relationship with Ilene, fostered by an understanding throughout the year that "we are a team and we are working together," has enabled them to bring their questions and concerns to the discussion without antagonism, defensiveness, or ambivalence. This happens because, according to Marc, "conversation is two-way. She offers advice and we listen. We offer advice that she addresses."

Particularly noteworthy is how Marc's explanation that "we are a team" is exactly the way Ilene describes her relationships with families. I have heard her say this in our interviews and conversations together, in her announcements at family events, to her students as they prepare for a family presentation, and during Alicia's family conference. This is a resounding message, because she believes it is true.

At the conclusion of the family conference this October evening, Ilene, Alicia, Marc, and Isabel talk about their goals for the year ahead. This is when the meeting truly feels collaborative. Together, they decide that they would like to support Alicia's literacy development and see her make progress in instructional reading level. When they talk about how to support her, Marc and Isabel discuss how they will support her at home: looking for new books to refresh the home library, taking trips to the local library, reading more often with Alicia, and having conversations with her about what she has read to develop her inference skills. Alicia commits to spending more time reading at home and trying to make greater use of the classroom's lending library. She admits that sometimes she gets "bored with reading," particularly when the book choices "are not that fun or they're books I've read already." Ilene promises to support her in the classroom, helping Alicia look for books that reflect her interests and "having conversations with Mom and Dad to let them know what she's interested in reading." The adults praise Alicia for her growth socially and emotionally. Her friendships and interactions have improved dramatically over the past year and this has allowed her to have "more focus in the classroom," according to Ilene, and gives "us space to focus more on her academic progress," according to Isabel.

These moments—where children are held and supported by the families who love them and the teachers who educate them—are rare. Ilene conducts family conferences that include the student because she believes they should be centrally involved in the goals that teachers and families set for them. As she said, this is not "something we're doing *to* the child." It is also evident that in meeting with Marc and Isabel, Ilene wanted to hear from them. She wanted to support the efforts they were making at home for Alicia, but she also wanted to learn about their hopes and aspirations, their expectations and concerns. That, according to Ilene, would only enhance her success as Alicia's teacher.

"AN ORGANIZER AT HEART"

This sense of working together, encouraging a sense of agency, and standing together in support of Alicia is what Ilene describes as an "activist" orientation to working with families. This is rooted in her years as a community organizer. After a year in college, Ilene recalls the urge she felt "to be more actively involved with trying to change the world." During her first year of college, Ilene decided to move to Louisville, Kentucky, to work with white racial justice activists Carl and Anne Braden. The Bradens organized white southern support for the civil rights movement through their work with organizations such as the Southern Conference Educational Fund. They were staunch supporters of desegregation efforts in the South, mobilizing national support for civil rights efforts and building multiracial coalitions that set out to end racial discrimination and dismantle white supremacy. Ilene knew the Bradens through a family connection and decided to work with Carl Braden as his assistant. Carl passed away that spring, and his wife Anne maintained the invitation to Ilene to work in Kentucky. Anne was planning to organize the boxes and boxes of leaflets, newsletters, and campaign materials that had accumulated in the Braden attic over the last twenty-five years. The Wisconsin Historical Society was collecting these papers, and Anne needed some support. Ilene recalls:

> After I finished my first year of college, I rode the bus down to Louisville in June. And it turned out that the Louisville schools that fall were desegregating just like Boston had been the year before, and all hell broke loose. I mean, there was a very similar scenario to what had happened in Boston the year before. There was a revival of the Ku Klux Klan for the first time in forty years in Kentucky. So it wasn't the time for activists to be organizing their attic . . . It turned out that neither Anne nor I was very good at organizing papers either. I was an assistant to Anne in whatever she needed and ended up becoming extremely involved for the first two years that I was there

in the movement to support the right of black children to attend previously segregated schools.

Over those years, Ilene supported the work of pivotal organizations such as the Southern Organizing Committee for Economic and Social Justice and the Kentucky Alliance Against Racist and Political Repression. Much of her work, however, was rooted in Louisville where they organized for school desegregation, challenged police brutality and the death penalty, and mobilized communities around issues of race and racism. She recalls:

> My role was largely behind the scenes, helping to make things work. So when I was in the South, I occasionally spoke at a school committee meeting or a rally, but my major role was being one of many people to do the work that would help create the force that we needed to build in order to accomplish our goal, which in this case was—initially was—doing what we could to protect the safety of the children who were going into communities where they were not welcome ... My experiences were totally rooted in the belief that what's most important is being part of a movement that is fighting against racism and injustice.

Ilene took these experiences back to Boston, where she worked as a union organizer, representing workers on grievances, running strikes, and organizing campaigns to protect workers' rights during a time when companies were shutting down plants, slashing wages and benefits to maximize profits, and consequently undermining the stability of workers' families and communities. Throughout countless one-on-one meetings with workers, Ilene developed a commitment to supporting the worker, the community member. In fact, throughout her civil rights activism in Kentucky and her union organizing in Massachusetts, "a central message was that securing the objective you were fighting for mattered more than anything else."

Just as the "major role" of her work in the South was "to do the work that would help create the force" that was needed to accomplish community goals, she describes her "primary goal" in working with families as "bringing together the adults who care about these children in ways that support them fully." Fostering self-determination for her students and their families is a driving force of her social justice commitment. She explains:

> One of the things I learned from my years of organizing, both in the South and in factories, is that . . . ownership of the goal is critical. And so in my classroom, it is really critical that I approach teaching and learning from a perspective where it isn't my goals that I'm setting, but the goals of the children and their families, developing collective goals for the year. What is it that we want to accomplish? The goals don't just grow out of some standard—state standards, or even my best understanding as a teacher—but are collectively generated and derived. We talk about what each one of us needs to do in order to accomplish these goals. Having that kind of mutual ownership of the goals makes a big difference in what we're able to achieve in a year's worth of time.

Ilene understands that individuals build power when they mobilize around common goals. When a company stripped its workers of the insurance benefits they had for years, Ilene and union workers organized a wildcat strike and walked out of the plants to demand reinstatement of those health benefits. These experiences taught Ilene "that your strength comes from community and comes from the unified force that you're able to mobilize together." Ilene believes that working with families is just like mobilizing allies: "I guess I kind of feel like I'm an organizer at heart before I'm even a teacher. And so the way I teach, so what I learned from being an organizer, is that you achieve your best outcomes when you mobilize your allies. And in the context of schools, families are the most important allies that we have."

BUILDING A CLIMATE OF RESPECT TOWARD FAMILIES

Ilene has always been committed to the authentic engagement of families, and she has been recognized for her efforts. She was a founding teacher at the Young Achievers Science and Mathematics Pilot School, where she helped to create an institutional framework for family engagement that flourishes to this day. Across her twenty-year career as a teacher, she has worked in different schools, promoting a climate of family-school partnership everywhere she goes, and working with her colleagues to develop innovative and authentic forms of family engagement in schools. In fact, all of the Boston teachers in this study know Ilene. Across schools in the district, she is seen as a resource and mentor. Some teachers learned how to conduct family conferences from Ilene; others took her advice in planning family presentations. In the growing community of Boston teachers who are committed to family engagement and beyond, Ilene is a well-known and highly regarded colleague.[1]

When Ilene joined the staff of the newly founded Dudley Street Neighborhood Charter School two years ago, she was invited to work as a teacher leader who would coordinate the school's family outreach efforts. The school was created in partnership with the Dudley Street Neighborhood Initiative, a community organizing group that is locally and nationally renowned for its mission of empowering local residents to create a vibrant, high-quality neighborhood in a part of the city that has been historically neglected and marginalized. About half of the school's students reside in the surrounding Dudley neighborhood. Consequently, the school seeks to be rooted in community and connected to families—considered the school's "most important partners" (www.bpe.org/dudley-street-neighborhood-charter-school/for-families/)—with a goal to secure "the participation and engagement of every parent/guardian."[2]

Family engagement was the part of the school's mission that teachers would likely be least equipped to practice. Since "family engagement is not something that many teachers have significant training in when they enter the classroom," according to Ilene, there is a need to support and develop teachers in their work with families. Teachers at the Dudley Street School were expected to engage families meaningfully and well. While all teachers are "open to developing partnerships with families," they may "have different amounts of experience doing it."

When the school first opened, Ilene developed a daylong training session for all staff that was focused on family engagement and would help set the tone for their work with families. Since then, she has designed orientation sessions for new staff to integrate them into the school's vision and practice around family engagement. She also supports teachers on schoolwide family engagement goals that they set collectively throughout the school year. For example, when the school sets a goal to conduct family conferences with 100 percent of families, Ilene works with teachers and the principal to help them communicate with families creatively and problem-solve for those that are more challenging to reach. But, as Ilene explains, this is "not just about learning how to be successful in getting families to attend and become full partners in conferences, it is also about supporting teachers to do this time- and labor-intensive work." When conferences are often thirty minutes long, "we have to be creative about when and how we plan them so that teachers don't feel burned out or overworked after a long instructional day."

Families often spend years connected to a school through their children, but these years are spent with an array of different teachers. These educators may each have their own ideas about the role of families or their capacity to support their child's learning or work as an "equal partner," as Ilene suggests. While one positive experience with a teacher like Ilene may be an incredible opportunity for collaboration, what happens when, the following year, the family returns to a teacher that is disinterested in engaging families? What is the point of building a sense of advocacy and partnership in parents if it is not a continuous part of their experience in the school? Ilene explains that this dilemma was "central to being part of this school community—I knew that we could build a culture around appreciating families and acknowledging that we can learn from them." Just as we understand the value in creating shared values around teaching and learning, we should also encourage schools to have shared values in their engagement with families.

CHANGING HEARTS AND MINDS

It is a hot, sunny day in June, and the second graders in Ilene's class are wearing colorful dresses, polo shirts, and slacks, with multicolored beads and sparkly headbands adorning their faces. It is the school's Step Up Day, and we have all just come inside—sweaty yet jubilant—as this young crop of children has been anointed the school's third-grade class. Family members and children file into the room for a publishing party. We all know the routine, so we spend the next hour on the floor, gathered around children who read us their very best work. One young girl, who has gotten to know me on the occasions I've spent in the classroom, waves me over and tells her mother that I'm a "book author too," but that my books "are a little less fun since they don't have pictures." I laugh heartily with her and join the group with a genuine sense of appreciation that this young author is so proud to share her work.

After we spend some time reading and sharing stories, we turn our attention to Ilene. She has prepared awards for each student; as the children come up to accept their awards in turn, they also get a hug from Ilene. There is loud cheering and applause; as children return to their families, they jump into a parent's arms or shout, "I love you, Mom!" There is warmth and affection radiating from this room, and I feel grateful to be sharing this moment with them.

Just when I think we are finished, Ilene makes some closing remarks she would like to share with "this remarkable group of young scholars" and their families: "Now these fabulous scholars and their extraordinary families are stepping up to third grade. Thank you for sharing your children with me and for the terrific partnership that we have had, which has been absolutely what has made the difference in the wonderful growth and progress that all of your children have made. So please, let's applaud families!"

After another round of applause, Ilene invites the families, as she does on many of these occasions, to share their own thoughts and feelings about their child and the classroom community. Around the room, parents express their gratitude for Ilene and their intense pride for their children:

> "I want to say that I'm very proud of the effort that she put in and the fact that she stuck with it and kept going. I really appreciate Ms. Carver's support in helping her be the scholar that she is."

"I am so proud of my daughter—to see her grow in her reading and how she has learned to be responsible, her homework and everything."

"More importantly, Ms. Carver, you have made a difference and supported them and that is something they will carry with them for the rest of their lives."

"Ilene keeps reminding us that this is a collaborative effort. Every family in the room and those that couldn't be here, we have all worked for this together."

"A lot has happened this year. When she came to this school, she didn't know anything and now, she is reading—adult books, no less. And I have to thank you for the difference you have made in our lives. We have really worked together on this and we couldn't have done this without you."

While Ilene has continually told me that she believes parents are equal partners and the most important allies in supporting children, I realize that these parents and caregivers believe this to be true of *her*. This is her most remarkable accomplishment. While we may believe in a family's capacity to ensure that homework gets completed or to send their child to school with lunch and a warm coat, there are often limits to what we believe families—particularly in urban, marginalized communities—can achieve. Many schools focus on improving parent turnout without offering a true space for their stories to be heard. We focus on giving information but don't solicit their feedback or ask for their insight. As a result, parents may go through the motions, but their ideas about the hierarchy between schools and families go unchallenged. In Ilene's classroom, however, their beliefs have been genuinely transformed.

2

MEGAN LUCAS
Transforming Practice

On the first day of school, five-year-old Asia woke up with endless questions for her Aunt Carlene: Who will pick me up from school? Is my teacher going to be there when we get there? Is she nice? Will she know my name when she sees me? These were typical first-day jitters, but they were punctuated with a nervousness that had not abated since the start of summer. On the heels of a tumultuous six-month personal journey and a summer spent together, Carlene and Asia were acutely aware of the challenges of Asia's transitioning back to school. An eager student who loved school, Asia had not met her new teacher yet. She had many questions about what the day and experience would be like and could not shake her nerves that morning.

As Asia and Carlene walked hand in hand toward the classroom, a young, smiling teacher called out the young girl's name. Megan Lucas was to be Asia's kindergarten teacher and, upon recognizing Carlene, whom she had met previously, she stepped out to greet both of them. After a warm introduction, she welcomed Asia into the classroom and began to show her around. Together, they walked through the space, explored the new classroom environment, and began to put Asia's belongings away in her cubby. Both women knew, however, that the return to school as well as her aunt's departure would unnerve and upset Asia. Noticing some worry as Carlene prepared to leave, Megan drew Asia's attention to a book about animals she had saved for her. This kind and simple act distracted Asia and helped settle her into the new environment. It was, as Carlene recalls, a "moment of comfort for us both."

Throughout that day, Megan sent text messages and photos to let Carlene know that Asia was doing all right. During those early weeks, some days were better than others. In particular, Asia would grow anxious about whether her aunt would come to pick her up at the end of the day. When she noticed this fear and anxiety, Megan took a moment aside with Asia to call or text Carlene and confirm that she would be there at the end of the day to pick Asia up from school.

Transitions to new classrooms can be fraught with anxiety, particularly for young students who are still new to the routines of school. However, in Asia's case, recent trauma in her personal life was creating intense emotions—a deep sense of insecurity and vulnerability. While families and teachers traditionally meet for the very first time on the first day of school, Megan and Carlene met over the summer for a home visit. When Megan sent home a note requesting that she and another teacher at the school conduct a home visit, Carlene recalls she was "a little skeptical about doing it." In the end, she decided that there was no harm in agreeing to do so: "She came and knocked on the door and came in and she just wanted to know how she could help and get to know my niece Asia. All she wanted was to get to know our family and know how she could help Asia in the classroom. She was there to listen to me, not tell me what to do."

During this conversation, Carlene shared what her niece was going through. Asia had been living with her grandmother in Washington, DC, because she had tragically lost her mother, father, and brother. At the same time, she was separated from her sister, who went to live with another family member. This was traumatic for Asia on many levels: she had never been separated from her sister and was simultaneously grieving the loss of her parents and brother. Just when things seemed that they could not get any worse, they did: Asia's grandmother passed away, prompting Carlene to relocate from Pennsylvania with her family to live in her mother's home with Asia. The change and trauma made for a tumultuous year for Asia. Carlene was concerned about Asia's return to school, given her issues with separation, grief, and loss.

Experiencing devastating grief herself, Carlene felt lost, disconnected, and distraught. She "was not in any state to connect with a teacher," but she agreed to the home visit for Asia's sake.

Megan remembers how sad and disengaged Carlene was at that home visit: "Knowing what she had gone through, I couldn't imagine making that connection with her without the warmth and privacy that a home visit provides." Carlene adds, "I'm not sure if I would have ever shared all this information with a teacher I had just met, someone I knew nothing about," but when Megan came into her home and made a sincere request to learn about their family and understand how she could support Asia, it felt like the "right time and place" to share Asia's story.

During the home visit, Megan also had the opportunity to learn how much Asia loved school. Asia was an avid learner and a curious reader, and school had been a place where she felt happy, confident, and secure. Megan also learned that Asia loved to pore over books about animals. If it weren't for that conversation, Megan recalls, "I wouldn't have known about the most essential things about Asia. What better person than a family member to get tuned into the child, their likes and dislikes, their experiences and apprehensions about school, the things that bring them joy?"

UNDOING THE TURNAROUND: REBUILDING AND HEALING IN THE CONTEXT OF SCHOOL REFORM

Megan, a white woman in her twenties, is in her sixth year of teaching. She met Carlene during her second year at Stanton Elementary School in Washington, DC. While they both look back fondly at that first meeting in Carlene's home and the relationship they have developed by working together over the years, they are also the first to admit that the school underwent a tumultuous transition.

Megan arrived at Stanton after completing her first two years as a teacher in Prince Georges County, Maryland, with Teach For America (TFA). She was ready for a change and committed to teaching in urban schools, but was new to the community. Woodside, the small residential and industrial community in Southeast Washington, DC, where Stanton is located, is almost exclusively African American. Part of the larger Anacostia neighborhood, Woodside is often portrayed in the media as one of the most "persistent pockets of crime," poverty, and violence.[1] Generations of poverty, inadequate public housing, insufficient social services, and underresourced schools have diminished the overall quality of life in Woodside. While outsiders may see only the violence, singularly portrayed in the media, those within it call the community home. I met numerous parents who attended the school as children, and for some, their parents did as well. As in many other communities, the school—despite its issues—was a core resource and community institution.

When Megan arrived, Stanton was in the midst of a dramatic overhaul. The school, along with five other low performing DC public schools, was slated for a turnaround effort in 2010, initiated by then mayor Adrian Fenty and school chancellor Michelle Rhee. The district brought in a Philadelphia-based nonprofit charter company, Scholar Academies, to guide the school's restructuring process.

Changes were swift and dramatic. The school, long known to the community as Stanton Elementary School, was renamed DC Scholars Stanton Elementary School.[2] Scholar Academies removed the principal and hired a new leader. Older, veteran African American teachers who were known by the community were replaced by a young corps of teachers—predominantly white women—from TFA. These changes came during the summer without parent or community input.

Regardless of how accustomed we have become to this "turnaround" story, the dramatic removal of the teaching staff stunned families and set the stage for an intense uphill battle for collaboration. While those on the outside might view Stanton solely as a place in need of reform and intervention, parents and community members felt a sense of loss—what sociologist Eve Ewing, in her study of school closings in Chicago, describes as "institutional mourning."[3] When Stanton staff reached out to families through a series of summer ice cream socials and expressed their willingness to work with parents to create a PTA, they were met with disregard and contention. Teachers were surprised at the negative response because, as Megan reflects, "we just neglected what a shock that would be to their system."

This was partly due to teachers' incomplete and superficial understanding of the community. What they knew was that revolving groups of substitute teachers were the norm in some classrooms, that altercations broke out between parents and teachers on school grounds, and that students openly defied teachers in the classroom. Their response was to "push those issues aside" and create a high-intensity academic environment for all students to be successful. There would be new demands on families too, as Megan explains: "We came in asking them to wear these specific uniforms, have an extended school day, their kids were going to do all this extra homework, the parents were going to come in for conferences, the parents were going to have to come up to the school if the kid was doing something that was aggressive or violent."

With new policies and practices in place, Stanton educators readied themselves for an uphill battle that they believed would ultimately end in school improvement. In reality, a terrible year ensued. Megan remembers the combative environment between teachers and families: "The community as a whole, my perception of them . . . was that they really just cared about their individual student and making sure that their kid wasn't in trouble. And so any type of interaction was always like, 'No, my kid couldn't have done that. No, my child didn't do that.' Or it was my fault if their child did something." Melissa Bryant, a fourth-grade math teacher and teacher leader for family engagement at Stanton, also recalls how distressing that first-year environment was:

> Parents never smiled, people weren't happy; it was just a very sad place to be and parents only ever came up with the intent of arguing or fighting, just automatically assuming this teacher doesn't like my child, this teacher is doing this, this teacher is doing this, I don't like it, I don't like it, I don't like it. And coming up to school to just always be negative, every interaction was negative all the time . . . I think we were all just trying to survive—parents, teachers, kids, everybody.

As she encountered challenges with students, Megan began reaching out to parents to address student behavior. Every phone call or conversation with a family member became a combative one. That year alone, Stanton suspended 267 students in an elementary school of 350 children. Parent attendance at school events was abysmally low, which only reinforced teachers' ideas about parents' lack of caring. To add insult to injury, Stanton went from being one of the five lowest performing schools in the district to *the* lowest performing school at the conclusion of the first year of turnaround.

With all eyes on Stanton, it was obvious that adjustments would have to be made for the following year. The school's turnaround attempt was failing. The district had just begun a partnership with the Flamboyan Foundation to develop the Comprehensive Family Engagement Partnership Pilot. The project was designed to support and launch schoolwide efforts to build trusting relationships with families and engage them as partners in supporting students' academic success. Pilot schools would agree to a series of trainings to implement schoolwide practices such as home visits and parent-centered programs. Four DC schools were chosen for the pilot, and Stanton appealed to be added as a fifth school partner. Susan Stevenson, executive director of Flamboyan Foundation's DC office, recalls the organization's initial hesitation in working with Stanton. She and her staff were unsure about the school's readiness given its significant challenges: "While we felt that we didn't know them that well, they convinced us that they would take this on and we bowed to the urging of others to do it."

This top-down reform was not the ideal way to bring in a new schoolwide family engagement strategy. Teachers were undoubtedly hesitant but felt they had few options. Megan remembers her mixed feelings as they headed into a new year with new expectations:

> For me, because that first year was so horrendous and so terrible, when the people from Flamboyan and the Parent Teacher Home Visit Project came and said this changed their relationship with families, I believed them, sure, but the whole concept was scary to me. Asking someone who I have never even met to come into their home, and they don't even know me. They have no reason to say yes

or trust me. I don't know how I would feel if it were me, and I'm not a parent. So I was really, really scared. But when they said it was going to work, I was like okay, I'll try anything, because the first year was so terrible.

"BRINGING HUMANITY TO OUR WORK AS TEACHERS"

Stanton's new partner, the Flamboyan Foundation, was founded to develop educators' capacity to effectively engage students' families. It became clear that schools needed to support building relationships with parents, so Flamboyan sought out compelling and successful models across the country that could form a comprehensive family engagement strategy. Helen Westmoreland, Flamboyan's deputy director, describes how important it was to the organization to "package the deep relationship-building piece," one of the greatest challenges schools face in this area, "with the academic partnering work" that highlights the importance of student success.

Building Relationships with Home Visits

For the relationship-building piece, Flamboyan looked to a promising model out of Sacramento, Parent Teacher Home Visits (PTHV). PTHV begins with the understanding that schools must break the cycle of blame between families and school staff by "building trust and respect, instilling cultural competency and increasing personal and professional capacity for all involved" (www.pthvp.org/). PTHV trains educators across the country to conduct home visits, bringing teachers and parents together in settings that are comfortable for families to spark genuine conversation about the child and build trust. Rather than using the home visit to address a problem, make an assessment of a family situation, or determine services needed, PTHV's home visit is designed to bring parents and teachers together as equal partners in a unique setting to develop a sense of trust and common purpose in supporting the child socially, emotionally, and academically. Teachers conduct home visits in pairs to ease teachers' sense of insecurity and anxiety. The focus of the conversation is on listening and getting to know the family—their hopes and dreams, their expectations and experiences. These conversations, Flamboyan believed, would help build one-on-one relationships that could heal past wounds and build trust and understanding.

Flamboyan invited parent and teacher trainers from the Sacramento organization to Stanton in May of Megan's first year to introduce the remaining staff to the concept of the home visit. Many teachers had already decided not to return. Of those who were committed to stay, most were unconvinced that the emphasis on family engagement would change the school. Megan recalls that teachers felt defeated. "We were all soaked in our own tears, sweat, and blood," she says. Despite the frustration they may have felt with the new family engagement initiative, however, most teachers saw their current efforts as a dismal failure. What else were they to do? They listened to testimony from parents, teachers, and high school students who had participated in home visits. Megan recalls the initial reaction from teachers was mixed: "First, we thought, wow, this seems really, really simple—just getting a parent to say yes and going and talking to them—but it also seemed really scary because so many parents still felt hostile toward us and we didn't know how they would receive it."

Despite their reservations, teachers were determined to try something new and wanted desperately to create a better relationship with families. Working in pairs, they reached out to families during the summer "over and over again" to meet with them in their homes. Megan remembers, "It took a while for parents to say yes to us, and other families were just not interested." Raquel, whose daughter Dion was a student in Megan's classroom, explains, "people associate home visits with negative connotations . . . when a teacher or someone from a school or school official comes to your house, it is not good . . . so a lot of people are like, 'Oh, I don't want [teachers] in my home, I don't want them to know what I'm doing; they are coming to judge me.'"

After repeated requests from teacher teams, some families agreed to open their homes to the teachers. As the home visits began, other parents in the community noticed teachers walking down neighborhood streets and into neighbors' homes. This created quite a stir in the community as parents began talking to each other about the home visits. As word got out, others become curious. Carlene recalls:

> Neighbors started to ask me why were these teachers going into people's homes and I would explain to them about the home visits and ask them, "Why haven't you had your home visit yet?" I think some people thought they were from CPS [Child Protective Services] and stuff like that. But then news started to spread and people are telling each other that the teachers were not judging us and wanted to work with us. And then people warmed up to that idea and, next thing you know, people are asking, "Why *haven't* I had my home visit yet?"

Trina, whose son was in Megan's class the year I visited Stanton, also remembers feeling more open to the idea of the home visit after Megan's explanation. The sole purpose was to get to know her and her son in their own environment, in a space that would put the family at ease "versus coming to the school where you feel like you have to tip-toe around certain things."

Teachers' perceptions were changing as well. For many teachers, it was their first time in the neighborhood and in a student's home. Melissa Bryant remembers how unusual it was for teachers to be in the community and inside students' homes. Many teachers "just didn't know how they felt about the whole thing—some uneasiness, some fear, especially if you weren't familiar with these kinds of communities." Megan recalls:

> But the community as a whole, when I think about the physical community, the Woodland community, where a lot of our families live, I was nervous to enter the community at first, to just walk around for home visits. I was afraid that I was going to see things that would make me feel uncomfortable. Not afraid for my well-being or for my safety, but more so afraid that I would see a living situation of one of my students, and I wouldn't be able to get past that to continue to hold them to high expectations.

Once teachers entered these homes and began connecting with families, though, they began to realize their fears were unwarranted. Megan found herself focusing on the family members and the ease with which she could have a conversation in someone's living room or kitchen table: "What I found was that the second I stepped into a home and the second I'm sitting down with the family, whatever's going on around us is not a part of the conversation. It's always about the people who are involved in that child's life, and that allows me to set even higher expectations for the students because it's like, 'No, now I know I have a partner in this work.'"

The Flamboyan Foundation recognizes that for educators to enhance and hone their family engagement skills, they must have a system of supports. In their partnership with the District of Columbia Public Schools (DCPS), Flamboyan seeks to foster cultural shifts, creating a school environment that is built upon trusting relationships between educators and families. This takes time, and it requires resources. To its partner schools, Flamboyan "provides training, coaching, and tools while schools create a family engagement leadership team to support the practice of effective family engagement within the school" (flamboyanfoundation.org/). Training sessions and professional development for faculty provide contextual background, research support, established guidelines for new practices, and testimony from parent leaders and facilitators who are often former teachers.

These professional development supports throughout the year, as well as the coaching that is available, provide educators in a partner school with opportunities to understand the benefits of engaging families, to ask questions, and to receive support when they face challenges. This ensures that experienced trainers and facilitators are available when a school has the will to engage families but has not yet established the staffing, resources, or sustained practices to be successful. Teachers are also paid stipends for the home visits they conduct during the summer to recognize the time they invest into the relationship-building process.

These are the kinds of supports that must be in place for educators to take the leap of faith in reinventing family engagement. For Megan, the support she and other Stanton teachers received was "invaluable in that it both helped us to see what was possible but also to understand that there was a deep knowledge base and expertise about what we were doing that we had to gain." While she initially had some reservations about the home visits in particular, with the support of Flamboyan, the visits were a transformative experience that taught her the true value of engaging families. As she reflects on her experience as a teacher, Megan is humbled by how much humanity these conversations revealed:

> I think that as teachers, we have a tendency to believe that we are responsible for making a difference in that child's life or that we can help them be academically successful. It's not that I believed parents weren't important but since we had such a hard time communicating with parents and there was so much hostility, I think we had given up on the belief that this needed to be work done together. These home visit conversations, they strip away all the baggage, and we are left as adults who care for and want the same thing—to support and care for that child together. It brings a sense of humanity to our work as teachers.

"THEY DON'T CARE WHAT YOU KNOW UNTIL THEY KNOW THAT YOU CARE"

These experiences illustrate how essential the groundwork of one-on-one relationship-building is. In any school community, but particularly in communities that have historically been marginalized by schools, educators cannot assume that parents are ready to engage, trust, or collaborate with teachers from the get-go. During her first year at Stanton, Megan noticed a recurring pattern in her interactions with parents when she called to talk about behavior issues that arose in the classroom: "Our first year at Stanton when I would call a parent and talk to them about something that happened, a student could say, 'No, Mom, that never happened.' The parent has no reason to trust me. I am new, I am calling her for maybe the fifth time that week and telling her the exact same story, but the child might not act like that at home or even if he does, the parent has no reason to trust me or believe. She really doesn't care what I have to say."

Megan assumed that parents would be on her side. Her training, experience, and possibly just her status as a teacher alone would give her the credibility she needed. In hindsight, she realizes her "naïveté": "I assumed families would see my passion, how much I cared about their children, how hard I was working and how much time I was investing, and they would just take to me and respect me because of that, but I was sorely mistaken . . . I learned the meaning of the phrase, 'They don't care what you know until they know that you care.'"

While school climate was far from perfect when Megan and her colleagues arrived, the abrupt firing and removal of the schools' teachers and administrator "completely broke any sense of trust that did exist." To make matters worse, the new staff came into the school with high demands and new expectations "without doing any of the getting-to-know-you part."

Without this trust, parents "will feel like they need to stand up for their child" in an environment where they are unsure of educators' motivations and judgments, according to Carlene. Raquel adds that in situations where a child and a teacher have different accounts of a problem or issue in the classroom, "why wouldn't the parent believe their own child if there is no trust or respect with that teacher?" Repeatedly unanswered phone calls, in this context, may be a family's way to avoid confrontation. These parental responses, often seen by teachers as a *lack* of caring for the child, may, in fact, stem from a family's wish to maintain their dignity and respect.

Over her years as a teacher, Megan has learned that it is her responsibility to "prove to my parents that they can trust me." That requires reaching out to families and seeking their stories and experiences. During these conversations, she learns about a parent's aspirations for their child. She gains insight into how that child views school and the learning styles that work well. She also becomes privy to a family's personal circumstances: parenting arrangements, cultural dynamics, and personal situations that influence a child's experience in school: "When a parent knows that I understand where they are coming from—whether it's their financial situation, their home life, how many children are in the home, that they are a single parent, whatever they need me to understand about life at home—that allows us to build trust."

Getting to know families and listening to their stories, however, is only one part of building trust with them. Megan explains, "They have to know who I am as a person to trust me with their children." As a young middle-class white woman working in a predominantly black community, she feels she has an even greater responsibility to open up to families and let them get to know her:

And I think that, especially as a white woman and younger—because a lot of the time I'm younger than them or even the same age as them—teacher, it's really hard for them to trust me at first, because I don't know those struggles. I haven't been there. I haven't gone through that. So I have to build that camaraderie and empathy by finding a shared source of inspiration and it always goes back to their child. I just do my best to be honest and open and aware of my limitations: "I can't understand everything that you're going through, but I will help in any way that I can and I will take part in as much as you will let me."

As a young novice teacher, she felt insecure about her lack of experience and "didn't really like saying how long I had been in the classroom because I did not feel like it was enough." Not a parent herself, she wondered if parents would question her ability to work with their children. Guided by these doubts, Megan thought it best to keep her personal details private and keep the interaction with parents "purely professional." While she used this guardedness to maintain an untainted image—a strategy that many teachers may relate to—it also slowly built a wall between her and her students' families.

When she began her training for home visits, Megan realized that while listening was important, it was essential for her to share her story as well:

I think [I share] the things that have been important to me . . . So talking about my family, talking about even growing up in Florida and coming to this area, and just owning that I don't really know a lot about DC or I know only as much as somebody who's lived here for six years. And then I've had a lot of conversations with parents about [how] I'm the first in my family to go to college, so that's always been a huge, "Wait, what?" moment for them. I think that they probably assume that my parents went to college and that my parents probably do something really awesome. And my parents are really awesome, but they also waited a while to have kids, so they're kind of part of that generation that didn't need to go to college to necessarily have a career and they're small-business owners so . . . it's untraditional, I guess, in a lot of ways.

Megan is the first to admit that this level of trust and openness is not always simple to achieve. Some parents take a while to open up to the idea of a home visit, and some families maintain a formal distance with her longer than others. Despite her invitations and appeals, Megan says, "they don't believe [me] a lot of the time at first. They're just like, 'Okay, you're just saying that.' So you do have to continue to go back to that and prove it. But that doesn't always take as long as you would think it would, especially when you're consistent and you're authentic in wanting to get to know people."

Ultimately, Megan believes this authenticity and consistency exists in the "shared source of inspiration"—the child. Whereas before parents may have viewed her appeals as her simply trying to gain their support for her teaching agenda, she hopes that now they view their aspirations as similar to hers. She explains, "When I call a parent and ask for their help, they know that I am asking because I have really done everything that I can do and now I am asking for their support in stepping in."

In reflecting on that first day of kindergarten for Asia two years ago, Megan realizes that Carlene's hope for a smooth transition became her own concern that morning as well. As Carlene did her best in preparing Asia for school that morning—making sure she was well fed, was nicely dressed, had her school materials ready, and felt a sense of support—Megan did her part by choosing a good book, planning a warm welcome and tour around the room, and keeping an eye out for them that morning. Their shared source of inspiration was Asia, and the two women had just begun to work together to support her.

SEEING EACH OTHER DIFFERENTLY

During the first summer that Stanton partnered with the Flamboyan Foundation, teachers and staff conducted over two hundred home visits. The experience was positive, and teachers began the new school year with feelings of excitement and uncertainty. The home visits cultivated teacher-parent relationships in the community, but what would happen when everyone returned to school?

After a few weeks, Stanton held its annual back-to-school night for families. Melissa Bryant recalls the dread she felt when that day approached. In the first year of the turnaround, fewer than thirty family members attended, and the evening was riddled with arguments and complaints from the community about teachers and new school policies. That experience was etched on the minds of teachers as they prepared for the evening a year later. They hoped for a slightly larger crowd because of the positive experience with home visits over the summer. They put out fifty chairs and awaited the families' arrival. Thirty minutes before the start of the program, those fifty chairs had filled up and teachers began to bring out another set of fifty chairs. At 5:30 p.m. when the program started, all two hundred chairs had been put out. Teachers gave up their seats to parents, and the room was filled with a standing-room-only crowd. Melissa recalls the awe that teachers felt. As the program began, the teachers were unsure what would happen. Why were all these parents here? She recalls, "We're looking at each other like, 'Man, something's about to go,' because, you know, when it first gets good, you don't believe. You don't believe."

But something good did happen that evening. More than two hundred family members came to listen to what the Stanton staff had to share about the upcoming school year. When ringtones went off, they were silenced. Crying babies were hushed. Parents wanted to hear what the principal, Caroline John, had to say. She started the evening by welcoming families, talking about their expectations as a staff, and introducing classroom teachers. When the communitywide program concluded, families left for their children's classrooms where they were greeted by teachers they had met over the summer. The mood was light and parents seemed happy to be there. It was obvious to Melissa that evening that "they wanted to be at the school."

Seeing Families Differently

What happened during that first month of school? How did the relationships created over the summer generate such a positive reaction from families? How could a school broken down from distrust and antagonism begin healing so quickly? Melissa recalls thinking, "Could this really be working?"

During Megan's first year at Stanton, she was puzzled at how unresponsive parents were about their child's classroom behavior. At the time, she couldn't imagine why they were so disinterested. Once she began getting to know them, however, she understood their actions differently:

> That really changed the way that I saw parents because they really did care about behavior, they really did care about all of the things that I cared about; they just did not really care about me until they got to know me. And I think that makes sense. I was kind of on a little bit of a high horse—I want all these amazing things for your kid and I am working so hard, super-long days, and how can you not see how hard I am working? But when I step back and think of it from their perspective, I can see how it would probably look like I am just asking them to do my job for me. I am asking them to manage their kid's behavior, I am asking them to do their kid's homework, I am asking them to read at home with their kid. They had no idea what I was doing in the classroom.

She began to see the network of adults who cared for a child, the relationships they had with siblings, the jobs their parents were managing, and the great lengths they would take to talk with her outside of school. Each family, as she got to know them, presented a different set of experiences that she would adapt to. She knew that Raquel would have difficulty getting to school events with seven children and no reliable transportation. This meant that Megan would try to hold parent meetings with Raquel on alternative days so that she could attend parent meetings for her other children. For Raquel, these adjustments were meaningful: "For her to know my family size and the obstacles that I overcome daily, just being a single mom and having the highest expectations for my children, she knew that being there for my kids in the school was important to me. She did whatever she could to help make that happen."

Megan also learned that parents held teachers in high esteem, because education was a core value in their families and communities. She remembers her surprise when she learned that parents may have disengaged from her because they were nervous or intimated by their child's teacher. "It literally never occurred to me that parents would see me in that way." Because she experienced her own nervousness and anxiety about meeting parents' expectations of her, this became a point of connection.

Seeing Teachers Differently

Home visits not only allow teachers to gain new perspectives into families and communities, they also allow parents to see a more human side of their child's teacher. As a young white middle-class teacher, Megan often found that her students' families did not always know how to connect with her initially.

Carlene admits that early on, she didn't think she had much in common with teachers. They seemed inaccessible to her, so she would come in and out of the school briefly with Asia each morning and afternoon. After they got to know each other, Megan invited Carlene to come in and help Asia get settled or to stay for a moment and catch up. Carlene felt welcomed by this gesture.

Some parents have had experiences in their past as students that reinforce this idea that teachers are uncaring or inaccessible. I first met Jason, whose son is in Megan's class, during a classroom presentation for families. He described to me how much he learns about Megan as a teacher by being able to see her interact with his son and other students in the class. "It's not just by her telling us who she is, but that I get to see what kind of person she is when she's in the classroom and the families are there to be a part of it." As a student, Jason never felt a connection to his teachers; they seemed disinterested in their jobs and dismissive toward students. He never interacted with them much outside of class, so this is one of the first times he has "gotten to know a teacher as a person, not just an authority." To him, "it makes a difference when you can make that connection." Similarly, Carlene sees teachers in a different light now: "Teachers are just normal people. They're here for the same reason that parents are here for . . . They love the kids like they're their own. They care for our kids and they want them to get a good education too and to grow up to be a teacher or a lawyer or a doctor or whatever they want to be."

According to Raquel, when teachers and parents see each other as equals and partners, "that starts to open the lines of communication and build that bond." Without that communication and bond, teachers support students without regard for their families and the full lives they live outside of schools. This leads Megan to ask, "If I don't know about a student's life outside of school—with their families, the communities they are part of—what exactly do I know? It is such an incomplete picture that I have to admit I'm not doing justice to that child."

MOVING FROM RELATIONSHIPS TO COLLABORATION

One afternoon in February, thirty-three first-grade parents are seated together at cafeteria tables in the school's multipurpose room. They are learning how to decode multisyllabic words the very same way their children would in class. Together, they are reciting the students' "Chunky Monkey Rap," which reminds them to sound out the "chunks" in multisyllabic words. Parents laugh together through the recitation of the rhyme and as they work in small groups to follow the instructions and mark the smaller pieces of a multisyllabic word. Megan and two other first-grade teachers walk around the room. They stop to answer questions, settle light-hearted disputes among parents, and sit down to check in with a small group of parents. The atmosphere is light and informal; everyone is having a good time.

This is the second of three Academic Parent Teacher Team (APTT) meetings. Spread out over the academic year, the APTT meetings are a clever redesign of the parent-teacher conference. While parent-teacher conferences can be short informational conversations during which the teacher does most of the talking and the parent does most of the listening, the APTT meeting is designed to be informative, interactive, and engaging.

At Stanton, grade-level teams plan the content of APTT meetings. At times, parents across grade-level classes are invited to a session run by the team; other times, the sessions are smaller and conducted in individual classrooms. The ninety-minute sessions focus on a few academic concepts that students are working on in the classroom. Teachers lead parents into activities—similar to the ones their children would use in class—that illustrate those concepts and develop academic skills. The sessions are interactive, often asking parents to work in pairs or small groups to solve a set of problems or practice a skill or concept. These activities and materials are given to parents to use at home with their children.

On this particular day, teachers gave parents worksheets to be used inside sheet protectors and with erasable crayons. The materials were designed to encourage home use in busy working families. By practicing the activity with other parents, they became familiar enough with the concepts to understand the instructional goals and to continue the activity with their children at home. In each APTT session, teachers describe the overall goals of the class but also prepare individualized data on each student to help parents understand how their child performs in relation to peers. Parents and teachers set a goal for their child on that skill and the activities are designed to support and encourage development of the skill at home. When parents review the materials prepared for their child, teachers walk around to discuss the data, answer questions, and help set goals for the next sixty days.

Since this is the third year of the schoolwide program and the second APTT meeting of the academic year, many parents are familiar with the process. Megan sits down with a parent who reviews her child's data, and they are both overjoyed at the progress her son has made in reading. "All that reading you've done together at home has really paid off!" Megan proclaims with a warm hug. The mother explains that for too long, they had been taking out books from the library that were too difficult for her son to read, and the books that Megan has been sending home are helping: "When you started sending those little books home and I realized that was what he needed, it became so much easier to help him with his reading."

Across the room, every conversation I overhear reflects very specific points of knowledge about a child's academic progress. Megan and her students' families have been tracking growth, discussing challenges, and exploring solutions together. These are not general conversations of progress or development. They are discussions about book titles, Fountas & Pinnell (F&P) reading levels, journal writing, new reading interests, the need for new math games to replace ones that have gotten tiresome, new home space devoted to homework, and scores on last week's assessments.

The APTT model was developed by WestEd researcher Maria Paredes in 2000 to foster interactions between parents and teachers centered on collaboratively supporting students' academic goals. The model sought to develop working relationships between teachers and families while also encouraging social interactions among parents. When developing its comprehensive family engagement strategy, the Flamboyan Foundation thought the APTT model would dovetail successfully with the home visit program. For this, too, the organization provides support through facilitated trainings, coaches, and professional development and scaffolding as teachers plan their sessions.

While the home visit creates a personal relationship and connection between the teacher and the family, the APTT meetings, according to Megan, "help us move into a yearlong conversation about supporting the child academically." Through her experiences with the APTT model, she has come to view parents as "experts on what their children need to be able to do in school": "I have high expectations and hopes for what my students accomplish in that year they have with me, but I couldn't make it happen without the collaboration I have with their parents. Over the years, parents have come to expect APTT meetings, and it has led to years and years of parents becoming experts on what their children need to be able to do in school."

She works closely with parents between APTT meetings to discuss how the children are developing at home and in the classroom. There is room to discuss discrepancies between what they see; there is cause for celebration when children make progress; there are conversations about the books that children check out at the library.

It is easy for parents who want to support a child's learning to struggle with the details of that support at home. Megan described the challenges specific to families with beginning readers because it is difficult to know, during a visit to the public library, which books are appropriate for a child. While teachers have a clear sense of a child's exact reading, that does not translate clearly into the volumes of books a parent and child will encounter on a library bookshelf. This is a rich two-way dialogue, not a didactic informational session.

COLLABORATION THAT SUPPORTS STUDENTS AND FAMILIES

One of Megan's most consistent desires in engaging families is to develop and maintain "open lines of communication." It's a phrase that comes up frequently in our conversation. It is essential to the two-way dialogue that she wants to promote with parents. For this reason, Megan chooses, from the very first home visit, to share her personal phone number with families. School phone lines are infamously ineffective in delivering messages to busy teachers. Similarly, busy parents may not be able to easily answer a daytime phone call for a conversation. As a result, Megan and many of her families choose to share mobile phone numbers and text each other at convenient times throughout the day. While some teachers may feel that they need to create distance between their personal and professional lives, this form of communication allows Megan to have an element of control over how and when she receives messages and calls from parents: "Texting really is the most common way for me to talk with parents throughout the year. And that is also because by the time I get home, I don't really want to talk on the phone . . . I will do quick calls to parents if I really need to . . . Texting was a great way for me to start bridging that gap between me and families and then sharing data once parents are really invested."

One afternoon as we sit down to talk about this, Megan shows me her phone and scrolls through the text messages. I see listing after listing of parents, grandparents, and family members that she communicates with regularly. As she opens an entry, I see a long-running thread of communication that includes questions about an assignment, updates about a child's day, pictures from a field trip, as well as kind and simple queries about the family. The messages and photos are endearing, but most importantly, parents have an open line of communication with her.

I must admit, as a mother of two children, I feel a tinge of jealousy as I scroll through Megan's text messages with students' parents and caregivers. Never having had interactions like this with my children's teachers, I wondered what it would feel like to receive these updates and reassurances as a parent. Indeed, I would understand this more clearly the following year with my son's teacher, Tracy, a young energetic woman who, like Megan, openly embraced the idea of communicating well and frequently with families. When Tracy asked us at the parent-teacher conference whether she could give us updates or send questions by text, I was excited at the idea that we could communicate so freely but admittedly wondered if she would follow through. Later that week, a notification from an unknown number popped up on my phone. I opened a text to find a photo of my son, beaming with two classmates as they held up a project they had made together. These windows into classroom life are rare for parents, and I felt a rush of gratitude to Tracy for that shared moment and the many that would follow.

Over the year, Trina has received countless photos, updates, and questions from Megan and has always felt able to contact her. The numerous parents I met in Megan's classroom have similar responses—they schedule times to talk, they receive photos from a field trip, clarify questions about an assignment, and learn about a child's progress. These myriad communications allow Megan to achieve the closeness she experiences with her families.

The ultimate goal of this ongoing communication, according to both Megan and the families I talked to, is the well-being and success of the child. Communication between Megan and students' parents often centers on academic goals and progress. APTT meetings begin a conversation about the instructional program and a child's academic achievement. Parents in Megan's classroom are well versed in reading levels and math outcomes. When a child struggles to meet a reading goal or math homework seems too easy, Megan and the family communicate about that. Trina remembers that when her son Carlton's reading levels improved, Megan noticed that his comprehension skills lagged behind: "She told me that this was normal but that the biggest thing was that we had to work on it together and he will get it." Megan sent home activities and information for Trina to work on with Carlton and encouraged her to talk to him about the books he was reading. These efforts supported the expectations Megan maintained in the classroom and "when there's progress and our work has paid off," Trina explains, "I know [Megan] will be the first to tell me about that."

In a Johns Hopkins evaluation of Flamboyan's Family Engagement Partnership (FEP), researchers found that improving teachers' capacity to engage families can lead to better outcomes for students and teachers.[4] Based on data from twelve elementary schools in DC, including Stanton, that were using the interventions developed by Flamboyan, the study found positive outcomes for students when teachers and families work together. Compared to schools with similar student populations, students in schools supporting systemwide family engagement practices were more likely to be proficient in reading fluency assessments at year's end and more likely to attend school on a regular basis. Significantly, school attendance has been shown to positively influence other student outcomes, such as graduation and later achievement.[5] The study went on to conclude that "these associations between school-level measures of FEP implementation quality and student outcomes suggest that a school's commitment to family engagement benefits all students attending the school, even those who do not directly participate in partnership activities like home visits."[6] These findings run counter to the traditional notion that educators alone will be key drivers to improving the educational outcomes for students. As Megan explains, "working alongside parents pretty much guarantees that I'll have greater success as a teacher. I have learned that I can't do this alone."

ENHANCING THE FULL AND COMPLEX LIVES OF TEACHERS

Megan will admit that one of the great challenges of teaching "is how exhausting and isolating it can be." A relational person, she is someone who relishes connection to others, and she has built a network of colleagues and friends who support her. Her relationships with parents have also been meaningful in this regard: "They are the people I lean on in this work—the same way I would lean on any kind of colleague at school that I am friends with as well. You know, I try not to bring a lot of my work, emotional work, home with me. But I do talk to my parents about [the difficult things that happened at school], the parents I am close to . . . the same way I would to a colleague."

Beyond the partnership in support of each child, parents have become a source of support for Megan through the challenging ups and downs of teaching. When Megan contemplated looping with her students and becoming a first-grade teacher after a dedication to kindergarten teaching, she consulted with a parent. The parent reassured Megan that despite the initial challenges, she would adjust to the new curriculum and dynamics of first grade. When Megan began the school year with thirty-one students on her classroom roster, Trina went to talk to the principal about the possibility of addressing the large classroom sizes. Along with Carlene, she argued that it was too large for a first-grade environment and pushed the principal to address the situation. Carlene made phone calls to the district, and even though the situation remained unchanged, Megan was grateful that "parents were advocating and supporting" her in this way.

Some of these relationships with parents deepen and extend beyond the time the child spends in Megan's classroom. She is invited to birthday parties, supports a family as they transition to another school, keeps in touch with older siblings as younger siblings enter her classroom, and consoles a family experiencing grief and loss. Megan explains:

> So I think I should say first that I've been really fortunate that I've been able to build some strong friendships with some of these women over the past few years—and all of the strong relationships I have with families. Of course, not all of them are friendships; some of

them are just like two adults working really hard and respecting each other, working to make a student grow. And they're great symbiotic relationships where we share and we talk and there's great open lines of positive communication, all those things that you would want. But then there are a handful of parents that I have become extraordinarily close to and I think it's because—I have to say it's not just me. These are parents who, as we've gotten to know each other, they've also opened themselves up to me so that a friendship could build and it comes back to just sharing things together.

Megan knows that skeptics will challenge the amount of time and effort she puts into these relationships with parents: "I get it, there's so much expected of us as teachers, this seems unreasonable to pile on something so significant and time-intensive." While the commitments to home visits and APTT are significant, to Megan the "return on that investment makes it all worthwhile." She may spend a substantial amount of time getting to know families over the summer or at the start of the year, but once those connections are made, those relationships facilitate and support her goals in the classroom: "A student's behavior always improves when they see their parent having a positive interaction with me. So many of my students know that they cannot pit their parent against me because we are on a first-name basis or I can text her right then and she will leave work for me because we have a strong relationship . . . Most importantly, they also believe that we are a united force to help them do their best."

Before she started building these positive relationships with parents, Megan spent considerable time throughout the school year trying to get in touch with parents, having the same repeated conversations about student behavior and missing homework. Melissa Bryant reiterates that teachers who are resistant to putting in that initial investment of time and energy may not realize that their seemingly minimal efforts exact their own toll:

You might be in a class where you have a lot of students who, behaviorally, are not there and they're not doing what you ask them to do, and you spend all your time calling parents trying to figure out how to do it, so you feel exhausted trying to find his mom . . . I don't have these problems, so while I put my energy and a lot of time into the other things, I spend no energy doing some of the other things where teachers constantly find themselves putting energy in.

Ultimately, "it is not an option anymore to leave parents out of the picture," according to Megan. Beyond the assumption that families are a valuable part of a child's life and essential to understanding the whole child, Megan believes her connection to parents gives her a fuller sense of purpose as a teacher. She explains, "I think it makes my job a lot easier because listening, having them hear my problems, or having them hear me out on something really makes me feel validated." This sense of fulfillment through her relationships with families also contributes to her long-term commitment to teaching: "I think it is also the reason why I've stayed in the classroom this long. If, for some reason, you said I couldn't talk to families anymore, I don't think I could do this anymore. I feel so loyal to this community because I have built such strong bonds to these families."

A NECESSARY CHANGE

When Stanton teachers began their family engagement plan at the end of a dramatically disappointing first year after the school turnaround, few were convinced that their relationship with families would lead to the school transformation that unfolded. If anything, teachers felt helpless and frustrated, turning to Flamboyan out of sheer desperation. Like many other educators, they believed the level of parent participation in a school reflected the values and commitment of families. With low turnout at family events and great animosity between teachers and families, certainly it seemed that students' families were the core problem. At the same time, teachers and administrators began to feel that their success would be achieved without families, possibly even in spite of them.

Teachers and administrators at Stanton, like Megan, feel differently now. Rena Johnson, the new principal of Stanton, believes the focus on family engagement goes hand in hand with the school's desire to be successful: "We can't do anything without families, we cannot do this work without families, we cannot educate students and put them on the path to college without incorporating families in that process. We only have our kids between five and seven years, depending on when they join us, and because our population is so transient, we have to make sure that we are incorporating families in our overall vision for their students."

Similarly, Megan believes, despite all the effort that educators may put into improving outcomes for students, "you are not going to be fully successful unless you have a relationship with your families." Ironically, this is the area in which teachers are least likely to be prepared "in spite of all the preparation [they] have on developing lesson plans, understanding learning and development, and managing behavior." Megan believes teacher preparation programs should emphasize the skills and dispositions for effective family engagement: "If you don't know how to talk to a parent and start that relationship to work together and see the way to improvement together, you will not be successful."

Susan Stevenson of Flamboyan believes Stanton's opening for success occurred when the staff developed robust ties to families: "They had everything else in place. They had good teachers, a good strong leader, they had discipline procedures and they had all the building blocks, but none of it was working because the parents were against them. And they felt that once they got the parents on their side, it was all able to work." Deputy Director Helen Westmoreland explains that the organization looks for partners who are "willing and capable." Success in engaging families requires key elements to be in place:

> Our approach has been to work with the coalition of the willing and capable—"capable" has increasingly been defined as schools that have those four other building blocks—leadership, strong teachers, strong curriculum and instructional practice, and strong school culture and discipline—in place. And then family engagement is the additional lever that makes the most out of those four ingredients and can send the school on a positive trajectory.

For Megan and Raquel, this is not just about changing a school environment for the better. As each woman will attest, their relationship has transformed them individually. Raquel sees herself as a change agent and advocate in her children's lives. No matter the challenges, she understands how to support Dion's education. She has learned how to talk to her children's teachers about her dreams and expectations for them. She understands how to monitor Dion's progress and engage her with learning activities at home. Megan's beliefs about children and their families likewise have deepened and changed through the relationships built with parents over the years. While the demands of teaching in an urban school are high, she draws inspiration and support from the parents she works with. She is now more effective in the classroom because students understand she works alongside their families and she accomplishes her goals with the support of parents. There's a sense of contentment and happiness that she did not possess before.

Two years after I met them in Megan's classroom, I watch these two women in front of a group of teachers and administrators one late afternoon. I know their commitment to family engagement is bigger than one school improvement plan. They are working with Flamboyan staff to train a group of educators from a new partner school. This is one of the first training sessions that school staff participate in, and the focus of today's session is home visits. A trainer has walked the educators through the home visit protocol and process, and now teachers and administrators listen to Megan and Raquel's stories of new bonds made through home visits. Like Megan years ago, they seem skeptical of what these visits will accomplish and have many questions. With only three days left in the school year, Raquel's relationship with Megan weighs heavily on her mind, because she has recently decided to send Dion to another school to join her brother, who is autistic. Raquel explains just what her relationship with Megan has meant to her. "Throughout this year, Ms. Lucas really touched my heart. I am a mother of seven kids who go to schools throughout DCPS. Being a parent and finding my way through the different schools is a real challenge." Megan looks to her as if she knows what will come next, and Raquel starts to tear up:

I have a child with special needs and kids who are preschool age, elementary, middle, and now one going to high school. I spend a lot of my time trying to find a school that fits my kids. I have been through a lot of schools in DCPS; many of them have made me get complacent with teachers. But then to find a teacher like Ms. Lucas who really cares about my kids—when she came into my home that first time for the home visit, she got to know my child and my family. And to be honest, I was curious about her too. We were both apprehensive.

As Raquel starts to cry, she says, "I'm the toughest woman in the world, but I feel so strongly about this. Not only is she my child's teacher, she is my sister and my friend. I don't know what we are gonna do without her." At that moment, when Megan gives her a hug and the room grows silent, I remember what Megan said to me earlier that day, "These families have changed my life. *I don't know what I would do without them.*"

3

CINTHIA COLÓN
Remembering Roots

Grabbing a book from her desk, Cinthia Colón hops up on a stool in the front of her classroom. She has dark hair in tight round curls that are neatly pulled back into a high bun. With dark wide glasses that frame her face and a scarf complementing her t-shirt, blazer, skinny jeans, and Converse low-tops, it is hard to disagree with a group of girls in her class who exclaim, "Ms. Colón is the coolest teacher!" She is dressed up yet casual, sleek yet approachable. Once they hear her calm, nearly hushed voice, the class moves from bustling activity to a quiet hum and then to silence. I am impressed but not at all surprised. This is Ms. Colón's seventh year as a teacher at the Young Achievers Science and Mathematics Pilot School. She is known by students, families, and colleagues alike to be kind, caring, and fun, but everyone knows she also does not mess around.

At Cinthia's prompting, the students begin to shift their seats to face the front of the room for a period of read-aloud. I am prompted to think that this will be a relaxed, low-key experience where students put their heads on their desks and listen passively. I am wrong. The book, *Second Daughter: The Story of a Slave Girl* by Mildred Pitts Walter, is one they have been reading since the beginning of the week and is based on the true story of Mum Bett, or Elizabeth Freeman, an enslaved woman who sued her owner in 1781 for her freedom. The book details not only the cruel atrocity of slavery but also the jarring contradictions of Revolutionary rhetoric about liberty amidst a time of legalized slavery. There are no students with heads down on their desk, no idle doodling.

Students are alert. Interspersed throughout the reading are illustrative teaching moments: Cinthia peppers students with questions such as, "What's the tone in the story right now? How is the author making us feel about this situation? What can we infer from the text? What's the big picture?" Cinthia wants deep and detailed discussion, so she probes for more: "What do you mean by that? Good, yes, but give me an example?" The text is challenging and the substance is intense; it's not easy for everyone to understand, but they are all trying to stay with her.

At the conclusion of the day's reading, Cinthia closes the book in her lap and takes a moment to look squarely at the group:

> Okay, listen, this is really important. This is really about the meaning of freedom. Can we really be fighting for freedom when some people aren't free? I really need you to focus with us, because this is what it means to read and absorb the story. There are the smaller things that are happening and yes, we need to keep track of that, but there is a big message here that, if we understand it, really makes us readers and thinkers. And that's what we're trying to do here, so that one day, you are going to be able to soak up all the stories and history around us.

CONNECTION AND A SENSE OF BELONGING

Like other moments I notice in Cinthia's classroom, this moment is one that echoes her own story. Cinthia Colón was born in the Dominican Republic, and when she was one year old, she, her parents, and her two older brothers "landed in Queens," joining others in her extended family. She has "too many memories" of schools being places where she was "quietly expected to fail or just ignored." In second grade, a teacher's words left a deep impression on her: "I remember my second-grade teacher saying 'you can't read,' and that made me cry. That's why I remember it, because it was hard to hear that from her—just making that statement about my ability to read. I guess I wasn't reading well enough for her and that was just the way it was going to be. I remember that exact moment." Then, in fifth grade, as students took turns reading aloud in her reading group, she noticed that while other students read with fluency and appropriate tone, she found herself, in comparison, "reading like a robot." No one talked to her about it; it hardly seemed to draw the teacher's notice, but Cinthia went home and began to read newspaper articles, magazine ads—whatever she could get her hands on. She read the paragraphs out loud and silently to herself, practicing her fluency again and again until she was satisfied with what she heard.

There were also teachers—though small in number—who supported her. There was a high school history teacher who asked her to join the yearbook club, because he sensed her isolation in the school. She recalls an "amazing" eighth-grade history teacher—one of the first and only people of color she had as a teacher. A "really mean" high school English teacher taught her how to read a book—to "really read, enjoy, and read a book." As she reflects on it now, it is astounding that it took so long for someone to "show me how important the love you have for literature can be."

But more often than not, Cinthia recalls a childhood in the United States that left her feeling that her home and school were distant and foreign. When she and her family arrived, they spoke only Spanish. Her brothers had attended school in the Dominican Republic, and while she was young when they arrived, she remembers that school "was a hard system to figure out," especially for her oldest brother. She recalls the hardships and her own amazement that they made it:

> And there were many times when my brothers and I probably could have steered in the wrong direction in our life, because things were not easy. My parents were always working, and so they were not as involved as my parents I have now in my own classroom. Not knowing the language was hard; I had to sort of fend for them many times, which kind of helped me get a little bit of grit and figure things out. But even with all the obstacles—financially and [with] moving all the time—we still made it. There was something about how my brothers and I navigated it without all that much support.

Cinthia also affirms how central her parents' love and support was. While they were not keenly aware of the specifics of the school culture and expectations, "they were always constantly working and never

ever spoke about how 'this is too hard' or 'we can't do this.' " From this determined "work ethic" came a sense of optimism and hope that fueled her: "I never heard negative language. I never had conversations in a household that revolved around what we can't do, what I can't do. I knew it was hard for my parents, but I saw them work through that for us. And even when I might be struggling, they always had the greatest faith that I could do anything." While the struggle to become integrated was real and her family became a source of hope and strength, Cinthia also recalls the tight-knit community that her family was part of. Whether it was extended family or Dominican neighbors and friends, there was always help and support nearby, and her parents were centrally involved:

> Somehow things are happening where whatever you need, your friends, your family, your neighborhood takes care of you. If you need food, there's food. If you need a ride somewhere, then my dad will figure out how to get a car from his buddy, or his buddy would give you a lift and it would work out . . . It was never like, "Well, I have this, so I'm just going to make sure I do this for myself." There was always a sense that my parents would be willing to help out, because the community was so important to us.

Cinthia's family, like many immigrant families, while simultaneously feeling disconnected to the broader society, had the intimate, resource-rich, and important connections that nourish and sustain individuals and families. Cinthia believes, however, that educators often fail to see the richness of these communities:

> Growing up in a place where you needed to depend on your neighbors and you needed to depend on family, that's always been a part of my life. But my teachers never saw that, and I think most teachers miss how rich and resilient our communities are. They see their students through such a narrow perspective—as someone who can't speak the language, can't read out loud with fluency. They are only seeing such a small part of our larger lives.

This leads to challenges in communication and general misunderstanding between schools and families, particularly when there are few meaningful opportunities for connection. While Cinthia's parents were loving and supportive and "provided everything we needed," they did not speak English and "were not really aware of the systems of how school worked and were not involved in that way." Even so, the schools she attended had few, if any, opportunities for families to be a presence in the building: "When school was done, like when the bell rang, everyone emptied out from the school. You had kids lined up in uniforms on the street, and buses would load them up or parents would be picking them up. But that was it—no parents in the school." As Cinthia recalls, there was no parent outreach, no programs for schools to provide information to families. The parent-teacher conference was the one connection each year between her family and her teachers; every year, she would attend with her mother to translate the conversation. And in those moments of conversation, she recalls very little of substance was communicated: "I don't ever remember my mom or any teacher interacting besides the very basic, 'She is doing fine; here is her report card. She talks a little bit too much sometimes in the back, but she is fine. Let me know if you have questions.' And then it's over."

"It's a Blur": Developing a Sense of Belonging in a Climate of Exclusion

What are the effects on children when school and family are, as in Cinthia's account, distant and estranged? For Cinthia, particularly in the elementary school years, when her linguistic and cultural fluency was forming and evolving, she remembers little:

I started school in New York, and my mom tells me that I went to day care, but I don't remember that at all. And then I went to a school . . . in Queens, and my brothers had gone there for a little bit. The thing with [this school] is that I only remember the schoolyard, my first day of kindergarten, and one first-grade teacher. I remember her strictly because I think I was learning how to read in first grade, and it was hard. She kind of helped me, she gave me a little bit of support, but I don't remember all of her. And then second [grade], third [grade], I don't remember much at all, all the way to fourth [grade]. So my entire elementary life was a blur.

This is disappointing, because she feels those years should be "the most memorable part of your life as a kid." In fact, her friends can "memorize all their teachers' names, and I can honestly not even remember their faces, [much] less their names." When I ask her to tell me why she thinks this is, she explains that it must be the lack of connection:

> When I think back on my childhood, I can tell you what was happening in my life, at home, and what I was interested in, but when it comes to school, there was just no sense of connection there. In your lifetime, you must have at least thirty adults from kindergarten to high school who could know you, and then in high school, you have at least four for each grade, so we're talking, at the very minimum, thirty to forty adults who could shape and mold you. You could remember amazing things about that time in your life, and I don't. It doesn't make me sad. It just makes me realize that I have no memory of that time in school, because I wasn't connected in any real way to anyone.

She explains that this realization—and her refusal to accept that as a reality for children like her—"totally just changed my world." It was one of the driving forces of her decision to become an elementary school teacher and has shaped the kind of teacher she has become: "Looking back, as a kid, I can't live like this. I shouldn't live like this. And I knew, when I was older and I looked back into this emptiness, this blur, I knew that I can't live like this and the kids I am going to teach cannot live like this."

Numerous studies have documented the phenomenon that schools and families may be "worlds apart" and that educators should seek to bridge the two disparate worlds.[1] Whether this distance is caused by differences in language, culture, or social class, or exacerbated by contrasting definitions of parent roles and family involvement, there is a recognition that schools and families can be in conflict.[2] Routinely, schools rely on parent education programs and supplemental outreach to create connections, but these programs are often focused on "fixing" families and teaching parents to adhere to the school's expectations.[3] Students are often asked to be cultural bridges between home and school, or at the very least, expected to engage in cultural brokering.[4] Cinthia's story shows us that it is often the school, not the family, that needs fixing and that teachers should also be on the frontlines of this transformative work:

> Part of my growing process—both with my parents and then seeing my brothers navigate this—was understanding how to play this game, this idea of power language in code-switching. I picked that up by the time I was nine years old. I knew this is how people speak who are here, and this is how I need to talk when I am here. I figured that out, I saw it . . . I knew the schools were not going to try to figure out my family or where I was from. It was a different world there and I knew that if I wanted to do well, I had to learn how to adapt, and in some ways, be the person they expected me to be. But this is absolutely not what I want for my students and their families. It took me all these years to realize that where we needed the most adapting and adjusting was in the schools themselves.

"MY STORY SHAPES MY TEACHING": LEARNING FROM TEACHERS OF COLOR

It is clear that many aspects of Cinthia's childhood and education color her motivations and goals as a teacher. As with her white friends who have fond memories of their childhood schools, Cinthia wants her students—of all backgrounds—to feel they have a connection to her and to their classmates. "I want them to remember moments of joy, the times they struggled and persevered, and the support they had from others in our community. These memories will make them feel fully seen and recognized, and their peers and teachers will make an imprint on their lives," she explains. Cinthia's experiences as a woman of color and a Dominican immigrant have powerfully shaped her motivations to teach, her aspirations for her students, and her relationships with their families.

Becoming a Teacher

In college, Cinthia knew that she wanted to remain connected to her community and support what she saw as some of the key needs. She also understood the tremendous influence that her family and community had in supporting her throughout her education. Many of her peers and friends encountered challenges:

> I saw drugs; I saw violence; I saw shootings; I saw it all, right at my doorstep, like in my building, it was there, and I used to think, why? Why didn't my brothers get involved in this? Why didn't I get involved? It was such an easy thing to do, right? Of course, I think my parents were key, because really those are the only people we had to guide us, and then the outside world. And so, I was like, "You know what? I want to be that for people, because I know that you can really take a bad turn, and it's not really your fault. It's just your environment, and it's what's there and what you see as the opportunity in front of you, and I want to help out."

Motivated by this reality, Cinthia aspired to work in the criminal justice system, but after working in various positions as an undergrad and after college, she became disappointed with the kind of impact she was having. She wanted to make a difference earlier in children's lives and discovered teaching as a path to achieving that.

She came to realize that one of the key sources of support for her was her community: her parents, her extended family, and other adults in the Dominican community. But she also saw the tremendous potential of schools to be spaces that could nurture and support young people like her and her brothers. Beyond the "academic knowledge" of schools, Cinthia also felt that it was important for young people to understand the world around them. Paulo Freire (1970) identifies this dual purpose as learning how to "read the word" and "read the world":[5]

> No one ever told me the truth until I sort of figured it out when I was eighteen, and I was like, "Why didn't someone talk to me honestly about how the systems work and why I am in the position I am in?" If I had this knowledge about the world by the time I was ten, I would have navigated this world completely differently and been so much more aware of the moves that I have to make. Being successful in life is in some ways like a game, you know, but someone has to help you see how the rules of that game work.

The rules of the game, for Cinthia, are what Lisa Delpit calls the "culture of power"—the often unspoken systems of power and privilege that enable white students and their families to become successful in society.[6] As Cinthia considered the next part of her professional journey, she came to the sudden realization that to help youth of color become successful, she could "become a teacher who brought knowledge about disciplines and knowledge about the world" into her classroom and into their lives.

Beyond the understanding she sought to bring to her students—a critical perspective of the world around them—she felt it was important for students of color and immigrant students to feel a sense of connection to her as well. As she explains, "It's the sole reason why I chose this path to teach, because growing up like they did, I didn't see myself in my teachers at all." Having had so few teachers of color herself yet remembering the deep impact they had on her, she felt it was "important for students—no matter who you are or what your experience or background is—to see yourself in your teachers, the adults who you see as your role models." Cinthia explains:

> It's just really important for them to hear my story, because for a lot of kids, they feel as if the teacher is like this magical person and that I'm not human. I feel that I have to make it real for them, but I also have to show them that I can understand how they're growing up. I think it's important for them to know that in some ways, I grew up like this. My story may not be exactly like yours, because we're all a little different. There have been tough times in my family just like you have tough times, and you have to persevere through them, but I can try my best to understand you and make you feel heard.

Promoting a New View of Students and Their Families

What Cinthia wants for her students is rooted, in part, by what she felt was missing in her own K–12 education:

> So I don't want students to come in my room and think that they have to just sit in their own world the way I did when I was younger. It's awful. I want them to open up and realize that they can contrib-

ute, that they are allowed to have a conversation about what they are seeing, feeling, and that we all want to see each other as whole people, on a more personal level. Your hopes and dreams, your fears, your families, how we feel about each other, how we are treating the woman in the cafeteria, all of that.

She believes that in urban schools, especially in schools that educate students of color, there is an expectation that students must learn to follow and to adhere to strict rules and demands. This is motivated primarily by educators' beliefs that "these students must be controlled in order to be successful." As a result, "student voice and agency—these things that must be taught and supported" are lost among a school's priorities:

> I feel like sometimes kids aren't allowed to voice what they're feeling or thinking. It's just "Line up, come to the rug. This is your spot [on the rug]." We want students to conform to schools, how we define school, and we don't often give them space to tell us what's on their minds. This is why I'm big on this idea that when you go forth out into society, you do not have assigned seats. I walk into a place and I immediately start to be a responsible citizen.

Student voice and agency is an important life skill that must be nurtured and encouraged in schools, and Cinthia believes it is critical to a student's sense of independence and autonomy in the world. If students are consistently instructed to follow directions and do what the school determines is best for them, it will be difficult for them to have ownership of "all the little decisions that we make in everyday life."

Nurturing students' sense of self and connection in the world is, for Cinthia, "a part of how we begin to see students more fully." This is what drives her view that family engagement is essential:

> I think that so many times, we see students in these really limited ways—how do we get them to do well on these assessments, reach a certain level of proficiency, stay on their spot on the rug. All of that becomes our emphasis, and we don't see them as full human beings. They have questions about the world, they want to know about each other, and they are part of these rich communities that we of-

ten know nothing about, and they are part of these families that we see in this limited way of "What can you do for us; why are you not helping this child be better?" Did we even ask you what you know and love about your child?

These incomplete views of students are common practice, as educators focus primarily on children as academic learners, and more recently, through the lens of social and emotional development. Even so, the inquiry into youth is bound by the school building's walls and there is little curiosity about children's families or communities. This lack of curiosity and knowledge is treacherously coupled with an abundance of assumptions and prejudice toward families and communities, particularly in urban schools and communities of color. Cinthia's own experience as a student reflects this pattern. She understands the rich tapestry of experience that is embedded in family and community: "If I think about how important my family was to me and how they shaped who I am today and every minute of my growing up, it is impossible for me to think that I can educate these kids without knowing their families. How would I do that? It seems so incomplete, and beyond that, it's a recognition that we are satisfied only knowing part of the picture."

Through her connection with students' families, she has come to see them as "big supporters of their children, partners in this work together, clear windows into seeing their children more fully." What she sees of students, particularly in the early part of the school year when she is "still figuring them out," is often complemented by the "stories and windows into the kid that parents share." These early connections with families are important, because as Cinthia explains, "I can get to an awareness of a student so much earlier in the year if I'm in conversation with their family."

But while meaningful conversation and communication with families are essential to her practice as a teacher, they're not enough. Cinthia also believes that parents should be present in the school and in the classroom, because it allows students to see the adults in their lives—parents and teachers—in similar ways: "There's something warm about having a parent in the classroom, and I think [students] seeing me interact with their parents in a certain way helps them kind of understand that I am not the end-all-be-all for knowledge, and that we work together. That there isn't this separation or hierarchy between the adults who support you in school and the adults who support you at home." Cinthia finds ways to have parents become a presence and resource in the classroom, whether they are working with a small group on math problems, organizing the classroom, or just being part of the classroom experience. For Janet, whose son Trey is in Cinthia's classroom, this was new: "I've never been in any other teacher's classroom before, and Ms. Colón is the only teacher who allows me to do that. The school is usually just getting [parents] in there when they have some kind of showcase or something. I was surprised when she told us that we were welcome to be in the classroom or help out, and she was just so open about it too—like, 'Anytime you are free, just come.'"

Although Janet works full-time, she has some flexibility in her schedule on Wednesdays, so she spends a couple hours in Cinthia's classroom "helping out and getting a feel for the classroom community." She describes the first time she was in the classroom:

> [Cinthia] invites me in here and said, "Come in and see what's going on," and then on Wednesday morning, I wasn't working, I just come and sit and see how she's talking to the kids, how she's teaching, how she's doing everything. I just went in, sit, see how everything was going. I just stayed in the back, and she do her thing. I just came, and I was just her assistant. I was just there to mainly pay attention, to see what Trey was doing and stuff, but it was good, because I came and I learned so much more than that.

This experience also allowed Janet to get a sense of Cinthia as a teacher and as a person. This was important to her, because "these teachers spend more time with my kids than we do." Prior to her experience with Cinthia and at other schools, she felt there was "a wall" that kept parents at a distance, and it was difficult to get more than a superficial understanding of them. As she spent time in Trey's classroom, though, she began to develop a deeper sense of Cinthia: "It was good, because you see what she does; you know she's a good person. It is easy to see teachers for their faults, and maybe you just don't trust them or maybe you don't know them at all. But to go in, and really see how she teaches, it was good. I felt like I could see how much she supported all the children, not just Trey. I could really get to know her, and it made me want to support her."

Parental presence in the classroom is not a novel concept, and while Cinthia encourages it, she also believes there are ways families can be more actively engaged in student learning. Particularly in subjects like history, social studies, and humanities, she feels that the experiences of students' families can be an important touchstone. She feels that it is important for students to see their life stories reflected in the curriculum: "I see these families as having rich stories that can help us learn and that can teach us about the bigger issues we study. But more importantly, I think it's important for students to feel as if they are somehow reflected in what we do and learn in school." This year, Cinthia invited family members to come and share their migration stories. She felt that families' experiences with migration in particular would be an important dimension to learning history:

> I decided to have parents and family members come in and share their migration stories. I knew that this makes some of the parents nervous about having to speak in front of the kids, and I could tell that a couple of the parents were very hesitant. But I just wanted the class to learn that the stories of their families were just as important as anything we could read in a book and, in most cases, you will remember those stories and the larger issues we study because they are the stories of your friends' grandparents, parents, and siblings.

When teachers are disconnected from the full lives of students, the only window into the child becomes the academic and social life of the classroom. With this partial and incomplete view, it becomes easier to dehumanize students—to see them solely for the unmet literacy goals, the challenges in math problem-solving, and the distractions they may cause in the classroom.

For immigrant students or students of color like Cinthia as a young girl, this lack of knowing is compounded by an estrangement that can lead to a sense of isolation. As human beings, we long for connection and a sense of belonging; it shapes our experience and forms our memories. We remember those who have made us feel seen and heard. In particular, students' affective relationships with teachers can promote this sense of belonging.[7] Unfortunately, in urban schools and among students of color, lower levels of school connectedness persist.[8] When Cinthia recalls nothing of her school experience, it is most likely because there were so few moments when she felt seen and heard and that she belonged.

Students can feel seen and heard when their families are present in the classroom. When Cinthia invites parents into the classroom to share their stories, she asserts that the cultural literacies and experiences of students' families and communities are central and must be preserved: "So often, we tell kids to come to school and learn this material and then turn your back to the stories of your family. I won't allow that. Those stories belong in here."

"SHE FEELS FAMILIAR TO ME": COMMON GROUND AND SHARED EXPERIENCE BETWEEN TEACHERS OF COLOR AND STUDENTS' FAMILIES

Beverly Bosant has three granddaughters who attend Young Achievers. One day, she enters Cinthia Colón's fifth-grade classroom and takes a seat at the front of the room. She is present on this day to share her story—a story of migration to the United States from her native country of Jamaica. She recalls that experience:

> Well, my granddaughter Jasmine, she asked me, "Mimi, can you come to school and tell my class how you ended up in this country?" . . . And so I came and I told them the story of how I came up to this country. I was thirteen at the time, and I think the kids could relate to me because it was only a little older than them . . . They had a lot of questions for me. They asked me where Jamaica was; they wanted to know the national colors. They wanted to know how I felt as a child coming over here and like I described earlier, it wasn't pleasant, but it opened my eyes, and it allowed me to see a different kind of life, because the life that I had in Jamaica was totally dif-

ferent from the life that I have up here. Here, I was granted more opportunity.

As Beverly shared her migration story, she also shared the trials and challenges she faced—the difficulties in leaving friends and family behind, mixed with the great joy and anticipation of reuniting with her mother, who had left for the United States four years earlier. She described the challenges in school, the language barriers that seemed to confront her at every turn, and the need to be emotionally strong when faced with discrimination and bullying: "Kids can be cruel at times when they don't understand the language barrier and the fact that you are from another country." She also noticed a particular affinity when it came to the other Jamaican students in Cinthia's classroom:

> There were some other students, a couple other students in the class, whose families also migrated here from Jamaica. So now they realize they have this commonality between them, like "Oh, my family is from Jamaica too." So they were able to make that connection as well, because I don't know, before that, how often they spoke about their backgrounds and where they are coming from. It definitely opened up the conversation more knowing we had these common factors, because all of a sudden, these kids are saying, "Well, my grandma came from Jamaica too and we did this and dah-dah-dah and we eat this food and yeah, we eat that curry chicken," and all these other things, so it opened up that dialogue with them where you have this common factor now. And they were excited to know that there were kids with families that are similar to mine in that sense.

Emphasizing Shared Experience and Sense of Belonging

The experience that Beverly, her granddaughter Jasmine, and the Jamaican students in Cinthia's classroom share is an important point of connection. Beverly feels that this invitation to share her story allows Jasmine and her family to feel recognized and appreciated: "I am hoping that my kids and my grandkids and the kids that I talked to in class will see that it is okay to come from another country and to have a different background, to have a different language, to have different cultural beliefs, and still make it and be whatever you want to be." Cinthia understands the value of this connection, the meaning it can hold for students, as she considers the void and lack of shared experience with her own teachers growing up. As she reflects on her relationship with families like Jasmine's, she discusses what it means for students when she shares her story and how it must feel to see themselves in a teacher:

> There's something to be said when you can see yourself in families—although the Jamaican family is not Dominican, we share the islander mentality. We're all from the Islands, so it doesn't matter what country, we're going to connect in this third-world kind of way. There is so much about our families and communities that we don't really have to explain or justify. And to have a teacher who understands and appreciates that side of you, that's important.

She believes that this common experience can make it easier for parents and caregivers to respond to invitations to be involved in the school. While she understands that long work hours are a reality that prevents many families from participating as much as they may like, she also understands that it matters *who* is asking. Families have a view of Cinthia, as a teacher who works with emergent bilinguals in the Sheltered English Immersion (SEI) program, that may feel familiar to them:

> It helps that I'm an SEI teacher, and most of the families are either Dominican or Puerto Rican, because there is just this level of understanding, like your child is exactly how I grew up: Spanish-speaking household, came here to the country either recently, or when they were one, or two, or they were born out there—whatever it was— like, that's my story. Your parents are working tons of hours. The reason they come and see me is because they have a relationship with me. I can communicate with them. I speak Spanish . . . that's part of the reason why they almost *have* to come to the school, because I feel like they can't use excuses like, "Well, I can't communicate with the teacher," [or] "Well, I'm afraid. I feel a little weird coming." "No, you don't. Your kid's teacher is pretty much you—pretty much sounds and looks like you. We're the same people; you're like my mom, you know?"

Janet, Trey's mother, describes this familiarity and the shared experience as immigrants as a point of trust and connection with Cinthia: "She feels familiar to me." She believes that her connection with Cinthia has much to do with what she assumes is a common experience and a shared sense of the values and priorities in their household: "I'm from Jamaica, and Ms. Colón is from [Dominican Republic]. We're not Americans. We are Americans in some ways, but we're not Americans in other ways. I feel comfortable with her. I know that she understands how kids are, and she is familiar with the students. I think she sees a little bit of herself in them, and they feel the same way about her. In a way, you just don't have to explain what we are expecting of our kids."

Trey, an active and energetic young boy, can sometimes need some redirection from his teachers, as is the case with many elementary-school-age students. While Janet doesn't "always feel that teachers understand how to deal with him or maybe don't understand how to work with him," she and Trey have developed a successful working relationship with Cinthia. After "many conversations about Trey—what he has to offer, what he enjoys, and how he needs some structure," she trusts that Cinthia has her son's best interests in mind when she encounters some of his excitement and activity. One morning, Janet received a phone call from Cinthia, who wanted Janet to talk to Trey. He was having some challenges that morning, and she thought a conversation with Mom would help him work things out:

> Trey was having some issues that morning, and with that phone call, she nipped it in the bud, like "we're not playing with him." And that was exactly what he needed that day, and she knew it. And she knew she could call me and we would work together. And that worked, because we had a relationship and an understanding—she knew me and how important it was for Trey to be cooperative, and I knew that everything she told me about Trey was going to be the clear truth.

Building Trust: A Listening Approach

I ask Janet if she was at least mildly frustrated to get a phone call from Cinthia in the middle of her workday. Without hesitation, she responds "no." She explains that there are "multiple layers of trust with Ms. Colón" that have been built over time: "First of all, I trust that she knows what she's doing in the classroom and that she can handle the situation with Trey. She's a good teacher, and she's not calling me because she can't do her job. But the other layer of trust is that I trust her as a person, as someone who knows my son and our family. I can believe her when she tells me that Trey needs a moment with me to regroup." Janet knows that some teachers may use the phone call to a parent as a threat to leverage improved behavior with the child, and this can be, in turn, frustrating for a parent who feels that "teachers should be able to handle what's happening in your classroom." These conversations can also be overshadowed by a tone of condescension or blame. But in the situation with Cinthia, Janet recalls, "I wasn't thinking negative about that call, and I knew it had to be something for Ms. Colón to call me." In fact, Janet feels that Cinthia has "every right" to call her, and this recognition is rooted in trust:

> I am still a mom the whole twenty-four hours, so if Ms. Colón feels the need to call me to tell me—it could have been that Trey was doing something bad, but it could also be, "Why wasn't Trey's homework in today?"—she had the right to call me to talk about that, and that is the kind of relationship me and Ms. Colón have. It's not even a teacher-parent—it's just a person-to-person relationship where she could call me and talk to me, and it would be good for me.

While we often focus on the *kinds* of communication that teachers can have with parents and caregivers in schools, we do not always emphasize the centrality of trust in shaping that communication.[9] The trust that Cinthia and Janet have developed over time allows for their communication to be comfortable, easy, and productive. Janet recalls the many conversations about Trey and her family that shape her sense "that Ms. Colón cares." She explains: "These times we would talk and she would listen, and there was never any judgment and it made me start to feel comfortable with Ms. Colón . . . and sometimes we would talk on a personal level, like, for example, we had a little emergency in November. I have not spoken to nobody about it, and I can just find myself talking to Ms. Colón about these things that I wouldn't open up to others about."

These conversations—where Cinthia listens without judgment or intention—are a critical part of how she seeks to build trusting relationships with her students' families. She does not assume that her background or shared experience as a person of color can stand in for that: "Listen, I think it's so important for students and their families to see someone like me as their teacher, but that doesn't let me off the hook for really working on building that trust and getting to know each other."

She also understands that parents will bring in their own assumptions and negative past experiences in ways that shape their own trust of teachers and their willingness to hear them out: "A lot of parents assume that you will blame them for their child's struggles in schools, so I need to talk to parents and listen to them and let them know that we are going to work together. Parents need to know that you care. If they don't trust you to care, there's no working relationship there."

Too often, teachers center conversations with parents on student grades or academic reports. To Cinthia, this is clearly important and "there's always time for that," but she also believes that conversations can start with questions to parents: "How are you? How are you doing? How's she doing at home? What's new? Anything you'd like to share?" These questions can create a space for parents to share and speak. Too often, Cinthia adds, "as teachers, we are trying to figure out how we can fill that space in the conversation without giving families a chance to offer their insight. It requires a totally different mind-set and purpose to the conversation."

"PARTNERSHIP IS A MIND-SET"

When I ask Cinthia about the values that guide her relationships with families, she explains that it comes down to one central belief: "I truly believe that parents want the best for their children. I don't know how people can believe otherwise. Even if you can't offer it, even if you can't give them everything you want to give them, parents want the best for their kids. No one wants their kid to suffer; no one wants their kid to go to school and be punished because they're bad." She understands that teachers may not always have this view, particularly when they face overwhelming challenges in their classroom. Teaching without the collaboration or partnership with families is a solitary experience, and teachers can get discouraged as a result, which Cinthia believes leads them to question the support and intentions of their students' families. In her mind, this represents a "lack of knowing families": "I hear a lot of teachers who get really down, because they're just dealing with a lot. They start seeing a lot, and they start to ask, 'Why don't these parents care? Why don't they care? Why aren't they doing this?' 'Well, I don't think it's that parents don't care. I think parents do care, so what are you seeing that I'm not, or vice versa?' We are so quick to blame families and see them for what we see as their faults and shortcomings."

This deficit-oriented view of families does not go unnoticed by parents and caregivers. Some parents, like Cinthia's own family, sense a cloak of invisibility; others face more blatant forms of prejudice and hostility from schools. As a result, Cinthia finds that many parents are suspicious of school outreach efforts because they "assume that you will blame them for their child's struggles in school." These struggles—be they academic, social, or emotional—are undoubtedly aggravated and influenced by teachers who have low expectations of children in school.

Within the landscape of family engagement in schools, educators often look for programs and activities that can improve parent participation. What kinds of parent education programs can we create in schools? How do we improve our communication and outreach to immigrant and refugee families? Where and what time of day can we hold our events for families to be more inclusive, inviting, and accessible? How can we encourage parents and caregivers to attend family conferences? While these questions are important, they focus on *what* schools can do without being grounded in the *how* and *why*. As Cinthia explains, partnership with parents and families "is not something you do. It's a mind-set."

This mind-set begins with the belief that parents *do* care for their children and want the best for them, and it guides every interaction she has with families. In my many years as a teacher and researcher in schools, I have experienced the varying ways teachers respond to families, but one scenario is disturbingly common. A student struggles academically—perhaps she's having difficulties in reading. In a large classroom, this child may not get the support she needs to progress or feel successful, and this, in turn, can cause her to act out in the classroom. The teacher becomes frustrated with her behavioral disruptions coupled with the lack of academic progress. Without much knowledge of or interaction with the family, and feeling overwhelmed by the general challenges of teaching, this teacher could act on his assumptions or biases about families instead.[10] There may even be prior negative and painful experiences with families causing him to be suspicious of parents.[11] Add to that the possibility of racial bias and mistrust, and this teacher could blame the student's family for her troubles and begin shutting out the family in order to focus more intently on "improving" the child.

In a rich exploration of successful family engagement strategies, Anne Henderson, Karen Mapp, Vivian Johnson, and Don Davies identified four core beliefs that guided educators who were exemplary family engagement practitioners:

- All families have dreams for their children and want the best for them.
- All families have the capacity to support their children's learning.
- Families and schools are equal partners.
- The responsibility for cultivating and sustaining partnerships among school, home, and community rests primarily with school staff, especially school leaders.[12]

In many ways, this is the "mind-set" that Cinthia believes is necessary; it is rooted in specific beliefs about families—their hopes, aspirations, and abilities—and about her role and responsibility in engaging them.

Rather than blaming families and shutting them out, Cinthia knows that parents care about their children, are concerned about the challenges they face, and seek to support them. In reality, families may need clearer explanations about academic goals or improved access to available resources, but she has found that they "have always wanted to be involved."

When I ask her what she does to support her families, her response is simple: "Whatever it takes to help them support their child. We work together. It's not on the student; it's not on me; it's not on you. It's all of us in this together." If a student is struggling in her classroom, she sees the parent not as an impediment to the child's success or a reason for their struggles, but rather as an untapped resource and partner: "My responsibility is to support the student, but the family is a big part of that, so I see my job as working with parents to help them answer the questions we have together. How do they figure it out? How do they support their child? How do we support them to support their kid? Unfortunately, not every person has the ability to read to their kid every day for an hour or two. I have to work with them to figure out what's possible." At times, this means showing parents how to use online literacy resources on a home computer to keep their child engaged in reading. She may create an audio recording of a student reading aloud so a parent can work with her at home to encourage and track improvements. She relishes the opportunity to introduce families to new resources and finds that parents appreciate this as well.

Students often respond well to these connections between what they learn at school and at home, and for parents it is eye-opening. They often admit to Cinthia that "whatever the kid is experiencing and doing academically is sometimes a mystery" to them. Cinthia explains: "The only way I'm going to be successful in my job is if I have parents supporting me at home and supporting their students . . . if I haven't given them the tools, then I can't assume that they're just going to magically have it at home, or that they even know what they need to do to make their child be successful in that specific way."

This kind of partnership appeals to parents and caregivers as well. Jasmine's mother, Sandra, describes her relationship with Cinthia as "a partnership where we are working together for the greater good of Jasmine." She admits that schools are not always transparent or specific about the ways that parents can support their children, and that can leave parents feeling as if there is nothing they can do.

In the field of education, we can sometimes chase after magic bullets or quick-fix solutions to address the problems and challenges we see in schools. As schools and districts look to family engagement strategies to improve communication with families and enhance collaboration, it is important to recognize that change must be cultural. It is tempting to use the language of partnership to hone in on the physical interactions between parents and teachers, but it is more than a partnership—it is also a mind-set that shapes every encounter. We often focus too readily and singularly on *what* a teacher like Cinthia does without understanding *how* her *values* and *beliefs* shape the collaboration in the first place.

4

ANNIE SHAH
Engaging Community

What do we want?
JUSTICE!
When do we want it?
NOW!
Books, access, fairness;
we're marching to
raise awareness!
Millions for Copley,
but Chinatown—
NO LIBRARY!

This unified chant pierces the air one blustery January morning on the busy streets of downtown Boston. Passersby with steaming cups of coffee in hand gather along the sidewalk to watch the scene. Some stop to take a picture and others, on the phone, pause their conversation and shift their focus. They are all drawn by this chant, the steady accompanying drumbeat, and the marching line of young protesters. The children belt out each word in a high-pitched tenor, aiming to be heard near and far.

As the protest group moves through the crowded streets, they hold up colorful handmade placards declaring "Chinatown needs a library NOW!" "57 years is TOO LONG to wait!" "Reading = Freedom" and "We have access. They should too." The placards bobble down the street, adorned with bright images of books and bubble-letter writing and held high by small, mittened hands. As the young protesters move through downtown, cars and trucks honk their horns in support, and shop owners come out to applaud them.

Second-grade students at Boston's Young Achievers Science and Mathematics Pilot School lead today's march. The students began the morning in a schoolwide assembly focused on community service. The school has chosen today as a day of service in honor of Dr. Martin Luther King Jr. After hearing from community speakers, class groups were transported by bus to different community service projects across the city. The second graders, along with their teachers and a group of family members, began their trek downtown armed with their placards, handmade drums, bullhorns, and a petition signed by 1,001 supporters that they plan to hand-deliver to Mayor Martin Walsh.

Earlier in the year, as they embarked on a study of Boston neighborhoods through an exploration of the city's branch libraries, the second graders learned that Chinatown was the only Boston neighborhood without a public library. As dutiful patrons of the branch library near their school, they understood the treasure that a public library can be to children.

As they dug deeper into the story, students learned of the community's rocky history with the city regarding library services. While the first branch library in Chinatown was opened in 1896—first as a delivery station before being moved into a new municipal building in 1915—it was closed in 1938 due to post-Depression budgeting challenges. Community residents protested the closure but to no avail. After years of advocacy, the city finally opened a library reading room in 1951 but just five years later demolished the library to make way for the Central Artery construction project. City officials promised the community that a new library would be constructed. Despite the city's intentions and the eventual demolition of the library, the site was never, in fact, used for the path of the Boston Central Artery. Organizers in the Chinatown community spent decades pushing the city to make good on its promise and build a branch library.

Annie Shah, one of the second-grade teachers at Young Achievers, felt that this community history was exactly the kind of story that would "bring meaning and the idea of community justice alive" for her students. When the class learned about the Chinatown library, fifty-seven years after its 1956 demolition, they were "adamant in insisting that this was unfair, unjust, and unacceptable." Shortly thereafter, the students uncovered a *Boston Globe* article on the Boston Public Library's approval of a $16 million renovation of the central branch in Copley Square and were struck by its seeming injustice.[1] On their behalf, Annie reached out to community and youth organizers in Chinatown who had been instrumental in the campaign for a branch library. Soon after, the class began meeting with organizers in Chinatown to learn about the community—its residents and businesses, the rich history of community for Chinese immigrants, the neighborhood's evolving landscape, and the campaign for a branch library. Upon learning the community's story while making connections to their ongoing study of community activism, Annie and her students offered to organize a march in support of the library.

On this January morning, the students had begun their march at the symbolic Chinatown gate, where they gathered alongside Chinatown residents, community organizers, and some of the adults who had staged their own protest as youth years before. Now the group weaves through narrow city streets into the expanse of the Boston Common, crossing over traffic-snarled Tremont Street to the supportive honking of drivers, and finally into City Hall Plaza.

When students arrive at City Hall, a group goes inside to present the petition to the mayor and invite him to their space. He is not available, but City Councilor Michelle Wu comes outside to meet with the students and community members. Having learned about the march, another group of students, from the Neighborhood School in Boston, has joined the young students from Mattapan to stand in solidarity with them. Teachers set up a raised platform for students to stand and share their individual stories. Bystanders gather as the students make a personal plea to the mayor and city councilor, sharing their own experiences with books, libraries, and literacy. Annie crouches beside each student in turn, holding a bullhorn to amplify their voices. Carlos, one of Annie's students, steps up without hesitation with this call to action:

> If you love books, then tell Mayor Walsh we need to get a library in Chinatown. Hi, my name is Carlos, and I'm a second-grade student. I know libraries help people. I'm learning how to read better and not to read too fast and not get too confused with words. I like books by the author Mo Willems. The problem is that Chinatown is the only neighborhood with no library. I want Mayor Walsh to tell the builders to build a new library in Chinatown so kids in Chinatown have access to books.

Upon hearing the stories of Carlos and his classmates, Councilor Wu vows to deliver the message to Mayor Walsh and discuss the return of library services to Chinatown.

Recalling the event later, Christy O'Connor, whose son Declan is in Annie's class, says, "It was remarkable. It was emotional . . . The kids were so dedicated, marching down the street, shouting and yelling. It was incredible to see little kids like that rallying for a cause like that. They were doing it to be heard, and they really did turn heads."

LEARNING ABOUT COMMUNITY

When Annie Shah decided to take her students on an exploratory journey into the Chinatown library campaign, she knew that they would need to connect with key community members and activists. She contacted the Chinese Progressive Association (CPA; www.cpaboston.org/), a well-respected community organizing group in Chinatown with a long history of improving the living and working conditions of Chinese Americans. CPA was founded in 1977 to organize Chinese parents' participation and input into the Boston school desegregation process. Over the years, CPA has mobilized the community to fight for community control over land development in the neighborhood, accountability and justice for police brutality, workers' rights, affordable housing, and other community issues.

When Annie reached out to CPA about her students' interest in supporting the Chinatown library campaign, she was "primarily invested in learning about what had been accomplished and fought for over the years." She had no illusions that her second graders would bring public attention to a community project "without being completely aware of the love and devotion that had already been poured into this project" and learning alongside the community members and residents for whom this would matter most.

Building Community Partnerships

Annie connected with Kim Situ, a youth organizer at CPA. She knew that youth were at the center of the long-term campaigns for a library in Chinatown. From Kim, she learned that youth had conducted focus groups with seniors/elders, other youth, and working parents; developed partnerships with local organizations in Chinatown to build a broad base of support for the campaign; and highlighted the library's potential not only as a site to support community literacy but also to promote a sense of community itself. Youth and residents in Chinatown saw the library as a cultural space, community center, gathering area, resource center for immigrant families, and an educational treasure. Annie recalls, "That conversation with Kim really opened my eyes to how multidimensional this issue was," but most of all, "this was about social justice, community justice—my kids were really fired up about the justice and fairness in this campaign."

She and Kim felt that an important part of the students' learning should be grounded in the Chinatown community itself, so they organized a community tour for the entire second grade. On a cold December morning, I joined three classes of students, teachers, and parent chaperones on a field trip just over five miles into the heart of Boston's Chinatown. As our personal guide, Kim took us on a walking tour of historical sites and important cultural and community centers. Along the way, we visited the site of the original "delivery station" established in 1896 on the corner of Harrison Avenue and Marginal Street. The delivery station included a reading room with shelves of books lining the wall and a corner nook where children could read. We walked to the site of the Tyler Street municipal building where the library was moved in 1915. In its place, Kim explained, stands the Tai Tung Village, a residential apartment complex that provides subsidized housing for community members; she encouraged us to imagine the site a hundred years ago as a community library.

Kim, who has given many neighborhood guided tours over the years, explains that the purpose of the tours is to help the people who come through Chinatown to "have a deeper understanding of the community's histories and struggles." She adds, "Our tour is really focused on the history of organizing in Chinatown, and we want people to see how issues in the community were addressed by community members through organizing efforts." That was her focus with Annie's second graders as well.

To provide a more current context for the Chinatown library campaign, Kim also took us to the site of the 2009 temporary Storefront Library, a collaboration between artists, youth, and community members for an innovative use of community space. We stepped inside the previous site of the community-organized Chinatown Lantern Reading Room. The one-year project sought to establish a lending library, promote awareness of the library campaign, and generate community and public support for the project. The room still functions as a private reading room for the residents of the Oak Terrace apartments. As we explored the space, students remarked that it was "so small" and "just a little room." They wondered aloud, "Why does the library in Chinatown have to be so small?"

These experiences in the community and the larger conversation students have had with Kim Situ have made a deep impression. When we visited the Tyler Street location where the library once stood and where residential apartments now stand, Kim directed us to look beyond the building to the massive overhead Central Artery highway behind it, then told us of the city's decision to demolish the library to make room for Central Artery construction. She spoke of the broken promises made to the community. As the children gazed at the highway, imagining the library that once stood in the space before them, they peppered her with questions: "Why did the city have to build the road right here?" "Where did kids go to read books and get books?" "What can the people in Chinatown do to make the city keep its promise?" Kim responded:

Chinatown is always growing, always changing, and that's because of the efforts of the youth, the community residents, and all the people who really care about Chinatown. Yes, they tore down the old library, but we are working together to get it back—first with the storefront library and then with the reading room. One of the best things about being with you today is that you are here because you care about Chinatown too.

Kim's words resonated with the class. Annie recalls the conversation she had with the students when they returned to their classroom later that day. The central question became, "What can we do to help Chinatown get a library?" Annie explains:

When we visited Chinatown, my students were appalled that there was no library and that they were the only neighborhood in Boston without one. At that point, they had been enjoying the local library and looking forward to those trips every week. We had also learned about Frederick Douglass and performed the play about his devotion to literacy and freedom. So by now, the second graders had become real advocates of libraries, authentic advocates. They came to believe that libraries are important and knew in their heart that it wasn't fair that kids in Chinatown had lost their library and never regained it.

"The Community Is Our Classroom": Community Engagement and Student Learning

The importance of a library was not lost on the students in Annie's class, in large part because of their own experience with the public library in their neighborhood. Every Tuesday afternoon, Annie and her class make the trek to the Mattapan branch library where they meet with the children's librarian for a book reading and spend the rest of their time perusing the bookshelves, reading books, and, finally, checking out some books to take home with them. Each child uses their own library card, which Annie helped students obtain at the beginning of the year. They make the weekly trip throughout the year—rain, snow, or shine. As the year progresses, her students develop familiarity with the library, facility with book exploration, and a greater sense of independence as readers.

Annie's students know that the Mattapan library was born out of community advocacy too, just like the library in Chinatown. Newly constructed in 2009, the library boasts one of the largest collections of children's books in the library system. It is currently just a ten-minute walk from Young Achievers, but the previous branch site was outdated, underutilized, and lacking the basic necessities of a quality library. Mattapan, home to one of the largest young adult populations in the city of Boston, is also underresourced when compared to its more middle-class and gentrifying Boston neighbors. When you walk into the twenty-one-thousand-square-foot building today, you see adults and children, young and old, at all times of the day, using the precious space. Community members and youth, with the support of City Councilor Charles Yancey, pushed the city to rebuild the branch library in a more visible, accessible, and central location. With such a precious community resource in their midst, Annie says, "it's impossible not to consider building this resource into our daily lives as learners." Learning about the existence of the library sparked in Annie a desire to have her students get out of the school building and into a public space that would enrich their lives as readers and provide a precious opportunity for students to be out in the community.

These weekly trips were a complement to the other community-based projects that Annie incorporated into her teaching. The class took field trips across the city to engage in the social studies curriculum on Boston neighborhoods. For three years, Annie and her class worked with a public radio host to create a series of community-based public service announcements for the radio program. They went on a personal tour of the WBUR public radio station in Boston, and after months of editing and research, students entered a soundproof studio to record their very own PSAs. A producer edited the students' audio clips, and the PSAs were then integrated into the host's radio program each evening. Audio of the PSAs along with students' accompanying artwork became the key pieces of an art exhibition that Annie and the second graders set up at the nearby Boston Nature Center. She recalls, "It was truly amazing to see these second graders sharing the stories of authentic learning. It was truly a labor of love for all of us."

When I ask Annie why it's so important to have students learn in the classroom and in the community, she pushes back on my assumption that in-school and out-of-school learning are distinct and separate:

> You see, that's where the problem starts. We tend to think of everything we do in the classroom as related to academic subjects, the books on our shelves, the curriculum content that students need to learn about. But every day when my students step into my classroom, they are bringing in their families with them. They are bringing in their communities with them. And when they go to my bookshelf and look for a book, they aren't just looking for a good story, they are looking for something that speaks to them as human beings—in that fullness.

Whether we recognize it or not, learning in school, according to Annie, "should be a celebration of all things that happen out of school too." Rather than seeing the classroom and the community as distinct entities, she views the community as her classroom. She explains:

> I guess some people would say that it's important for students to be out in the community. We go on field trips for that reason. We might get out of the school and into the community a couple times a year, and we want to make sure that what we're learning is applicable, or maybe we see it as an extension—like, here's an example that tells us more—or even as evidence that what we are learning is true. But I would say that the community is our classroom, and it shouldn't be an option whether we take children into the community that surrounds us or not.

Annie's students and their families have become accustomed to seeing the community as their classroom too. Angela Jones, whose son Jayson is in Annie's class, accompanied the class on their trip to Chinatown. She loves the exposure that Jayson has to communities beyond the classroom. In fact, she describes the community as "an outdoor classroom." The excitement is long-lasting as she recounts the way Jayson sees Boston neighborhoods today:

> Some of these kids have never been outside . . . of their own neighborhood walking. They drive through neighborhoods in cars, but this year, they've gotten to go out and see so much. Now with Jayson, we go to the South End, and he can tell me where Martin Luther King used to live. He shows me where the South End library is. He knows, and I think that's awesome, because it just exposes him to so much more than what some of us parents would have.

Staying True to Community-Based Learning Amidst Increased Accountability in Schools

The trips to Chinatown and the Mattapan library are part of a larger yearlong study of Boston neighborhoods that Annie and the second-grade team have designed for their students. They visit public libraries across the city, meeting with librarians who tell them about the local collection and community. The public library in general, with its rituals, reading rooms, and staff, has become familiar to students, but they see each branch library through the lens of its local community and unique characteristics. So, when news breaks of the $16 million Copley library renovation, Annie's students know exactly what it means. They have been in the space, with its vaulted ceilings, enormous children's reading room, grand staircase, and bookshelves that span an entire city block. While library officials believe the central library is overdue for a building upgrade, Annie's students think otherwise from personal experience.

These experiences, "in and out of different communities in Boston," according to Annie, are "a beautiful part of student learning—learning about yourself, your city, the meaning of community, and the necessity of connection." She says that even in big cities that are brimming with ethnic, racial, and cultural diversity, it's important not to assume that everyone is connected. Add to that the larger narratives on race and community in cities like Boston:

We like to think that in cities like Boston and other large cities, we are all connected somehow. Our lives are connected through sharing space, being on public transportation, being close together in a dense urban environment, but it's amazing how we can still live isolated and segregated lives . . . And then we add to that these troubling narratives about certain communities, like the ones my kids live in. The only time you hear about these neighborhoods is when something bad happens in them, when we are talking about crime or drugs, and so I knew that was messed up, and my kids get the messages all the time. I wanted to get kids into those awesome places in their neighborhoods and outside their neighborhoods, and I wanted to figure out ways to make that public to people.

For this reason, Annie has always been committed to having her students experience the rich variety and diversity of Boston's neighborhoods through experiential learning. With the second-grade social studies curriculum focused on Boston neighborhoods, for many years this was not difficult to accomplish. This was the "blissful" period of time when Annie and her students visited community activists and organizations across the city, learning what made their communities unique, and creating PSAs and radio programs to spread the word. Annie recalls, "There was so much freedom then to learn outside of the classroom. It was really valued, and there was time, space, and resources for it."

But times began to change at Young Achievers with increased pressure on the school to bring up students' literacy and math scores. When the school decided to take on a new literacy initiative, Annie found the new demands to be overwhelming for teachers. "It requires a lot of preparation and teachers were always living on the edge of their cognitive demand, because there was so much to do and develop that was new," she explains. With the emphasis on longer periods of independent reading for students and the greater demands on teachers to plan the new curriculum, Annie felt the time for experiential education and social studies slipping away from her. These elements were "at the heart" of her beliefs in teaching—"to be inspired by the stories of community and individuals around you." She began to see herself at a crossroads:

> When the big focus became about literacy and independent reading, there was a sense that maybe we just wouldn't do social studies, at least in the way we had done it before. But that would have eaten up my soul, so I really wanted to figure out a way that we would still be able to study Boston neighborhoods and still do social studies while figuring out this commitment to literacy. That was when I came up with the lifesaving idea of doing a library study.

Annie knew that one of the lasting impressions on her students and their families over the years was the experiential learning of Boston neighborhoods. She realized that she would no longer be able to devote as much time visiting Boston neighborhoods simply to learn about community history, but the weekly trips to the Mattapan library did inspire in her a new idea. She explains, "Once my kids became adept at learning to use the library, I realized that we could visit other public libraries in the city and use that experience to learn about neighborhoods in Boston."

Annie, along with the second-grade team, decided that the study of community through public libraries would become the new curricula. They would visit the community spaces and experience the unique history and collection of each library through an exploration of its spaces, the children's reading room, and conversation with librarians. The team of second-grade teachers believed this new curriculum would marry literacy with the arts, experiential education, and social studies:

> I wanted my kids to understand the importance of literacy and to be able to read independently, but I also wanted to help them see what an important part literacy played in the struggle for freedom as well. So all of a sudden, I was imagining that we were going to visit these neighborhoods' libraries, learn about Frederick Douglass and other freedom fighters who made literacy one of the cornerstones to their activism, and in the process, our second graders would be inspired to read, talk about books, and most importantly, take ownership for that precious gift of literacy.

Community as a Space for Critical Multicultural Learning

While we may be tempted to focus on the community as a learning environment that benefits students, Annie explains that the community can be a place where teachers learn more about their students' lives, families, and communities as well. Especially in "urban school environments where teachers are driving in from their suburban homes and speeding right back as soon as the school day is over," Annie says the local community can be an unfamiliar place for teachers. There may be discomfort or fear, often unwarranted, that guide their hesitation or unwillingness to venture out into the community with their students. It may be, according to Annie, "far easier in their minds to go way out, like to Plimoth Plantation, than to go down the street."

The experiences in Chinatown were a critical multicultural learning moment for Annie's students. Like any of us who have little exposure to certain groups or communities, Annie's students learned to challenge their assumptions about Chinatown and about Chinese Americans/Asian Americans through their experiences. It took me a while to understand why Annie's students had started to call me "Miss Kim," when I came to visit the classroom. It is a common Korean surname, so I wondered if they had confused my name. When I asked Annie about it, she thought for a moment and said, "Oh, wow, I think they mistook you for Kim—Kim Situ. I think they have such little exposure to Asians sometimes that they get us mixed up." We took that moment to talk to the students gathered around me and explain that I was not who they mistook me for. I chuckled to myself as one of the girls said, "I thought you looked a little different."

In that moment, I recalled a few of the questions that students had for Kim the month before when we took the Chinatown tour with her. As we stood at the Chinatown gate at the end of the tour, Kim asked the students if they still had questions about Chinatown that she could answer for them. One boy raised his hand, looked straight into Kim's eyes, and asked, "Do kids in Chinatown watch TV?" Kim explained that kids in Chinatown are just like kids anywhere else. They go to school, they like to play in playgrounds, and, yes, they watch TV too. When I sat down to talk with Kim after the tour, she brought up that question to explain how often people's views are shaped by assumptions about Chinatown. They are often surprised to learn about the predominance of low-income community members, the challenges for workers, and the community's struggles to preserve and maintain the neighborhood. Instead, they are often familiar with the restaurants or the cultural environment, but don't know much about the people and the long history of the neighborhood. She explained, "I think those realities are very jarring for people who may not see it, because I think on the surface, you can walk through Chinatown, eat the food, get the cultural experience, and walk away never having to think about how people really live . . . I think people are also surprised at how much people have to fight to preserve the community and all the challenges that have come up over time."

Annie, too, brings up some of students' questions and expresses some regret that, in addition to the experiences with Kim, CPA, community members, and at the protest, there wasn't an opportunity for students to connect with other students in Chinatown:

> One of the most striking things for me when we were there for the tour with Kim was how little my kids knew about this community. We don't bring kids from different parts of the city together enough in ways that they can interact and get to know each other. I can see that my students had stereotypes and assumptions about kids in Chinatown, and it was important for them to be able to talk to Kim and ask questions of her, because she really helped them understand that while they lived in different parts of the city, they had shared connections. They like to read, they wanted libraries, they wanted playgrounds and parks in their neighborhood, they like to watch TV. This is why I think it's so important for us to take our students out not only into their immediate community but into the broader one as well.

Despite the overall diversity that can be found in large cities, increasingly neighborhoods and schools are becoming more racially isolated, due in part to changing school policies.[2] Researchers have aptly named this the "resegregation" of schools.[3] In a school like Young Achievers, where the majority of students are black, Afro-Latino, or Latino, there are few encounters with Asian Americans, and learning in the community can be just as much about human relationships and confronting bias as it can be about illustrating academic material.

THE IMPORTANCE OF LIVED EXPERIENCE

Annie is a petite woman with a big personality. Tucked inside her long, wavy black hair is a splash of color from her dangling earrings. Usually sporting a chic colorful top, trousers, and comfortable shoes, Annie looks like the kind of elementary teacher students want to have. High praise abounds from the second graders I have come to know in Annie's classroom; overwhelmingly, they describe her as someone who "makes learning fun and easy." Part of the fun comes from Annie's contagious energy and spirit. She is in her seventh year of teaching at Young Achievers, and her enthusiasm for learning is grounded in the deep relationships that she strives to cultivate in her classroom. It's not just what they learn that excites her; it's that they learn in connection and relationship to each other: "So much of what I love about teaching, what I crave about it at the beginning and end of each day, is how we relate to each other, how we learn from each other, and the sense of community that we are building every day."

In my role as a researcher, I have found that there are varying degrees to how people will connect, open up, and share their story with me. Annie is a superbly easy and pleasant person to connect with. I recall the very first time we met to talk about my research project. School had just been dismissed for the day, and we were sitting on the front steps of the school, off to the side, as students streamed out of the front doors, running to catch up with friends or walking in groups to buses that awaited them. Despite the noise and activity, Annie was focused singularly on me, on our conversation. She brought full honesty and openness to the discussion as we talked about public libraries, experiential learning, and engaging communities.

As I have seen countless times in her classroom, Annie listens fully, with her whole body, when she is engaged in conversation. She leans in so as not to miss a word, maintaining eye contact and utterly undistracted by all the surrounding activity. Her smile radiates warmth and kindness, and her deep, hearty laugh is never a solo act; it always invites others to join in. Many times, she has attested that she "loves to listen to people's stories." These are not empty words; each conversation is an opportunity for her to lean in and witness someone's story. This seems to bring her joy.

While it may be tempting to believe that Annie's goals for experiential learning and community engagement are attempts to make learning fun and enjoyable for students in the midst of an educational climate that is relentlessly focused on standardized tests and school-based learning, Annie's motivations are quite personal. Her experience as a teacher is undeniably shaped by her experience as a child of Indian immigrant parents, growing up in towns just outside of Boston where race and ethnicity were sometimes poorly understood and where families like hers were vastly unappreciated.

One afternoon, as we sit and talk in her colorful, sun-filled apartment, she shows me pictures of her family—her sisters whom she talks of as best friends, their children, and her parents. Family is a big part of Annie's life. She grew up twenty minutes north of Boston. Her parents own a jewelry store in downtown Boston, and she recalls spending a lot of time in the store's office as a child. At the time, the downtown shopping district and red light district were one and the same. While her parents wanted to protect her from those images, the experience in the city was a vivid and familiar part of her life: "We had a lot of experience going into downtown, Chinatown, and I remember my parents gripping my hands a little bit tighter and my dad covering my eyes because Chinatown was not really a great place back in the '80s. So I had exposure coming into the city, and it was a very familiar part of my life."

Back home, her parents were very active in the Indian community and through their temple. Annie says, "When I think of community, we had a wonderfully supportive Indian community that my parents were a very active part of. It was a source of kinship and friendship for many of us. But it was not just the geographic 'community' people may often think of." For many immigrant families like Annie's, these ethnic and cultural communities are a touchstone and provide many supports and networks that mainstream American communities may not.

In her suburban neighborhood, she and her two older sisters were among only a few students of color, and this sometimes created challenges for the girls growing up. The family did not always feel fully integrated in the neighborhood, but Annie has a deep sense of unwavering pride for her parents, who "worked hard to create a good life for their daughters." Still, this was the 1980s; predominantly white suburban towns were forming across the country, the result of residents fleeing cities that were becoming more accessible to communities of color. Annie's family was the only Indian American one in her community, and she recalls that her classmates and friends' parents weren't always friendly to her parents. She assumes that many people were confused by her family's presence and unsure of how to see them in a town that was mostly white.

Beyond more subtle signs of discrimination, there were blatant acts of racism as well, such as an incident in kindergarten that is Annie's first and most vivid memory:

> There was this little boy who tormented me in kindergarten. He would put pudding in my hair and torment me relentlessly. I remember one time he dragged me around the room by my hair, and the teacher was terrible. She saw this happening and didn't do anything, even though everybody had complained to her. I felt so abandoned by her, and there was no doubt in my mind that not only was I being singled out for being brown, [but] the teacher was absolutely refusing to deal with it because I was brown.

The teacher's shameful response was to tell Annie that she could sit out the next activity if she was bothered by what the boy was doing. His behavior fully sanctioned by the teacher's inaction, the boy continued to bully Annie throughout the year. This left Annie feeling "like I had to protect myself, because no one was looking out for me." She dealt with it the only way her four-year-old self knew how—to distinguish herself from the black and brown kids who were being uniformly tormented in the school. She remembers a pair of black twin boys in the kindergarten, the only other students of color. After being harassed by her classmates and neglected by her teacher, Annie disassociated herself from the two boys:

> We were the only brown kids in that classroom, but there was a part of me that didn't want to be associated with them, for God knows whatever reason I had in my four-year-old brain. I remember one day we were all trying to look at the pet hamsters in the other class-room, and I wanted to see too, so I was nudging forward. I remember this little boy who was tormenting me said, "You can't come over here; there is no black people allowed." I remember my first reaction was, "I am not black; I am Indian." Then I went over to that terrible teacher and she said, "Tommy, Annie is Indian; she isn't black!" I have to tell you that for years—I don't think it was until my mid-twenties that I let go of the guilt of feeling that. I felt that I had to defend myself, the need to rank myself higher at such a young age.

As she reflects on that time, it angers her to think about how systematically racist her classroom environment was at the time. From the presence of white children who bullied her and alienated students of color, to the inaction of teachers who neglected to respond with care and instead put children's social and emotional lives in danger, she recalls, "that whole year had a big effect on me, because, one, I was being treated badly, and two, as a defensive mechanism, I separated myself from the other kids who were brown in the room."

As a result, Annie felt "misunderstood." In addition to the racism that pervaded her peer and teacher interactions, she also recalls a profound sense that her family and cultural experience were irrelevant, unimportant. To make matters worse, false assumptions about her and her family prevailed. This experience, still vivid in her mind, guides her belief that students should be fully and wholly understood through their families and communities:

> Because of our immigrant experience, I always thought that my family functioned in a totally different way than all my friends' families functioned. Not only did I feel as though there was no effort

made by my teachers or my friends' parents to understand us, I almost felt like there was a misunderstanding, that there were assumptions about us. You can feel those things in subtle ways and I always felt that growing up. I felt very misunderstood. I didn't feel that way about my friends and their understanding of me, but I did feel that about their parents and about my teachers.

Over her experience in schools, Annie learned to deal with the situation around her. It "was never a positive experience," but she found a group of friends who, while they would not necessarily be able to relate to her, connected with her. "They were real friendships" that still continue to the present. Some of them—in particular, a white Jewish boy—felt a common kinship in "being tokenized in some ways. We made lots of off-color jokes growing up about being the Jew and the Indian, and I think it was the way to recognize it without having to deal with it seriously because we didn't know how to navigate that space growing up."

These childhood experiences have shaped Annie's ideas for her own classroom. She explains, "I truly believe that I would never intentionally want to recreate this in my own classroom." The classroom conflict she recalls is part of "a problematic tendency we have as individuals":

We can have these deeply ingrained beliefs about people and assumptions that guide how we see people, and we have never even had an opportunity to know them as people. And I think part of that stems from parents wanting their kids to be around others that feel familiar to them, but the problem is that we don't stop there. We don't recognize that we are also guided by faulty assumptions. And what we really need to do is go out and meet others and be in relationships with people. That's the only way to break these assumptions.

She goes on to explain that "learning about people and learning about cultures is certainly a start, but like I said, it's not enough." She is impatient with such inadequate approaches to multicultural learning, and it is this impatience that drives her to be out in the community with her students. She believes that only by cultivating relationships can we truly learn about others in meaningful ways. She likens this to her approach with her students' families and the centrality of human stories in building those relationships: "When I interact with a family member I learn a lot about their culture and I learn about their story, and that gets me really excited. That's what's interesting about life to me. I guess human stories are more interesting to me than anything else, and so I get to have these authentic experiences with families and kids where I can understand people more. I get to understand the human condition, the human story more." In libraries, at City Hall, with Kim in Chinatown, and in the larger community, Annie's students are not just learning about people, they are exploring human stories and building community.

BECOMING ALLIES: CREATING SPACES FOR TRUST AND BELONGING

Christy O'Connor's son Declan is in Annie's second-grade classroom. Every Tuesday, she accompanies Annie and her students to the Mattapan library. Over the year, she has gotten to know Annie and Declan's classmates well through their weekly excursions. When I ask her what she enjoys about the experience, she replies:

> I like to get a chance to know the community. I like to know their classmates and just be able to recognize them in the hallway and know them a little bit more than just hearing their names from Declan. The school has always been very welcoming and Ms. Shah especially, she has made me feel like my support and assistance is helpful to her. Being out in the community is so important for these kids. I know that Declan and I have learned a lot ourselves.

Having participated in some of the field trips with Annie's class, Christy underscores the importance of new learning in community contexts:

> I thought it was an eye-opener even for me, just learning some of the stuff as the kids were learning it. I was like, "Wow, I didn't know that." The trip to the main library was great. The kids were fascinated and just to see their faces, you could see how much they were

learning and that so much of this was new and changing their per-spective. Just to be out in the city and walking down the street, there was so much excitement . . . It was great to be engaged with the kids and to see her engagement with the kids.

Angela, Jayson's mother, also believes that the time in the commu-nity has made a mark on the students in Annie's class. She says, "Not only are they excited to be out in the community, [but] these are the experiences that are going to make learning real for them. It makes what you learn in the classroom so much more relevant." Annie's way of teaching has taught Jayson to see the world around him a bit differ-ently, Angela explains:

> She's just an awesome teacher. She made a really big impact on Jay-son; it has changed the way he sees the city and the community. When we are in the area, even if we're not near where we went, but just in the area, he notices things, and he just remembers a lot of the things that Annie taught him. I really believe that she has taught these kids to look out into the community and think about what it means to them and to make them feel that they are knowledgeable and can notice important things out in the world.

Coda

On a crisp, clear morning in Boston's Chinatown, the bright sun has brought a momentary respite from the otherwise cold and windy day. Children in puffy coats and colorful mittens, alongside parents, elderly Chinese residents, Asian American young adults, and many others, en-ter the China Trade Building on Boylston Street. Once inside, they move en masse down the large staircase to the central atrium. It is just before 11 a.m. on February 3, 2018, and a large crowd is gathering be-low. It is not long before the entire atrium space is filled—standing room only—and people begin to line the two staircases as well as the balcony space overlooking the crowd. After decades of community or-ganizing, led by Chinatown youth, the city is returning library ser-vices to Chinatown. While a full-service branch has been promised to the community in the future, today the Boston Public Library opens a small temporary services branch in the China Trade Building. Hundreds of people have gathered on this morning for the ribbon-cutting to celebrate both the library and a great community achievement.

A year earlier, Mayor Martin J. Walsh published an op-ed in the *SAMPAN*, New England's only bilingual Chinese-English newspaper. He discussed the importance of public libraries—the resources, programs, and services they offer to communities—and the key role they play in promoting democracy and access. But he also highlighted the role of the second graders at Young Achievers:

> Chinatown's library was torn down to make way for MassPike construction back in 1956. Since then, it has been the only neighborhood in Boston without a library. This was brought to my attention several years ago. About two weeks after being sworn in, second-graders from a Dorchester elementary school marched from the Chinatown Gate to City Hall one afternoon, sending a clear message: that a lack of a neighborhood library, a lack of a gathering place, a learning center and fundamental resource is an injustice.[4]

Annie would be the first to admit that her second graders were merely joining a decades-long organizing effort by Chinatown youth and community members, but one thing is clear: Young Achievers students sent a message to the mayor.

On this morning, I am standing next to Annie, her fiancé Keith, a parent named Gaby, her daughter Patricia, and Patricia's friend Keri. The girls, now in sixth grade, have an older, more confident look about them, but there's no mistaking that they are two of the students I came to know four years ago. As they stand on the steps watching Mayor Walsh and the surrounding children cut the broad ribbon, I am taken back to the images of colorful posters and the sound of loud, young voices chanting in unison:

> What do we want?
> JUSTICE!
> When do we want it?
> NOW!

Books, access, fairness;
we're marching to
raise awareness!
Millions for Copley,
but Chinatown—
NO LIBRARY!

As we gather around the library to listen to the speakers—the mayor, elected officials, community activists, and former youth leaders who are now adults—there is a poignancy in the diverse crowd. Carolyn Rubin, community activist and chair of the Friends of the Chinatown Library, proclaims: "When I look at this library, what I think about is the healing of an injustice that happened seventy years ago. I think about the strength and the resilience of an immigrant community that, despite all the pressures on it now, we are saying, 'We are here to stay.' And when I look out on this crowd, I see a cross-racial, multigenerational, native-born, immigrant-born community, and we are the future of Boston."[5] As the crowd cheers wildly, Annie, Patricia, and Keri hold their hands up in collective thunderous applause. I have a feeling that those sounds and images from the streets of Chinatown four years ago in January are on their minds as well. And in that moment, I recall something Angela said to me back then:

When I think about Jayson at that march, I think he felt like he made a difference, or that there's going to be a Chinatown library someday. I never exposed him to marches before, and what the cause behind them might be, so with that, him being exposed, him watching for something, it made an impact on him. And then with him seeing marches further down the line for other causes, he knew what it was for. He knew that people were marching for a reason, not just marching to be in the street or to be making noise. It made a difference with him. He knew that he had a reason to be involved and that he wanted to make a difference in other people's neighborhoods. I think he really believes that there will be a Chinatown library one day, and when that day comes, he will know that he had something to do with it.

5

JULIA FINKELSTEIN
Sustaining Culture

It is October in Boston. Autumn is under way, and so is the season of back-to-school nights. At the Young Achievers Science and Mathematics Pilot School, a steady stream of parents is filing in to a large and cavernous auditorium. The entryways are flanked by teachers and staff who welcome the families, many with children in tow. As they enter, some family members are greeted warmly by teachers they know from previous years; these conversations are sprinkled with family updates and questions about the children. The atmosphere is lively as parents fill the room and find other parents they know, embrace them, and start catching up. There is an air of familiarity and kinship in the room—a sense of community.

One young teacher, Julia, stands off to the side. As some family members enter the room, she greets them in Spanish. They, too, talk about the summer, the start of school, and children who are growing older. She then hands each parent a small device, which they take to their seat with them.

After a short while, the principal steps to the microphone in the front of the room to start the program. The room begins to quiet and everyone takes a seat. Parents with the small audio devices unwind corded earbuds, place them in their ears, and then switch on the device. Julia has taken her place in a quiet corner in the back of the room. She, too, switches on her device and begins to interpret the principal's opening remarks into a portable transmitter. As parents sit and listen to the presentations, Julia's voice carries them through the evening.

BECOMING A TEACHER FOR IMMIGRANT FAMILIES

Julia Finkelstein is a sixth- and seventh-grade ESL teacher at Young Achievers, in her second year as a teacher and at the school. She teaches in two different kinds of classroom environments typically. She teaches emergent bilinguals in a stand-alone ESL classroom.[1] She also co-teaches Sheltered English Immersion (SEI) content classes (English language arts, science, and math) with teacher colleagues, providing differentiated instruction to support students' language development.[2] In her position, Julia also works with many of the families that have been recently transferred into the school due to the closure of another school in the district that served many Spanish-speaking immigrant families. Through her interactions with these families, she found that while the school made many efforts to welcome them, language was a barrier that kept many of the new families from participating. Without fluency in English, parents were hesitant to attend school events.

On this October evening, she brings her prior experience as an organizer and interpreter to the school's evening program. In a school that wants to make all families feel welcome, she has been given the freedom to dream up new possibilities to make this a reality. Following Julia's lead, Young Achievers has begun to offer simultaneous interpretation for the Spanish-speaking families who have recently enrolled their children in the school. Julia and her colleagues have done their part to let parents know that the interpretation is available. As I stand by the entrance on this evening, many of these parents look for Julia or Ms. Rodriguez, the school's Family and Community Outreach Coordinator.

Julia's journey as an educator, as well as her experience with interpreting, evolved from years working within immigrant communities as an organizer. When she graduated from college and started working in rural North Carolina, she was intent on supporting immigrant workers' rights to humane and respectable jobs. She never dreamed she would become a teacher, in part because her early experiences in school were so negative. Between racist teachers, low expectations, and her frustration with the uniformity that schools demanded, Julia recalls this sentiment from a young age: "I had no desire to ever be a teacher. It was like, 'Get me away from school.'"

Out of college, Julia knew that she wanted to work in service of marginalized communities. As a self-described big-picture thinker, she also knew that she wanted to support work that would make an impact on a larger scale. She took a job as a local organizer supporting farm worker communities—working with undocumented families and Latino immigrant workers. It was a formative time for her, and the lessons she learned were born out of the relationships she built with individuals and their families. At the time, she was focused on improving farm workers' rights and workplace conditions. While these issues were tremendously important, she also learned that "people need to work in order to support their families [back home]." Julia explains, "I learned a lot during that time and it was also really challenging . . . I was visiting a lot of farm workers and talking to them, and I learned that their problems are so deeply entrenched. Here I am talking about improving their job conditions. They're like, 'Yes, we hear you. At the same time, conditions back in Mexico are worse and I can't afford to lose this job and take a risk because I have to send [money] home to my family.'"

As a young college graduate who had high hopes and ambitions to improve work conditions, Julia describes this moment as a seminal one, one in which "your bubble gets deflated." The farm workers encouraged her to listen and slow down. She found that many "little things" involving language and culture access confounded them. "There were doctors' visits, school meetings for their children, many everyday experiences where families needed some support with translation and having their voices heard," so she began accompanying them, offering interpretation. It wasn't long until they began asking her to teach them English.

Julia saw that these farm workers yearned to improve their English fluency, but their lives were full and they had no time to participate in formal language classes. More significantly, learning a new language could be an emotional process. She explains, "We attach so much shame and embarrassment around language because of not wanting people to laugh at you if you mispronounce something or while you're practicing." She found that the willingness to learn was great, but the obstacles were undeniably real.

What started as informal sessions with a couple of union workers at the end of the workday turned into group language classes as word began to spread. To make the language learning meaningful, Julia had to teach it with relevance and care: "I was always trying to figure out, 'How can I create this space where they trust each other and can make mistakes and we can laugh about it and have fun too?'" She opted against traditional English language texts; instead, they read the union handbook and the International Declaration of Human Rights and engaged in conversations "about real issues through the lens of language learning." She taught them to read the letters from their child's school. She incorporated community-building to combat the fear and intimidation of learning language. She threaded the class with the goal of personal empowerment that was so familiar to her as a community organizer.

Through the lessons and the interpreting, she began to see the intersectional nature of language and power. As immigrants, low-wage workers, and English language learners, they experienced marginalization at many turns—from doctors, their children's teachers, the cashier at the big box store, their neighbors. Her presence at their side as a white English-dominant woman could confound matters: "I began thinking about language and the intersection between power and privilege . . . being in situations like a doctor's office or place where I would be the interpreter and the doctor would just talk directly to me without looking at the person . . . I started to recognize how language can shift power dynamics in a lot of ways, especially in this country with English being the dominant language."

She began attending trainings for interpreters, joining a community of multilingual speakers who understood the skill of translation and the cultural context within which language signified power. When she moved to Boston to work with the Service Employees International Union, she became involved in an ESL program that integrated workers' rights, human rights, and citizenship education. Bringing her previous experience with farm workers in North Carolina, she and a coworker recreated the citizenship class curriculum to include topics on US government and history, all through the lens of immigrant narratives. Through the experience, she listened to the stories of her students and her coworkers, many of them immigrants too. They taught her about the social isolation that comes from migrating to a new place, the impact it has on families and relationship dynamics within them. The conversations imbued within her a respect for immigrant communities, a compassion for their experiences, and a yearning for their just treatment.

The Latino families she worked with were a close-knit unit. Class members were more likely to participate when they could bring their children. But she recalls, "two hours is a long time for kids" and "they could be bored out of their minds," so she gathered books, coloring materials, and other activities to keep them occupied. At times, she would try to integrate the children into the class, knowing that their English was developing as well.

As the families shared this language learning space, parents began to open up about the questions they had: "A lot of times, they would share with me that they feel uncomfortable coming to school or there would be [school materials] at home that they didn't understand . . . they also had questions of uncertainty, feeling like, 'My kids are growing up in this world that I don't understand, or they're using the internet and going on all these [websites] . . . and I don't know what this is.'" She tapped into the immense love and caring between the parents and their children as well as parents' deep desire to know and understand the language and culture in which the younger generation was immersed.

She also found a profound disconnect between these families and the schools their children attended. Educators didn't seem to have any connection to the families or any understanding about their experiences transitioning to the community. Very few meetings or interactions were translated, if Julia was not herself available, so the interactions were few and far between. However, the greatest flaw of these predominantly white institutions (e.g., schools and medical offices) was rooted in their perception of these immigrant families purely through the skills and experiences they had *not* attained and mastered: "There was the uncertainty that these families had about what their kids were experiencing, but what made the issue more problematic was that I could see how the doctor or the school didn't value them. Then, [when] you add the power and privilege that these individuals can wield, this became a very disempowering situation."

As she began connecting to the children of the immigrant union members in her class, she realized that she could become an educator who engaged families and understood the community: "I just really loved talking to the kids and asking them about their school experience, and from there I realized I want to not only understand how to work within a public school system and how schools function, I also wanted to have an impact with these young people by knowing their parents and recognizing how their families and communities shape them."

Could she become an educator who learned to create interconnectedness among immigrant students, their families, and their schools? This question shaped her induction into teaching.

LITERACY AND THE LANGUAGE OF INCLUSION

While charismatic leaders often become the face of community organizing movements and campaigns, the heart of the movement beats with individuals like Julia who build relationships, one by one, in living rooms, community centers, and local businesses. When we meet to talk about the project, it is consistent with every other interaction I have seen—with students in her classroom, a parent in the hallway, a new family at a school event. Attentive and engaging, Julia listens intently and fully. In an age when we can be increasingly distracted, she is unabashedly present.

A white woman among black and brown students in an urban school, Julia stands out. She is petite in height, sometimes outsized by her middle school students, who, through their close bond and affection, often come in close to make her laugh or get her undivided attention. She doesn't stand out because she's an outsider, though; she is purely outstanding to her students. The sight of her elicits excitement and fun-loving attention. Down the hallway, I can hear students call, "Ms. F!" As they walk by her open door and see her inside, they peek to see if she has a snack on her desk, to share a quick greeting, or to ask whether they can come visit her later.

At first, you may notice her quiet voice, which seems almost timid at times—not from lack of confidence, but instead, a seeming aversion to dominating a conversation. But as students attest, "When you get to know Ms. F., she is really fun to be around," and "you just know that she really cares about us, no doubt." They also know that she has "super-high" expectations for them and they must "be ready to work."

Teaching Emergent Bilinguals

Through her early interactions and relationships with immigrant families, Julia came to realize that "much of my world teaching was really recognizing literacy." Her notion of literacy is broad and expansive:

> I see the word in its plural form—*literacies*—because I believe it's a plural concept. We can be very literate in certain areas and not in others. Someone who has a wealth of knowledge around mechanical engineering could struggle with grammar construction of a sentence. You may have a literacy in an area that I know nothing about. So many of the adults I worked with had huge educational gaps or didn't have strong literacy in their first language, coming from a lot of different backgrounds, whether it was through poverty or war or that their education was cut off. But they were literate in fields and areas that I was unfamiliar with.

This is also the situation with the emergent bilinguals in Julia's classroom. While they work to develop language fluency and literacy, Julia also recognizes that they possess well-developed literacies that she, as a teacher, should acknowledge and utilize in the classroom.[3] They have experiences to share—as athletes, visual artists, musicians—and deep knowledge of the languages and cultures of their native countries. How do these beliefs shape her aspirations as a teacher? She values the theory of systemic functional linguistics, an approach she describes as "teaching grammar in context and teaching the functions of language."[4] That is, instead of learning the mechanics of language in isolation, her students learn language and grammar through a relevant context that adds meaning to their lives, as Julia explains:

I want to create authentic experiences to facilitate learning and the-matic units of study . . . when we did the unit on family recipes, we had this great authentic experience of talking about recipes in our families and where they came from, but at the same time, we were deep into the details of language and grammar . . . As much as I re-ally focus on the holistic approach and the whole child, when I get in the zone of teaching, I am a hardcore grammar teacher too. The mi-nutia of learning English can be really challenging, and I never lose sight of that and want to teach my students to be successful.

To understand and acknowledge the whole child, Julia believes she must go beyond classroom experiences. Families are an important part of a student's worldview, and during a time "when so much feels un-settled and unfamiliar, family is a space that can be constant and famil-iar." So how does she incorporate family into her work with students?

I visit Julia's stand-alone ESL class one afternoon and find that stu-dents are hard at work on a family history project that is part of a larger historical study of immigration to the United States. I sit with Robert, partly because Julia feels he needs a little more support and motivation to get through this phase of the project. While studying about immi-gration history and policy in the US, the students have also participated in a parallel study of their own family's history of migration. Each stu-dent has chosen to complete an oral history project on a family mem-ber. Many of the interviews have been conducted and now students must complete the arduous task of writing up the story. This task is even more challenging to a group of emergent bilinguals. Robert feels the weight of a long day and the strain of a longer-term project, so he seems to welcome the opportunity to talk his ideas through with me.

Robert tells me that he chose to interview his father and thought ini-tially that the interview "would show what I already know," he recalls. But this project surprised him. He discovered new layers, "new sides to the story," even about those things that he felt he knew so well—like their common love of drumming. Taught by his father, Robert found that the skill seemed to come naturally to him, but his conversation with his father helped him understand that it was cultural and familial as well. Drumming is an art form that has been passed down through generations of men and boys in his family; his great-grandfather taught his son, who in turn taught his son, Robert's father. When Robert learned drumming as a child, it was, in essence, a cultural tradition passed down through his family and a reflection of their Puerto Rican heritage. "That blew me away; I had no idea about that," he recalls.

That wasn't all Robert discovered. He learned that his father spent his teen years in the US, finding work to help support his family. He worked with his hands, building, maintaining, and repairing boats— a trade that he remembers with affection and still misses to this day. When Robert asked his father why he had never told him these things before, his father answered, "Why would you want to know? That is the past." That reply also surprised Robert—that there are things about his father that he still does not know; this, from a young person who admits wondering at the start of the project, "What is the point of this interview?"

This assignment is not easy for a group of emergent bilinguals, many of whom have conducted interviews with family members in their native language and translated the conversations to written responses in English for Julia. Now, as Robert attempts to write a piece about his father's journey, he is struck by the difficulty of the assignment. Julia is prepared for this moment and offers encouragement but also tactical strategies for constructing the essay. She walks the class through a series of "sentence starters," phrases to begin sentences or portions of the essay. She encourages them to return to their interview data so that they can look for the responses to the overarching questions of the narrative project. She spends time with each student, examining the interview responses, going over their written notes, and teaching them to match the content of the interview, the guiding question, and the sentence starters that will help them begin their written description. As she sits with each student, she talks through ways to tackle their particular challenges and struggles, and continues to redirect them to the instructional scaffolds that she has created for them to use.

Writing in a new language is difficult, but Julia has incorporated these scaffolds to help her students recognize that they are learning and making gains, even when it can feel like it's not enough. When I ask her about this teaching moment later in the day, Julia explains that "no matter what you teach, you will encounter students who have fears and anxieties about the learning environment. My students happen to have fears about learning a new language and acquiring a kind of fluency that seems really daunting and sometimes impossible to them." As a result, her repertoire of skills to support students not only must include academic scaffolding, but also must acknowledge the social and emotional challenges of facing new, and sometimes intimidating, learning objectives.

Recognizing Language as a Representation of Power

One of the uniquely interesting facets of middle school students, according to Julia, is that they are acutely aware of the world around them and their place within it. Developmentally, middle schoolers "are sensitive to how they are perceived and received by others." Julia explains that for many emergent bilinguals, there is a consciousness about how language is spoken and received: "There is so much shame around, 'Oh, you speak English with an accent.' It's easy for them to get wrapped up in that kind of thinking, because we really do devalue being bilingual sometimes and the focus is so much on being fluent in English. For students who are learning to speak the language, there is an additional burden of feeling like the language you are learning has to sound 'the same way' for everyone." When students think there is one way that English should be spoken and heard, they may feel shame while learning English and devalue their own families, culture, and native language.[5] Schools have, historically and in the present, assimilated young people by prioritizing speaking English "the right way," paying allegiance to a new patriotism and the cultural values, rituals, and behaviors of white middle-class Americans in ways that families actively resist.[6] These assimilationist goals, promoted by language policies in schools, have also encouraged or required students and families to shed their native languages and cultures in efforts to "become American."[7]

In Massachusetts, where Julia teaches, voters passed a 2002 ballot initiative, "Rethinking Equity and Teaching for English Language Learners" (RETELL), that eliminated existing traditional transitional bilingual education classrooms. Instead, emergent bilingual students—or English language learners (ELLs), as the law identifies them—receive nearly all instruction in English unless a parent requests and receives a waiver or the child is enrolled in a two-way bilingual program.[8] This instructional approach, Sheltered English Immersion, has changed the climate and practice in support of emergent bilingual students in the state. The initiative requires that teachers like Julia support her students not as emergent bilinguals, but as ELLs in an English-only immersion program. Restrictive policies like those in Massachusetts contribute to the sense that school is a "subtractive" force that seeks to eliminate existing cultural and linguistic assets and literacies.[9] Devaluing students' native language and culture certainly contributes to their existing insecurities and anxieties about learning a new language.

Driving her work with emergent bilinguals, according to Julia, is a recognition that language represents power. While many might think her job is purely to teach a new language, she explains that teachers who support emergent bilinguals have a more important role than simply teaching language fluency. They must teach students "how to use language as a tool and not see it as something that has control over you or is holding you back, but . . . how can you use this as a tool to open doors, have access and opportunity?"

When schools do not honor the assets and strengths of emergent bilinguals and instead focus purely on "what students can't do and how they can't speak English," it is harmful to students and their families. Julia explains that "you can't separate out the language, tradition, and culture that each person contains within them," so if schools are resistant to honoring the language(s) that students bring with them, then they are sending "a message that [students'] traditions, culture, and family don't matter."

This is a challenge for a teacher like Julia, who must teach within an educational model that explicitly values English immersion. There is no allowance in antibilingual education models for the sustenance and preservation of cultural and linguistic diversity, but, acknowledging our place in a vibrant pluralistic society, Julia seeks to find other ways to develop culturally sustaining pedagogy. Integrating family stories into the curriculum, to Julia, is a way of affirming and honoring their experiences. Through his project, Robert recognizes his father's story and, more importantly, it becomes a part of his learning experience. He and his classmates learn important lessons about migration to the United States through historical context, immigration policies, and the journeys of their own families. For emergent bilinguals, the story of migration is never far away and it is always relevant. Julia reminds us that education policies and practices relating to emergent bilinguals are powerful signals to families about their place and belonging in schools.

Confronting Race, Identity, and Family Engagement

As a white teacher who works with students of color, Julia believes that there is explicit work to be done in examining the culture of her classroom—that of her students and her own. She believes that it is important for her students to get to know her fully, and with this knowledge, they can begin to see her beyond her whiteness or her privilege. Understanding that her students and their families will have had a full range of experiences with white teachers, she is also well aware that she has to build a sense of trust with them that is centered on cultural understanding and recognition: "There are a lot of white women teachers, some of whom they haven't had the best experience with, so I'm also trying to really recognize that I come in with those levels of privilege and that it is on me to bring my full self and recognize that that's also there and that's not something—I can't pretend like I'm not white."

Too often, Julia says, teachers are tempted to skirt the issue of race, but "the reality is that most teachers are white and we are teaching in a system that is mostly students of color. The situation calls us to confront that." One of the ways that Julia best confronts that reality is to intentionally build information about her full self into the conversations and interactions they have in class: "I try to be honest and I like to share things with them and for them to get a sense of who I am and where I come from and why I do this work and why I care, because otherwise, I think especially in the context of this system . . . it's like, 'You're just another white lady teacher.'" When she signals to students that she wants to bring her full self to the classroom, "it doesn't take long" for them to realize that she encourages those interpersonal connections. Whether on issues of race or migration or family or community, she explains that students "are very open in asking me," and she tries to be honest by sharing of herself and her story, which in her mind "lends itself to building relationships and trust and community."

But bringing her full self to the conversation with students and families is only one part of Julia's aspirations as a teacher. As a white woman, she underscores the importance of learning from families about their culture and ways of knowing, particularly as immigrants from native countries that may have strikingly different values and traditions. Julia appreciates, for example, that many of her students' families bring a certain amount of respect to her from the beginning, because in their home countries, teaching is a valued profession. But she has also learned that families may bring differing views and perspectives on schooling and educational experiences as well. These conversations, however, "don't come from the first meeting" as Julia attests, "they come after you have built a sense of trust together."

Marisa is a parent who has established trust and understanding with Julia this year. Marisa moved to Boston from Santo Domingo five years before her daughter Teresa. When Teresa arrived, Marisa anticipated challenges in the transition but was unprepared for how intensely difficult it was. She recalls the first year being "very hard," a "shock" to both of them. Marisa was working two jobs, and Teresa—faced with a new school, a language transition to English that was fully immersive, the loss of old friends, and the difficulty of making new ones—was terrified and "miserable." Marisa recalls, "It was a disaster; it was very hard. She was depressed. She cried a lot." At that point, Teresa was so upset and unhappy that Marisa considered taking her back to the Dominican Republic.

Young Achievers teachers got involved when they learned of Marisa's concerns, and she received a phone call from a teacher who wanted to reassure her. Marisa still remembers this conversation with Cinthia Colón, who did her best to reassure and support her. Cinthia told her that the challenges were not "going to go away overnight," and in fact, it may even take three years for Teresa to make a fuller adjustment. Cinthia shared her own experience as an immigrant and as a teacher working with immigrant families, and tried to reassure Marisa that what she was going through was "just part of the experience" and that the most she could do was to support Teresa and try to be patient with the process. Cinthia also recounted various comments from Teresa's teachers about the strides she was making.

This connection with the teachers helped Marisa "to feel that they understand what we are going through, those important things that really affect how she is doing at school." The connection also gave her confidence that they could stay in this country and make a home and a life here. These are not insignificant contributions, and they are the result of relationships with families that sustain and preserve cultural literacies and experiences rather than replacing or marginalizing them.

Why were the challenges of adjusting to school in the United States so great for Teresa and other students like her? One reason, Marisa explains, stems from the dramatically different nature of the educational environment:

> It's totally different, so much so that the schools here resemble the universities there; that is, the way that they go to their classes, the way they interact, they do this or those presentations as you call them . . . presenting on topics and explaining. We would generally do that as part of professional studies in my country. School is a little simpler there—more at the desk, more about sitting in your chair and doing schoolwork and writing things . . . they don't interact as much.

Educators often believe that the greatest challenge for emergent bilinguals is in learning a new language and adjusting to a social environment where ELLs can be stigmatized, but Marisa reminds us that immigrant children come from a host of different native countries, all with their own unique contrasts to US schools. The cultural expectations of the school and classroom were distinctly different in the Dominican Republic. Ultimately, Marisa feels that the style of teaching and learning at Young Achievers has suited Teresa well and that she has "grown so much in the time that she's been here," but it was important for Julia to know and understand that the school environment itself was critically different.

It wasn't just the school and classroom that were distinct, however; there were different expectations about the relationships between teachers and students as well. Unlike the practice in the United States where teachers meet individually with parents during conferences, in Marisa's experience in the Dominican Republic, schools schedule parent meetings in groups for an hour outside of class time. She describes these meetings as gatherings of ten or more parents and one teacher, and the conversation focuses on general classroom topics, not on an individual child's experience. When Marisa was first asked to talk individually with her child's teachers, she recalls feeling "surprised and nervous" because it was unfamiliar, and she wondered what the meeting would entail: "They don't do what we're doing here now. I mean, I have done this a lot; I always come to [school] meetings by myself, and I feel fine, because [in the Dominican Republic], they give you a schedule for all the parents to meet together, see? That is, there isn't just one, for just one parent, like you do [here]. I've come here and I've talked to all the teachers, just me."

Julia's work with immigrant families is driven by her experiences in these communities; her actions and decisions as a teacher are guided by stories of migration, cultural border crossing, the importance of family, the social isolation of newcomer immigrants, and the guiding care and concern about a child's education. To her, there is "no choice" when it comes to integrating family and community realities into her work as a teacher, a point she made in a conversation we had at the beginning of the year, after the October back-to-school night. I spent that evening next to a mother, with a young child in her lap, who was using the headset that was streaming Julia's voice and translation. After the presentation, parents and family members began to disperse and head to individual classrooms. As the mother picked up her son to walk out of the auditorium, the audio box connected to her headset fell to the ground and slid under the row of seats in front of us. Noticing her hands were full, I went to pick it up and return it her, speaking to her in Spanish. She explained what the device was for and when I asked her if it was helpful, she replied in quite simple terms, "Without this, I would not be here." When I relayed this interaction to Julia a few weeks later, she, too, had a simple reply, "That's why this work is not a choice."

THE BEAUTY OF CONNECTIONS

Connecting Parents to Each Other

Early in her conversations with immigrant parents, Julia learned that families often experienced challenges in their transition to the US, such as learning a new language, adjusting to a new work environment, and acclimating to an unfamiliar community. When parents were juggling multiple jobs, working evenings, and caring for multiple young or school-age children, there was little time for new social connections. Julia found that many of her students' parents, particularly mothers, reported feeling isolated and lonely. Many mothers were either single parents and/or had little family support locally. While their children began to build friendships and connections among peers, social connections for newcomer parents were harder to come by. Julia began to see how much these parents would enjoy a connection to each other: "I remember I went to do a home visit . . . and [a mother] told me, 'It's really hard being here. I feel really lonely.' That was one of the first things she said to me right away. So . . . that's been present in my mind, so last year my goal was to integrate families a lot."

Julia recalls pondering how to foster these connections at the conclusion of her first year as a teacher. While her focus as a teacher had been primarily to connect with each family, she saw the value in having parents connect with one another as well. Such opportunities—even in a school like Young Achievers, which prides itself on its connections to families—were rare and not without challenges. Maria, a parent I met at one of the school's family nights, describes the difficulty, particularly for immigrant parents: "This school has so many opportunities for us to feel welcome. They have programs for parents in the evening, and many parents come to that, but it is not easy when you are new to the country. There are many parents who seem to know each other, and it can be hard to make a connection, especially if your language is not yet good enough. Sometimes, you can leave a program and feel the same loneliness you felt before."

The desire to encourage connections across parents lingered in Julia's mind amidst the goals of engaging families in the classroom, and an opportunity to act on these ideas emerged. Julia planned to accompany a group of students on a nine-day school-sponsored trip to Costa Rica during spring break. A group of her ESL students were committed to the trip. The school convened information sessions for families whose children would be going on the trip, but discovered that many of the Spanish-speaking families would not be able to attend an after-school presentation due to their evening work schedules or childcare issues. Julia volunteered to offer information sessions in Spanish for the Spanish-speaking families in the morning.

The small size of the group coupled with the shared experience of the Costa Rica trip "brought these families together in ways I didn't anticipate but that I was so happy to see," Julia recalls. "I wanted them to talk to each other. I wanted them to get to know each other," but "I wasn't always sure how to encourage that amongst them." As they began to talk about the trip, Julia recounts, the parents began to feel a sense of connection to each other:

> It's interesting, this is a situation where parents come together and they're talking about the trip and sharing their concerns and questions. One parent is really worried about their child swimming, and somebody else assures them, "Oh, don't worry" . . . in that moment, it wasn't centered around me making explanations to the parents. It was a group of moms and me sitting around a circle having a conversation about this trip, where everybody was part of the conversation. It was a really beautiful moment.

Marisa was one of the parents in this group. She experienced many unforeseen logistical challenges in preparing Teresa for the Costa Rica trip but found that the support of the other families allowed her "to feel that it was possible." She recalls:

> I was afraid for this trip, because you worry, you know? As a parent, you want to know that your child will be okay and at some point,

you just have to trust that the process will take care of itself. I am not sure I would have been able to go through it without knowing the other parents who were sending their children. And then it helped me, because my daughter was friends with their daughters and then I had the chance to get to know their families. As a parent, you do not always get a chance to feel that you can know the other families.

Through this experience, Julia felt parents like Marisa "coming together" in ways that she had always desired but not fully understood how to accomplish.

What were some of the lessons from being with the mothers who connected during the Costa Rica information sessions? How did this setting generate open engagement and dialogue? Clearly, these were smaller settings where Spanish-speaking parents felt free to ask questions and share their insight with others they might feel comfortable with, whereas they might hesitate to engage in connections with other parents during large schoolwide events and activities.

But there was also Julia's insistence that the conversation be parent-centered and not dominated by her voice or perspective. She encouraged parents to freely guide the conversation. While she did offer insight about the trip and information that was important for families, she also fostered a discussion that was rooted in parents' language, questions, concerns, and feedback. In fact, these connections led to parents supporting one another—providing an early-morning ride to the airport for a parent without a car and offering reassurance and encouragement as they faced the daunting task of sending their children abroad. Finally, there was a shared experience that connected them. Without introductions or time to get acquainted, parents often do not know enough about each other to feel connected; this situation brought these families together in ways that encouraged more connection. And while these goals for engaging parents—fostering small-group settings, creating parent-centered spaces, and identifying shared experiences— may be applicable in most communities, Julia also understood that she was engaging a particular group of parents; her efforts were culturally grounded. She recognized the common concerns and anxieties that these parents would have. She knew that as immigrant mothers and newcomers themselves, they would welcome the social connection to other parents with a shared experience and could express their potential to support one another as well.

Embracing a Relational Approach to Families Rooted in Listening and Appreciation

When I ask Julia why she feels motivated to bring parents together, an aspiration that is quite unique among her peers, she simply states, "Well, that's the message I get when I listen to them." In fact, much of what she explains about her family engagement practices comes from her experiences with families—with migrant farm workers and their children, and with her students' families.

One fundamental aspect of her communication with families is that it begins with light and brightness. She explains, "No matter who we're talking about, every kid, there is a light that they bring to the classroom, and it's my job as their teacher to not get too busy or distracted from noticing that." Julia believes it is important to reach out to parents from the beginning with these affirmations of their children. "Whenever I'm connecting with families and talking about students, I always start from their strengths and the gains that I see and what they bring." This positive approach to meeting and communicating with families allows teachers and families to develop a sense of trust as well. Marisa, who gained confidence about the Costa Rica trip through meeting with other mothers, explains what it means to her to have a teacher who appreciates her daughter Teresa in full and complete ways:

In the beginning, it was very hard for [my daughter], all of the struggle that she had when she was learning English and becoming part of the school. Now that she has been here longer, she feels more comfortable, but it is important to hear the encouragement from the teacher. She can feel frustrated, my child, because she wants to do her best, and I feel so thankful that the teacher shows me how well she is doing and gives me a chance to see her achieve things. I feel very satisfied about that and it makes me feel comfortable with the teacher.

These one-to-one conversations in support of children are not always focused on the positive, and often there are necessary, difficult conversations about academic or social concerns. But Julia believes that these conversations are easier when they build upon prior communication that has recognized a child's strengths and assets. This is, in part, how teachers can build a sense of trust with families. According to Julia, "the best way to support students is to feel like you are working with their parents, and you won't feel like you're working with their parents until you have established some trust with them. It doesn't always exist at the beginning and it's my responsibility to build it if that's the case."

To establish this trust, Julia tries to express to parents how valuable their perspective is to her and to recognize that they know their child in ways that are important, greater than her own understanding, and thus essential to her as a teacher. But merely asking parents for their input or feedback is not a simple endeavor, particularly if they are not accustomed to being asked by educators to share their perspective. Julia recounts her early experiences during family conferences:

> Parents are the experts on their children and so I want to know, "What do you notice at home?" or "What are they passionate about?" and "What do they enjoy learning about?" or "What do they like?" I always try to start the conversation with what they bring before immediately jumping into what's not happening or jumping into my own assessment as to what's going on. I want to know how they think the year is going and how their child is doing in school, just starting from that point of giving them the chance to speak first. And it's interesting because I don't think parents are used to that. I think some parents are uncomfortable at first because they aren't used to that. [They say,] "I'm not used to that. I'm used to you just coming in and telling me, 'Here are their test scores, here's what they're doing, here's what they're not doing, here's how they measure up to seventh-grade standards.'"

When teachers develop a sense of trust with families, Julia also asserts that the routine communication between parent and teacher "becomes much easier and almost effortless." Teachers who don't have relationships with families may feel that their efforts to communicate are intimidating, cumbersome, or an added burden and responsibility:

> When you have that base level of trust and you have that relationship, those kinds of little things or those quick check-ins—whether it's about behavior or grades or this—you don't have to feel like there's one more thing on your plate. When you have that relationship as that strong foundation, then that channel's been opened up so when things come up, you're better able to access that or navigate that relationship or you know what's really going on at home . . . You begin to understand situations within the larger scope of things.

Julia uses the example of one student, Lety, to explain what she means. Lety has severe allergies, and her complex health issues precipitated the family's move to the United States. Her condition had become so precarious, and the medical facilities in Puerto Rico so limited, that her mother Ayla decided to move them to Boston for better health care. Lety has regular doctor's appointments, and while her mother tries to schedule them outside of school time, Lety still is often late to school. On evenings prior to a doctor's appointment, Lety's mother will often text Julia to remind her that her daughter may be late. These simple messages are reminders to Julia that Lety is late for a reason. Julia explains, "You know even those little things, versus in the past where you're like, 'Ah, they're always late for school or absent.' I know exactly why she's absent. I know exactly what's going on." The early conversations between Julia and Ayla allowed Julia to understand the larger scope of Lety's life—her health, her parents' aspirations for her education—and to demonstrate a shared interest in supporting her. Julia explains, "There are so many points at which assumptions can be made, and those assumptions can misdirect our actions or our reactions. It's not just about building trust; it's about building understanding."

Rethinking Family Engagement in Middle Schools

Julia is unabashed about her embrace of families in her classroom, a rarity in middle and high schools. While many regard family engagement positively, most assume that it is a practice reserved for elementary schools. It is not surprising to see parents of elementary school children volunteering in a classroom, chaperoning a field trip, or generally present in the school, but adolescents, with their growing independence, may not want to see their families participate in the same ways. Middle schools themselves are structured in ways that make communication with individual families challenging and interactions with parents quick and sporadic. Unlike elementary schools, where children usually have one primary teacher, in middle school students have many different teachers, who in turn have large student rosters. While it seems reasonable to expect elementary teachers to be connected to their twenty-five students' families, it seems an impossible burden for a middle school science teacher, for example, to be engaged with one hundred families in a large public school.

This reality means we must find a developmentally appropriate way to engage families of middle schools students, particularly when studies show that there is a positive relationship between general parent engagement and academic achievement among middle school students.[10] Despite the growing independence of adolescents, positive parent-child relationships and parents' general support of children at home continue to impact middle school children's schooling in positive ways.[11]

Young Achievers is a K–8 school, and while some spaces like the cafeteria, gym, art room, and music room are shared by students across the grades, the middle school students also have a physical space apart from the elementary-age students. Being a middle school teacher in a K–8 school with a vision for integrating families has certainly affected Julia's ideas about family engagement. Prior to joining Young Achievers, Julia, like others, had observed that elementary school is a space where "volunteering in a class or going on field trips or bringing food in if there's a party, bringing cupcakes when there's a birthday" is accepted and sometimes expected, but it is "a different dynamic that doesn't always get translated to middle school."

In middle schools, parental engagement and communication usually involves one-way reporting on grades, information sessions for parents on the year ahead, and discussion of behavior-related problems that crop up. Julia argues, however, that even in middle school, "it is possible to communicate to parents about behavior and grades, and also to focus on the 'real relationship-building piece.'" Without this distinction, teachers may feel they are doing all that's necessary to engage families by reporting on grades and behavior, but Julia believes that these conversations are ineffective when teachers have not paid attention to the "relationship-building" and development of trust that must come first:

> We have to find a balance between what we all agree needs to be done—communicating about behavior and grades—and what we believe must be a foundation to that communication: building trust and real relationships. It can feel really challenging as middle school teachers, because our jobs are challenging and we don't have time and there are so many other commitments and sixty-plus students that you're working with throughout a day.

Building Trust Through Collaborative Family Conferences

It might seem unreasonable to expect a teacher to engage with more than sixty families, but Julia explains that middle school teachers at Young Achievers have devised a different way of engaging families, "because it's just not sustainable to be able to [build relationships with the family] of every kid." At Young Achievers, she and her middle school teaching colleagues plan family conferences as a team. To provide space and time for these meetings with parents, the school sets aside a full professional development day for family conferences.[12] Julia explains that there is a schoolwide expectation to value and meet with all families, so teachers find it helpful to have this time allocated in the schedule "to actually have the time and resources to focus when meeting with families versus teachers having to use PD time, their own lunch time, and before/after school to schedule conferences. Without admin allocating the time for conferences, it feels like more work for teachers and inevitably is always cut short, rushed, or distracted."

A middle school team may decide to meet together with families, so that the group can collectively have an opportunity to hear from the family and offer feedback across the different subject area classrooms. These conversations have the added benefit that teachers, being together, can gain insight into each student's experience with different teachers and in different subject areas and learning environments.

In other instances, teachers create stations around the room so families can move around and meet with each of them individually, allowing for more families to be scheduled simultaneously. One teacher, the advisor—or sometimes, as in Julia's case, the teacher who is most fluent in the language spoken by the family—remains a point person to encourage families to stay connected with the team. This assignment of a point person is rooted in a recognition that it is challenging for parents to manage communication with myriad teachers. Whether teacher teams meet collectively with families or individually in a room devoted to conversations with teachers across the team, what is important to Julia is that it is a collaborative effort. As a novice teacher, she learns immensely from the collective conversation and the insight of her colleagues: "I think that having that team approach, it's very unifying as teachers. I think that sends messages to families that we are a team of people who are committed to working with your student."

WHAT DO NEW AND ASPIRING TEACHERS NEED TO FEEL SUCCESSFUL IN ENGAGING FAMILIES?

I invited Julia, a second-year teacher, to be part of this project because I believe it is important for *all* teachers, not just those who are experienced, to integrate families into their practice. When I first met her, soon after she had been hired to teach at Young Achievers, I had a sense, given her prior experience working with immigrant families and her explicit commitment to engaging families, that she would bring a unique perspective as a new teacher. Julia's story is an important one, because she shows us that new teachers *can* effectively engage families, and in doing so they can become more successful teachers.

Intentional Support and Modeling

Julia completed her teacher training through the Boston Teacher Residency (BTR), a yearlong clinical teacher preparation program that is modeled on medical residencies. BTR residents spend an immersive year in Boston classrooms with a mentor teacher and simultaneously enroll in courses taught by BTR faculty. Julia recalls applying to the program due to "its commitment to the local community and educational equity," and she appreciated the "intense amount of time in the classroom" during her training.

While family engagement was not necessarily a focus of her training, she learned by example from one of her mentor teachers in the program, Susie. A fifth-grade teacher in an SEI classroom, Susie was not "necessarily a teacher that reached out to families all the time, but she really got to know the students and she really cared about them as learners." For Julia, Susie's presence and example were "inspiring." As part of her program, Julia was required to conduct a parent conference with her mentor teacher's assistance. What she learned from that conference still resonates:

> As we started the conference, [Susie] said, "You're the expert on your child. Tell me. Tell me who they are as learners, or what do you think their strengths are?" She really honored the parents. "You raise your child. You know them." I feel like she really showed me how to lead a conference, giving parents the space for them to share first or [asking] "What do you see as concerns?" or "Do you have any concerns?" or "What are you worried about with your child?" So really putting their voices first and as the centerpiece.

Julia also remembers that when Susie began to talk about the child, she shared concrete examples of what he or she was able to do in school. The stories were "detailed and specific," about how a child was helpful to other students during an activity, or excited about a particular topic in class. These accounts brought a level of interest and engagement from the parents that was palpable, and Julia remembers "soaking in everything, because it was teaching me how to be with families in an open, honest, and collaborative way." In her mind, the conference was unlike what she had come to know and expect. It concluded with an appeal to collaborate: "I just really love the way that [Susie] conducted that parent conference, where it didn't feel that it was about the grades. And of course after all that, [she asked], 'So . . . now that we know you voiced things you're concerned about, here's what I see. Okay, so now how are we gonna problem-solve together to figure out how to best support your child?'"

Clearly, Julia's interactions with Susie shaped her own ideas about effective family engagement, but she believes that it was through luck and circumstance that she learned from a teacher who had a family-centered orientation to the parent conference. If teacher preparation programs do not develop and support family engagement explicitly, teacher candidates will learn through the school context. As a result, what a new teacher learns will be "dependent upon your mentor teacher and what they're focused on and how they interact with families . . . They could be the kind of teacher who I've heard say, 'I just can't focus on that,' where it's a very conscious choice to say, 'Family engagement is not on my plate. I'm not doing it.'" This common misconception—that family engagement is a choice—inhibits the cultivation of schools that truly embrace and welcome families.

While teacher candidates may not receive any training or mentorship in family engagement, they often come to the classroom with clear conceptions of what it could look like. There exists a near-universal model of family engagement that often involves teacher-led parent conferences, bake sales, PTA meetings, and school open houses. Parents and teachers alike can get locked into a particular interaction they have come to expect. Julia explains:

> I think that for most teachers, the parent conference is immediately about teachers talking *at* parents. Then when we ask [parents] at the very end, "Do you have any questions or anything?" it's like, "Well, you've already obviously told me everything, so what could I possibly have to say?" It doesn't create a space for parents to be able to really engage when teachers just kind of go right in and talk to parents as if we know what's best for your kid.

This parent conference scenario does not have to be the case. New teachers are adept at reimagining classroom practice when provided the scaffolds and supports to do so. Communicating with and engaging parents, however, are the most frequently cited challenges among novice teachers and the area they feel the least prepared to manage during their first year.[13] Clearly, teachers need support in family engagement. Julia believes that, with proper support and training, new teachers will feel more competent and successful in engaging families. As part of their training, teachers could learn about the different ways schools engage families, be it home visits, parent programs, family conferences, or general communication with families. For structured and universal practices like the parent-teacher conference, Julia says, there could be greater support for new teachers as well:

> Even if it was just a framework for how you could structure or organize a parent conference. Just like we have that framework for mini-lessons, there should be a framework for parent conferences. And sometimes it's talked about, but it's not really explicit. Not to say you always have to follow a formula, but "Here's a way to think about it—make sure that you're giving parents the space to speak first," figuring out all these nuances.

As with the other elements of teaching that teacher training programs support and develop, they could also teach, model, challenge, and support family engagement. These scaffolds will allow teachers like Julia to come into the classroom with new ideas and address some of the most significant challenges new teachers face.

Understanding the Benefits, Possibility, and Sustainability of Family Engagement

Often overwhelmed by the sheer challenges of planning and executing instruction, novice teachers sometimes express resistance when asked to engage families. Julia explains, "I think oftentimes, we are focused, as teachers, on students first. So it's just like, 'I can only do so much. My students are my focus.' And I get that and that is very true—that's all that you can personally be responsible for. But I think it's wrong to say that we are focused on students instead of their families. I think it's about taking a more holistic approach, which is going to help you more in the long run." When tasked with family engagement, some teachers argue that the additional focus on families is too much. However, if successful student learning experiences are the goal, then engaging families is a necessary part of achieving that goal. Given some schools' lack of attention to family engagement, Julia endorses a "paradigm shift":

> I think that you have to recognize the importance of this mental shift—it's a paradigm shift. You have to realize that working and collaborating with families is going to help you lesson-plan. It's going to help you do these other things that are really overwhelming and daunting and that you feel you have to spend all your time doing. But in essence, knowing families and knowing those students—that's going to help you engage better with them; it's going to help you support them in their learning more.

This shift would mean that novice teachers, rather than postponing engaging families, would benefit from connecting with them. Julia says, "Reaching out to families at the beginning of the year and establishing that relationship is going to help you so that when things do come up and you need to call a family or you need to call when someone's in trouble . . . it's not like, 'Who are you?' And then you're just some teacher that's calling when there's something bad going on." At the same time, this partnership also allows Julia to work with parents in collaborative ways to support their child's learning and growth. She explains, "When you are working alone, it's easy to feel that every responsibility is yours alone, but when you communicate with families and work with them, you feel that you are doing this together. I can honestly say I have had so much more success as a teacher because I'm working with their families."

Julia believes that families are integral to her development, success, and sustenance as a teacher. It may be hard for some educators to see beyond the "phone calls, text messages, hallway conversations" sprinkled throughout her day. It may seem tedious, laborious, and distracting, given the sheer weight of responsibility that every teacher manages. But "beyond the tasks of engaging families," Julia notes that there is immense reward. The sense of partnership allows her to feel more successful as a teacher, more confident in her decisions, and more hopeful about the long arc of her career as an educator. Most importantly, she feels satisfied in her progress, motivated by what's to come, and joyful in the relationships she has built. This sense of contentment among teachers receives little recognition and attention, yet as a novice teacher, Julia believes it is key to her commitment to the profession and the sustenance of the "joy and hope in teaching as well as a belief in the possibility of what lies ahead."

6

New Hopes and Possibilities Through Culturally Sustaining Family Engagement

Every teacher experiences moments of joy in the classroom and a true sense of hope and possibility in their practice. These are mixed in with moments of frustration and a sense of demoralization as well. To be a teacher today requires a great sense of purpose and a deep belief that you have something to offer in shaping and influencing the next generation, because the challenges are significant.

There are many ideas and propositions for how to deal with these challenges. School reform efforts seek to influence school leadership, enhance the classroom learning environment, address the social emotional lives of young people, and develop standards and curricula that meet the evolving needs of students and of career, college, and industry.

DEMYSTIFYING THE RELATIONSHIPS BETWEEN SCHOOLS AND FAMILIES

This book proposes that we also pay close attention to the relationships between schools and families. To create schools that truly promote culturally sustaining pedagogies and practices, we must encourage teachers to cultivate relationships that are rooted in trust and recognize the full range of resources that families bring. As the teacher and parent narratives in this book show, there are steep hurdles to address first. Parents and teachers are not always ready to see each other as partners.

In my conversations with parents, I heard painful accounts and troubling stories of broken relationships and traumatic interactions between parents and teachers. In fact, many of the difficulties teachers faced communicating with parents stemmed from a parent's unwillingness to trust or enter into a relationship with teachers. Trina, a parent in Megan Lucas's classroom, recalls how hard it was to come to the realization that she could actually work with teachers: "So many times, you feel that your child is just at the whim of these teachers who maybe aren't that invested in your child. Or you have heard some of the ugly things that teachers say or the ways they treat your child. You just get so tired of that, and you don't know who you can trust anymore. Even when a kind teacher reaches out to me, my instinct is to be cynical—'Oh, this is not going to stay this way.'"

Parents describe some of their interactions with teachers as "horror stories," or "something I would be ashamed to share with my child." Through their own experiences as students, parents can harbor past trauma and resentment toward teachers who "gave up on us" or "never believed we would amount to anything." Some of these interactions are subtle—a disparaging comment or a statement of antipathy about their job—but some are hostile and antagonistic. Thus, parents do not always enter relationships with teachers with bright-eyed hope, optimism, and reverence for their abilities and expertise. Rather, some parents could be hypersensitive to how their child is treated. Misgivings about a teacher can turn into negative feelings quickly.

Some teachers have no idea that parents will come to them shaped by previous negative encounters. They may feel their own defensive posture mixed with a wish to be appreciated and recognized. Their desire for recognition, coupled with unawareness of parent anxieties, may create a relationship that is fractured from the start. Teachers may wonder, "Why don't these parents respond to me? Why don't they care about their child's education?" Similarly, parents may ask, "What does she want from me? Why should I call her back when she is probably going to complain about my child?"

As mentioned in the introduction, in the 1930s sociologist Willard Waller described parents and teachers as "natural enemies."[1] Parents, as the primary caretakers of their children before they enter school, believe (with good reason) that they know their child best. This wealth of knowledge about and experience with their child becomes questioned or irrelevant when the child enters the classroom and the teacher becomes an established authority. While parents may be singularly focused on their child's well-being, a teacher attends to that child within the context of the class as a whole. This contrast between what a parent knows and what a teacher knows often results in conflict. It is exacerbated by a school's insistence that interactions between teachers and families center on the interests of schools. Waller explains: "Parent-teacher work has usually been directed at securing for the school the support of parents, that is, at getting parents to see children more or less as teachers see them. But it would be a sad day for childhood if parent-teacher work ever really succeeded in its object."[2] In this way, parent-teacher interactions become a mechanism for communicating in one direction—from teachers to parents—about the expectations and priorities of the school.

Schools as Marginalizing Institutions

Are parents and teachers truly natural enemies? Clearly, the experiences reported by parents in this book point to a relationship that is too often broken. Teachers admit that parents don't return their calls or that parents become confrontational when they share concerns. To say that they are natural enemies, however, assumes that teachers and parents are innately inclined to work in opposition and compete for authority and expertise.

This opposition is not exactly what the families and teachers in this book describe. Instead, they share stories describing schools as *marginalizing institutions* that distort the interactions between teachers and parents in harmful ways. We may be tempted to see schools as institutions that promote opportunity and support young people in pursuing their hopes and dreams; certainly, this is the goal. But schools are cultural institutions that oftentimes reflect, reinforce, and reify the illness and inequity of the larger society. Systems of structural oppression such as racism, poverty, economic segregation, and anti-immigration policies

157

are replicated in schools unless educators are explicit about an intention and vision to implement antiracist and anti-oppressive practices. This is our past and it bleeds into the present. How do these teacher and family narratives describe schools as marginalizing institutions?

Schools are sites of past trauma

Narratives of parents, caregivers, and teachers reveal that schools can represent oppressive environments and can exist as sites of past (and present) trauma. When parents step into a classroom for a parent-teacher conference, their expectations and interactions with a teacher are colored by misgivings, anxieties, and what Sara Lawrence-Lightfoot calls the "ghosts" of past experiences with schools.[3] These experiences and the psychodynamic response that they elicit for parents and caregivers, when unaddressed or unrecognized, can limit the possibilities for positive, honest, and open communication between parents and teachers. Rather than seeing parents through this resistance or unresponsiveness, a commitment to healing-centered engagement assumes that the interaction is the symptom of a deeper harm, not confrontational defiance or disrespect.[4]

Schools are designed to keep parents at bay

From the dismissive receptionist in the main office to the lines on the school blacktop for dropping off and picking up children, schools often make parents feel that they must justify their presence. While these measures may be rooted in safety or efficiency, they point to the many ways that schools dictate exactly when and where parents can or cannot be present. Even during times when parents are invited into the school, there are structures in place to limit their movement and interactions. A middle school open house may allow parents eight minutes in each classroom for a short presentation, after which point a school bell rings and parents are quickly ushered out to the next room. The few minutes in between sessions make it nearly impossible for a parent and teacher to interact in a meaningful way. These kinds of guardrails can diminish a parent's sense of welcome and familiarity in the school.

Schools prioritize professional expertise

Increasingly, the education of young people has become highly professionalized. Learning standards and objectives, mandated curricula, and district-sanctioned programs shape and influence teaching and learning as well as school management and organization. All of the teachers in this study reported the high demands and expectations that districts place on them through the cycle of new programs and initiatives, each requiring a new knowledge set. The intense pressure on teachers to meet these revolving expectations, as well as the high-stakes nature of standardized tests, prioritizes professional expertise and minimizes the experience and expertise of families as less than professional. Additionally, when teachers are struggling to keep up due to external pressures, they have less time, energy, and patience for engaging families.

Schools enact decision-making with limited participation from families

Decision-making in schools rarely involves the participation and viewpoints of students and families, especially in low-income communities of color. That is, school leaders often make decisions—even ones that impact families, such as contracts for afterschool programs and methods for engaging families—without input from students, families, and community members. If a parent finds a family program to be disappointing or in need of improvement, there is often no way for that parent to offer feedback beyond contacting a teacher or administrator on their own.

School staff do not reflect the cultural diversity of the communities they serve

Even in schools that primarily serve students of color, the proportion of teachers and administrators that are people of color remains low.[5] While the community may be linguistically and culturally diverse, schools are primarily staffed by monolingual white educators with little knowledge of the language, culture, and life experiences of students and their families. Schools may seem like unfamiliar places when the teaching staff does not represent the community. Local, community knowledge is unlikely to be part of the expertise of educators in the school.

When schools become marginalizing institutions, students and their families are dehumanized in the process. Rather than honoring and valuing their culture, traditions, values, and experiences, schools can fail to acknowledge them or reject them altogether. Deficit approaches to teaching and learning assume the languages, literacies, and cultural ways of knowing of communities of color as liabilities rather than assets.[6] As a result, the linguistic and cultural practices of students of color are eradicated and replaced. The current trend of "no excuses" schools rests on the presumption that a child's background, living context, and life circumstance do not and should not matter. While no child should fail to access a quality education due to their background, the details of their families and communities *do* matter. The challenges we see in our schools today are a relic and reminder of the racism, marginalization, and oppression that wreaked havoc and violence on communities in the past.[7] The past most certainly bleeds into the present.

Schools as Grounded Institutions

In our most aspirational notions of education, on the other hand, we may see schools as sites of liberation, belonging, connection, and individual transformation. The narratives of the educators and families in this book call for schools as *grounded institutions*—schools that are rooted in and reflect the full lives and experiences of students' families and communities. Through home visits, family conferences, and regular communication with families, these teachers are continually learning about families and the larger community, understanding their experiences, and building relationships with parents and caregivers. What they learn in these conversations, visits, and interactions in turn shapes how they design their curriculum, how they approach and communicate with families, and how they understand the role of partnership in supporting students. How do their narratives describe schools as grounded institutions?

*Schools celebrate the diversity of communities and strive to be
unique, not uniform*

Rather than believing there should be one way to engage families,
grounded schools recognize and celebrate the languages, literacies, and
cultural ways of being of communities of color. Becoming effective
at engaging families requires being adaptive, responsive, and unique,
not uniform. Founding principal Dawn Lewis expressed this vision for
Young Achievers:

> Schools can be so absent of the families and communities they serve.
> It can sometimes lead you to believe that our goal is to create one
> version of a school that will work no matter where you go, but this
> doesn't work. We have always believed that the families and this
> community are at the heart of all we do. We should know them, we
> should partner with them, and we should learn about the commu-
> nity too. This is our responsibility as educators. It should be at the
> heart of everything we do.

Schools view successful family engagement as an issue of educational equity

Too often, arguments for family and community engagement are centered on the importance of honoring and valuing communities. Inherent in this argument is an assumption that schools can be a mechanism
for promoting a pluralist society. There is an implicit benevolence in
this framing—that communities of color get their share of recognition
and celebration. These teachers, however, believe that engaging with
students' families is an essential element in being a successful teacher.
It is not an option; as our society shifts, so does the "culture of power."[8]
These teachers recognize that our school communities require teachers who can ensure equal access, representation, and opportunity to all
families.

*Schools build a web of connections that cultivate relationships and
trust with all families*

Educators too often make the easy connections to parents who are
present in the school or who extend their own invitations to support

the classroom. Instead, like the teachers in this book, educators should strive to build connections to *all* families, even those who may seem hard to reach. Using outdated and inappropriate definitions of family engagement can create a fundamental disconnection between families and schools, especially with families who are poor, of color, economically distressed, immigrants, and/or limited English speakers. It may be more accurate that schools—programs, practices, policies, and school personnel—are "hard to reach," not the families.[9] New modes of family engagement are necessary to create a complex web of relationships that connects families with teachers, school staff, administrators, and each other. In schools that work with traditionally marginalized communities, this is paramount and must be part of a larger effort to engage in dialogue across difference.

Schools invite meaningful two-way conversation with families

Teachers build connections with families not merely to report on what occurs in the classroom but also to obtain feedback and develop meaningful and productive ways to collaboratively support students. When Annie Shah reflects on her own experience at Young Achievers and what she has learned, she has come to understand that the work of engaging families is much more wide-ranging than she initially imagined. It's more than the phone calls and communication with parents that most schools expect, focused primarily on what teachers report to parents:

> We talk about what's at the root of the things that are important to us. It helps us understand that there are values or goals that guide what we do. I would say this should be true of a school. What is at the root of its interactions with students? I believe that what anchors us [at Young Achievers] is that we believe that the school should be a welcome place for families, but being welcome is not enough. How will families feel welcome here? They have to have relationships with us, be able to come to us when they have a question or something to share about their child. What we teach has to be grounded in the kinds of experiences that students have and the ones that they still need to explore. Everything we do should matter based on what

we know about our students, their families, and this beautiful community . . . we can't just report information to families; we have to be able to receive it from them, process it, and work with it.

Schools recognize and dismantle the pervasive problems of lopsided power in schools

In a seminal 1993 article that is still relevant today, Michelle Fine wrote that "parents enter the contested public sphere of public education typically with neither resources nor power."[10] The busy hum and full calendar of school activity is little influenced by parents, especially in marginalized communities. This presents a lopsided dynamic where educators and administrators exercise unilateral power—"power over" parents. To fear parent power reflects a "unilateral power framework of winners and losers."[11] Within this framework of power, teachers are not always winners either. The constant churn of new policies and programs goes on without the input of teachers. If teachers and parents can see themselves as allies and partners, there is a possibility for building collective power in schools. In contrast to unilateral power arrangements, teachers and parents can take a more relational approach, centered on the "power to" act collectively and share leadership and decision-making.[12]

Teachers emerge as collaborative leaders who are deeply invested in families and communities

The solitary nature of teaching can pose challenges to individual teachers but can also impact the collective voice, agency, and leadership of teachers within a school. Teachers also sense that they have little influence in policy decisions that impact their lives in the classroom. By establishing relationships with parents, dismantling traditional barriers to collaboration, and working collectively to improve students' educational experiences and outcomes, teachers emerge with a greater sense of leadership and agency in schools. Opportunities for teacher leadership, particularly outside of classrooms, are poorly developed, and this presents a missed chance for equitable system change and improvement.[13] By working alongside family and community partners, teachers build upon their experience and expertise to map out new possibilities for equitable school-family relationships.

Schools become spaces that sustain the cultural experiences of students of color

Many would agree that Ilene, Megan, Cinthia, Annie, and Julia are, at the core, culturally responsive teachers, or teachers who engage in culturally relevant or responsive pedagogy. That is, they view the cultural literacies, languages, and experiences of their students' families not as deficits or liabilities, but as key resources in the community that educators must recognize, appreciate, and understand.[14] Conceptualizations of resource pedagogies such as these have made a deep and lasting imprint in educational research, policy, and practice, encouraging educators to re-envision the classroom and embrace the language and culture of students across categories of difference. These frameworks challenge the marginalizing nature of schools and directly seek to transform the school itself so that it reflects students' cultural literacies, languages, and experiences. This is at the heart of what these teachers do.

But they are also doing more. They seek to disrupt and dismantle the dominant white cultural narratives and curricular practices in schools, particularly as these relate to family engagement. This is a different kind of commitment to students' families and communities, because it is explicitly concerned with cultural preservation and sustenance. The commitment is also unique in that it is not singularly focused on the teaching and learning dynamics within the classroom. Their focus, at least not in the framework of this book, is not on curriculum development, teacher-student interactions, or restorative practices in classrooms, but at the same time, it is. Teachers center family conferences on the experiences of children and families; they bring in parents to develop empathic and collaborative approaches to addressing a student's behavioral challenges; they work families' life histories and cultural traditions into classroom projects and learning experiences. Their steadfast commitment to engaging students' families and communities and the authentic relationships that they cultivate flow into all they do as teachers.

At the same time, teachers must recognize the reality of students' communities as well as the social and political world that shapes and influences their families. While schools push to understand the experiences of Latinx, Asian American, African American, and indigenous families, educators must refrain from seeing these communities as cultural monoliths. Through sustained relationships with families, educators can recognize the distinct experiences of refugees, immigrants, and asylum-seekers as well as the myriad narratives of Vietnamese American families, Korean American families, first- and second-generation immigrants, undocumented students, and students from mixed-status families. When teachers and family members cultivate relationships of trust and understanding, educators can also move away from the potentially harmful assumptions and generalizations that oversimplify diversity within a school.

Consequently, sustaining culture requires knowledge and understanding about the cultural experiences of communities, as well as the recognition of the diversity within them. The scholarship on culturally sustaining pedagogies recognizes the centrality of *honoring* students' families and communities, yet advances the idea that schooling should be a site for *sustaining* the cultural practices and experiences of communities of color.[15] This distinction—between honor and recognition and then sustenance and preservation—is an important one in understanding family engagement as well. Without diminishing the ways that schools celebrate families (e.g., through multicultural potluck dinners or invitations to parents to talk to students about cultural holidays such as the lunar new year), we must expect and do more. We must work toward a model of culturally sustaining family engagement: definitions and modes of engaging families that sustain the cultural practices and experiences of communities of color while also inviting their experience and knowledge about children, families, and communities.

This concept of culturally sustaining family engagement is derived from myriad theoretical insights and contributions, from the early calls by Gloria Ladson-Billings to develop and support educators who must be culturally responsive, to the more recent conceptualizations of culturally sustaining pedagogy by Django Paris and H. Samy Alim and the many other scholars who have contributed to our critical understanding of teacher practice.[16] In our discussions of resource pedagogies—be it culturally relevant or responsive education or culturally sustaining pedagogies—we must be clear and exact about the relationships between teachers and students' families. While there is a recognition that honoring families and valuing communities is paramount, there is less direction about *how* educators will make these connections with parents and caregivers in communities of color, immigrant/refugee communities, and poor communities. In order to sustain the languages, literacies, and cultural ways of being of students' families, teachers must learn and understand them in the first place, but how? Our understanding of and ideas about family engagement are key.

The five teachers in this book reaffirm this commitment to recognizing, appreciating, and sustaining families' languages, literacies, and cultural ways of being, and they have devised explicit and comprehensive ways of making connections to families. These connections, in turn, shape the kinds of classrooms they cultivate—the curriculum, the participation and role of parents, and the ways students engage with the community. They encourage a conceptualization of schools as grounded institutions and a model of family engagement that is culturally sustaining. Given the entrenched views that exist about families and schools, this, in many ways, requires that we relearn the concept of family engagement altogether.

RELEARNING FAMILY ENGAGEMENT

> *Teaching is unusual in that those who decide to enter it have had exceptional opportunity to observe members of the occupation at work.*
>
> —Dan Lortie, *Schoolteacher: A Sociological Study,* 1975

There is power in tradition. The universal forms of parent involvement we as adults and children have come to know cripple our imagination for what is possible in engaging families and communities. Teachers communicate with families in ways that feel familiar if they have grown up in US schools; parents interact with teachers in the same ways that they imagine their own parents and caregivers did when they were young children. The routines and practices of family engagement have changed little over decades. Most schools have not attempted to be innovative and imaginative, but family engagement can be an exciting and transformative part of our reimagining of schools.

Creating schools that are grounded in families and communities requires that we unlearn those universal approaches, moving beyond the familiar bake sales and parent-teacher conferences. Dan Lortie, in his oft-referenced book *Schoolteacher: A Sociological Study*, discusses the impact that a teacher's childhood experience in school can have on his or her teaching practice. Through thousands of hours observing teachers and their methods, Lortie found that teachers engage in what he calls an "apprenticeship of observation." Students see teachers "front stage and center like an audience viewing a play," consequently learning about teaching as a practice that is "intuitive and imitative"—learned through uncritical observation rather than through "explicit and analytical" instruction in teaching methods.[17]

With this dominant context of acculturation to education, teacher educators explore the inherent challenges they face with preservice teachers, who may approach their work in classrooms with deep-seated beliefs and assumptions about classroom practice that are challenging to disrupt or replace during their teacher education courses.[18] These "folkways of teaching," according to Margaret Buchmann, can become "ready-made recipes for action and interpretation that do not require testing or analysis while promising familiar, safe results."[19] Without knowledge of alternatives, new teachers may fall back on what seem to be reliable strategies based in one's apprenticeship of observation. Add to that the unchecked assumptions guided by individual and institutional racism, and the fallback practices can be damaging and harmful.

These theories, while important, tend to portray teachers as lacking much agency in developing their craft. The narratives of Ilene, Megan, Cinthia, Annie, and Julia illustrate that teachers can reflect on their past experience and author their own critically informed goals as teachers. When teachers are taught to develop habits of reflection and a sense of cognitive control over prior school experiences, this exploration is more likely to occur.[20] Without these opportunities, teachers will fall back on these traditional strategies, quite simply because they are uncertain about how to proceed.

Routine can be the enemy of innovation and creativity. The teachers in this book show us that leaving behind tradition presents a true opportunity for growth and transformation. In the words of sociologist Sara Lawrence-Lightfoot, "Trusting relationships between parents and teachers grow out of a freedom of expression and a truth-telling that rails against the constraints and dullness of routine."[21] How, then, do we break from tradition and envision a model of family engagement that encourages bold, honest, and transformative conversation?

Repair Relationships: Building Trust and Healing

Across the city, parents have been mistreated, distrusted, and neglected by teachers. This is the reality we face as teachers, and it affects all our interactions with families, but the complexity of that past experience and how it affects us now—that is what's most poorly understood.

—Ilene Carver

The narratives of the teachers in this book provide an abundance of strategies and program ideas that will hopefully inspire in readers a renewed interest in bolstering family and community engagement in schools. Teachers may try family conferences. Schools leaders may become curious about how their teachers could conduct home visits to build relationships with families. Administrators may hold family programs and events in Spanish, while offering simultaneous English interpretation for the small group of English-speaking families. School districts may hire family/community outreach coordinators to support the development of family engagement in schools.

While these programs and ideas can certainly light the way forward, we can't merely waltz in with them. As is often the case with education reform, we risk focusing on *what* is needed—new people, programs, initiatives, and curriculum—without attending to *how* these changes must be cultivated and *why* they're necessary in the first place. In this study of teachers committed to families and communities, these questions of *how* and *why* are critically important. Continuing this section's opening quote, Ilene says, "We can't race in with new ideas if we don't change our mind-set and beliefs about families. I can't just focus on the fact that this parent isn't calling me back. I have to assume that there's a reason why, and as uncomfortable or challenging as it might be to work through that, I will, because I am ultimately committed to understanding how that family and I will work together."

At the center of these teachers' narratives are the intimate stories and experiences of the families they have gotten to know. In a family's living room during a home visit, across a child-sized table for a family conference, or in a quiet moment in the classroom at the end of a long day, families entrust these teachers with the hard truths and crushing reality of the pain, trauma, and indifference they've faced in schools and with teachers who have marginalized them.

The field of family engagement has sometimes overlooked the role that racism, classism, cultural bias, and power has played in the relationships and interactions between families and schools. Inattention to the cultural experiences of families and the cultural values privileged in the school and by teachers will result in parent engagement programs that fall flat or fail to generate community interest. Ultimately, parents will be blamed for the outcome.

Even in Dan Lortie's explanation of the apprenticeship of observation, it should matter who the student is, what their experiences are, who their teacher is, what kinds of beliefs the teacher espouses, and how those beliefs are enacted in classroom practice. Teachers do not blindly follow the actions of their past if they are taught to critically observe and reflect on the issues of race, culture, and power that permeate interactions between teachers and families. In fact, most of the teachers in this study chart paths for themselves that signal protest, indignation, reimagination, and justice.

Acknowledging harm

Healing is the process of being sound or healthy again. It assumes a state of brokenness and acknowledges harm that must be repaired. Schools can be spaces where the harm of racism, classism, and xenophobia is present—sometimes rampant—but remains unaddressed. Ilene, Megan, Cinthia, Annie, and Julia's relationships with families describe a family engagement strategy that is centered on healing. Their efforts reflect an understanding that relationships between parents and teachers are fractured by years of unhealthy, sometimes toxic, interactions and the ill effects of racist attitudes and discrimination or deficit views about families. The strategies they employ to build trust, cultivate relationships, and integrate families are shaped by that understanding.

So what are the keys to healing parent-teacher relationships? First, it is important to understand and identify the harm. When parents report negative or traumatic experiences with teachers in the past, they share these stories with a sense of hurt, indignation, and protest. These strong feelings are, however, in essence, an act of love; parents use the language of care and protection to describe their reactions to mistreatment from teachers. Dion's mother, Raquel, describes the importance of "shutting down a conversation that is unjustly harsh against [her] child" and Trey's mother, Janet, admits, "I don't always trust what a teacher says about my child, especially if I don't get the sense that they know or understand him."

It would be overly simplistic, racist, and biased to describe these two black mothers as angry and antagonistic, but I can imagine that parents, especially parents of color, who act in this way—in defense of their children—have been characterized in this manner. When teachers like Ilene describe parents "who don't return my calls or won't pick up the phone when I call," she does not blame them for their inaction. Rather, she and other teachers recognize that when parents build walls, they are protecting their children and families from potential harm and mistreatment. To say that their lack of participation reflects a lack of caring or disinvestment in their child's education couldn't be further from the truth.

How do teachers respond to these acts of resistance? It is one thing to understand a parent's response and to take it as an act of resistance or devotion to their child, but it is another to endure the conflict and the emotional response it may stir up amidst all the other pressures of teaching. In schools that create systems of support for teachers in regards to family engagement, veteran teachers like Ilene, school staff like Abby Rodriguez, or administrators like Jinny Chalmers at Young Achievers provide formal (e.g., workshops for new teachers on engaging families) and informal (e.g., conversations to support a distressed teacher who is experiencing a challenging situation with a parent) support. These are some of the necessary building blocks to antiracist and anti-oppressive education in schools.

Embracing positive two-way communication

Teachers in this study understand that how they begin a conversation with a parent matters and, thus, they start with positive communication. It is a common conception that when a teacher calls home, there is bad news to report. As a first-year teacher, I recall that when I decided to call my students' families in the first few months with an affirming report, I was met every time with hushed silence and anxious anticipation. Parents inevitably wondered, "What has my child done? How will I respond to this teacher's claims?" Likewise, all five teachers found ways to make the first communication with parents one that reflected appreciation and affirmation of their child.

Beyond the first conversation, these teachers also sought to continue their communication with families with consistency and frequency. Subsequent conversations could be brief but reflected a desire to generate continuity in teacher-parent communication. Teachers wanted to let parents know that they remembered early conversations, wanted to keep the lines of communication open, and most importantly, genuinely cared about their children. According to Ilene:

> My first interaction and every subsequent conversation with a parent reflects a deep sense of caring. I think it's much easier to say that we want these conversations to be positive, and we certainly don't want them to be negative. But what's always on my mind is, "Do they know that they are important to me? Do they get a sense that I care about their child?" Part of that comes from a willingness to listen to parents, to ask them questions, invite them to support me and give

me feedback on what I'm doing. But it's also reflected in my desire to keep that conversation going and to continue to make them feel that they are important.

With this consistency, parents begin to have a wholly different response when teachers call or reach out to them. According to Janet, a parent in Cinthia's classroom: "At this point, when I hear from Ms. Colón, I feel completely at ease. Over all the times that we have talked in person or on the phone or by text, we just now have a history of working together. I don't feel threatened or nervous when I hear from her, and I know that whatever we do talk about, it is going to be improving the situation for Trey; I have no doubt about that."

When considering parent-teacher communication, we traditionally focus on what teachers communicate to parents. This is usually the focus of parent-teacher conferences and the stance in school events designed for families. What this implies to parents and caregivers is that the most useful knowledge about a child's education originates at the school, but in the case of all five teachers in this study, they place a high premium on listening to parents as well. Through home visits, Megan "zeroes in on the family to hear their story and to listen to their perspectives on their children." Similarly, Ilene believes that the primary purpose of a family conference is to listen to and learn from a child's family members, not to give a report on a child she has known for two months. And when she invites family members into the classroom for a presentation, she devotes part of the time to soliciting comments and feedback from family members who are present. These teachers, thus, establish parent-teacher communication as a two-way endeavor.

Creating new forms of communication is important as well. Gone are the days when teacher communication primarily took the form of phone calls home and teacher notices and newsletters tucked into student backpacks. These can largely be ineffective because parents are not always free to answer calls from school during the day, and newsletters are not individualized for a student's experience and do not always make it home. These five teachers develop new and evolving forms of communication with families. From beginning-of-the-year parent questionnaires, to the novel engagement style of APTT meetings, to the use of text messages to ask and answer questions as well as share images and videos of students at work, teachers are finding novel and diverse ways to communicate with families that work for them and are preferred by parents.

Healing is a form of transformation. In their relationships with families, educators—in urban, suburban, and rural schools alike—have perpetuated the argument that schools know what is best for students. That case has bred insecurity and distrust among parents and crippled schools' efforts to build parent participation. But some schools do not want to increase parent participation, especially those in which educators are influenced by troubling and faulty assumptions about parents. Distrust and prejudice are likely most heightened in school environments where black, brown, poor, and/or immigrant children are present alongside white and/or uncritical educators.

The strategies employed by the teachers in this book are grounded in the premise that their expertise and training do not automatically grant them the privilege of trust from students' families. According to Megan:

> When we realized that we didn't have the trust of parents and we understood that we wouldn't be able to accomplish anything significant without their trust, I think I just understood that everything we were doing was a sham. I mean, we had good intentions, but these parents did not trust us at all. We realized that every single way we reached out to them had to be colored by that assumption—that they didn't trust us and that we wanted to earn it.

Beyond the assumption that trust must be earned, teachers in this book uniformly believed in the value of parent knowledge as well as the essential nature of their partnership. The relational work with families was at the core of their practice. According to Ilene, "for as long as I am a teacher, I will partner with families. I can't do one without the other."

The relationships, collaboration, and partnership between parents and teachers is a type of healing and transformation for teachers as well. As previous chapters have noted, despite the buzz of activity and the great number of children in a classroom, teaching can be a solitary act. And while teachers have colleagues in their building with whom they can discuss issues or unpack challenges, there is little time in the school day to do so, and as Julia explains, "everyone can be focused on their projects and classroom." She describes what her relationships with parents have meant to her:

> As a new teacher—and even for veteran teachers, I imagine—we don't have much opportunity to talk through the questions we have about what's going on in our classroom. I am lucky because my position has some collaboration built into it, but the life of a teacher is more solitary than we imagine. Working with parents, though, has completely changed that for me. They make my job fuller, more exciting, and they are the ones who can offer me the best feedback and conversation on the questions I have about their child. It is sad that we don't encourage teachers to see this part of their craft as important, because it has been transformative for me.

The routine, solitude, trauma, and harm of school environments dissipates hope. To transform schools from marginalizing institutions to institutions grounded in families and communities, educators must recognize the key role of healing. In *Hope and Healing in Urban Education: How Urban Activists and Teachers Are Reclaiming Matters of the Heart*, Shawn Ginwright explains that where there is harm, there must be hope, but hope can be built only through healing. We must first recognize that "structural oppression harms hope," then understand that "healing is a critical component in building hope."[22] But Ginwright also emphasizes that building hope is an important form of political activity. In dismantling unfounded assumptions and prejudice that marginalize families and carving out new relationships of understanding and collaboration, educators and parents establish a greater sense not only of hope but also of solidarity.

Renew Perspectives: Bringing New Voices into the Conversation

With more intense efforts to foster family engagement in schools, leaders must widen their perspectives on those who can lead the way. There is an abundance of literature on the perspectives of parents and those generally of teachers, but the narratives in this book show that leaders should explore and learn from the voices of teachers of color and new teachers.

Teachers of color

Annie's and Cinthia's motivation for engaging with families stems, in part, from their own negative experiences as immigrant children in US schools. Teachers who had little knowledge or interest in their families' experiences misunderstood, neglected, and harmed them. Their childhood experiences support the narrative that schools can be marginalizing institutions. Annie recalls, "As an immigrant kid, there was no interest in my family's story, but there was a strong expectation that we should get on board with whatever the school had in mind for us."

Annie's desire to bring her students into the community and to bring the community into her classroom is based on her observation that the divisions and fractures in society bleed into schools. Her firsthand experience with this reality "shapes every aspect of my life as a teacher":

I feel that there is so much that I am learning and growing as a teacher, but I can honestly say that my experience as a person of color in this country, and in a predominantly white teaching force, provides me with insight into the kind of teacher that I want to be. I think that those of us who have gone through this system, been harmed and hurt and misunderstood by it, can help show why this work is important and how it can be carried out. I think that so often, we look to experts for solutions. And when we ask teachers, we don't acknowledge that we are a teaching force that is so predominantly white, even in cities like Boston where most of the students are kids of color. We [teachers of color] can relate to our students in ways that are eye-opening, and that perspective, that empathy, is so important in the work that we do. I know that for myself, there have been many times when I meet a family or see one of my students struggle with feeling isolated, and that just fires up in me a sense of how important it is that I'm here. And the struggle that I told you about before, those things, as painful as they were at the time, they helped me understand what kind of teacher I want to be.

As with Annie, the social isolation and the struggles Cinthia faced growing up are the genesis for what she rejects in her classroom. Without teachers who understood her family's experience or schools that embraced her family and community, she developed the necessary skill of code-switching, which allowed her to navigate the distinct worlds of home and school. In her practice as a teacher, she wants her students to see those boundaries between home and school blurred. Grandparents, parents, and other family members have a place in Cinthia's classroom, signaling to students that their experiences matter:

> I think that for me, to learn how to be in different environments—code-switch—that was a survival skill that I picked up because I was very tuned in to what was acceptable and what was not. But that process of navigating those environments was confusing and probably exhausting. And when you are code-switching, you are in some ways acknowledging to yourself that you have to hide a part of yourself or at least know that it's something you can't be very open about. I should have had adults who could understand what I'd be going through so that they could help me figure it out without it taking a toll on me or making me feel that my family or my community was different.

Teachers of color can provide valuable wisdom and experience. They carry with them a sense of purpose and necessity in their engagements with families and communities that white teachers may not understand or may explain away. Teachers of color can reinforce that there is no room for complacency and acceptance of the status quo. And while a school's surrounding community may be a mysterious and monolithic entity that causes fear or anxiety for many white middle-class teachers, it is instead a place of love, close-knit community, friendships, supportive networks, and extended family for teachers like Cinthia.

Like schools, teacher education programs and school transformation efforts should be grounded in the linguistic and cultural pluralism of our communities. As aspiring educators of color enter teacher education programs, their experiences should be heard, celebrated, and sustained. This should not mean, however, that they carry the burden and responsibility of this learning process on their shoulders, as can be the case in many multicultural education settings. Rather, their experiences should not be marginalized but instead recognized for the important role they play in decentering whiteness in teacher preparation programs. Likewise, in school transformation efforts, their perspectives should be central to decision-making. Scholars and practitioners must create space for teachers like Annie and Cinthia, whose perspectives can light the way toward a model of family and community engagement that is culturally sustaining.

Novice teachers

Veteran teachers like Ilene can share lessons learned over her career as a teacher as well as her experience as the parent of two children in Boston Public Schools. Indeed, during our conversations and interviews, I felt immense gratitude for learning from her struggles as a parent in schools, and from her multitude of experiences with parents. Her family and community engagement strategies were clearly refined over the years and through the lessons she learned from her relationships with families.

It is not unusual for educators to look to experts and experienced teachers for guidance in vexing issues of school practice. But Julia's story—as well as the early teaching experiences of Annie, Cinthia, and Megan—illuminates the twin necessity of exploring the experiences of novice teachers. We learn different lessons from them. Their experiences with family engagement often highlight their early enthusiasm for innovation, the palpable struggles that teachers can encounter, and their calls for support. Their enthusiasm to connect with families may be diminished by their more experienced colleagues' hopeless and pessimistic attitudes toward parents. To develop comprehensive approaches to improving family-school relationships, researchers and experienced teachers alike need to hear from the full range of teacher voices.

Julia recalls how much she, as a newly hired teacher at Young Achievers, embraced the school's emphasis on family and community engagement. As a former organizer in immigrant communities, she understood how important it would be to connect with students' families. She recalled how invested parents were in their child's education and success and how much they wanted to connect with their child's teacher in positive ways. Similarly, Annie remembers her strong desire to build relationships with families. She had core beliefs that the connection was important. In contrast, Megan's situation was unique: she was teaching in a low performing school that was under intense pressure and scrutiny to improve. While her efforts to engage families were more externally directed, she, too, describes "a willingness to do whatever it took to create a better school and to allow our students' lives to feel successful."

New teachers come to their jobs with optimism, hope, and enthusiasm that can be invaluable. Novice teachers place a high value on personal connections, perhaps because they are more likely to experience isolation, have few existing connections in the school (with teachers or families), and feel that they have the most to prove. A 2005 study of new teachers found that they consistently believed in the importance of connecting with and engaging parents to support their child's educational development.[23] In fact, eight out of ten new teachers surveyed strongly agreed that effective teachers need to be able to work well with students' parents. Early in their career, young teachers are open to the idea of connecting with their students' families. They show us that teachers enter the profession with curiosity about family engagement, an interest in forging connections, and a willingness to invest their time in developing effective strategies to engage families.

"This should not be a mystery. We need support."

Despite their willingness and enthusiasm to build connections, unfortunately, new teachers also report low levels of support in family and community engagement strategies.[24] Consequently, they feel inadequately prepared and unsuccessful in their attempts to engage families. In fact, they consider their work and engagement with families to be the greatest challenge they face—greater than insufficient resources and maintaining order and discipline in the classroom. Not surprisingly, they feel deeply unsatisfied with their relationships with parents.

When Annie joined the faculty at Young Achievers, she, like many other new teachers, felt unsure that she had "the concrete knowledge that I could engage families and what that could look like." While she believed that connecting with families was central to her work as a teacher, she acknowledges that she was neither skilled nor trained to engage families in meaningful ways. Julia, however, recalls the "great luck" she had in being assigned to a mentor teacher "who valued her relationships with families." She recalls: "I remember when I watched and learned from her, I had so many more questions about how to talk with parents, how to talk to them about challenges, how they would see me, and how to ask them about their experiences without feeling like I was being intrusive."

These experiences raised questions about family engagement, but Julia's teacher training program did not provide much formal guidance on the subject: "I don't remember there being a space to flesh out those questions and think about the possibilities. When we did talk about family engagement, the discussion was not that deeply engaged and it always left me feeling a little bit unsatisfied."

Julia and Annie, as well as Cinthia, are graduates of the Boston Teacher Residency (BTR), which made clear attempts to support teachers with knowledge and experience in family and community engagement. As a program committed to training teachers in the Boston Public Schools, the residency training, according to Annie, valued families and communities and this alone was important, even if she did not always get the answers to her questions: "I don't think that BTR provided experiences that helped me hone skills, but they communicated with me in subtle ways that made me know that BTR thought it was important, and I, in turn, really hung onto that."

Eager to learn, Annie recalled many of those experiences as formative in her development as a teacher, but like Julia, she feels that the topics raised more questions and could be covered more deeply. While it may be tempting to cover family engagement simply and superficially, Annie warns, "there is no script for this work. I think that one of the dangers right now in education is that people want a script or a quick fix and in this work with families, there simply is no script or fix. The real question is, How do you authentically harvest these relationships, these ideals for yourself, and how does that look for you? You can get great ideas from other people, but in the end, you have to own this work to have it continue."

In contrast, for Megan, discussions about family engagement were absent from her training in Teach for America, as was the case for many of her colleagues at Stanton. While she acknowledges that professional development in schools can be helpful, she feels strongly that novice teachers and preservice teachers should be supported in family engagement before their assumptions about families set in:

> I think it is something that you need, especially teachers in training, you need to get them while they are fresh and excited, not a few months into the school or in their second year of teaching where they have already started to build these assumptions about families. A new teacher focuses on the newsletters sent home and never returned, behavior charts that are not returned, and the phone calls that are never answered. They are just burnt out a lot of the time. And so I think if [teacher training on family engagement] happened before they even started teaching, teachers would have an entirely different orientation to families from the beginning and their work with families would have a greater impact. They would be open to the work because they haven't started to build up any of those walls or assumptions yet.

Teachers should be ushered into the profession with opportunities to examine theory, research, and practice in school-family-community partnerships. Megan explains that too often, the strategies and ideas of family engagement are "unclear and unspoken." Given the centrality of family engagement in her practice as a teacher, she argues, "This should not be a mystery. We need support."

Increasingly, teacher education programs are designing ways to engage and incorporate communities into the praxis of teaching. Centered on the belief that community knowledge and experience are critical to a teacher's practice, these programs create immersive summer experiences in urban communities for aspiring teachers who may lack experience in urban schools, invite community members and mentors to serve as instructors in teacher education programs, arrange neighborhood walks and tours facilitated by community members, organize visits with community-based organizations, and invite panels of community members and residents to engage preservice teachers in discussion about community-based teaching.[25] These models aim to cultivate community teachers—educators who possess knowledge of students' cultures, families, and communities and who draw upon that knowledge to provide high-quality learning experiences for students.[26] Unfortunately, these types of programs are the exception, not the rule.

These innovations in teacher education are important in cultivating community teachers, but preservice teachers should also have ample opportunities to learn how to communicate with parents and build relationships of collaboration and partnership. Preservice teachers need practice communicating with parents, conducting family conferences, and integrating family and community life into their classrooms. As in all other aspects of a teacher's training, they should be exposed to the new innovations and advances in the family and community engagement.

In the same ways that immigrant families, communities of color, and poor families may be kept at the margins of school decision-making, so, too, may novice teachers and teachers of color be marginalized in their professional communities. To create a culturally sustaining model of family engagement, school leaders, researchers, and teacher educators must look beyond the dominant perspectives of professional communities—to the novice teachers who enter the profession with hope and enthusiasm for engaging families and to teachers like Cinthia and Annie whose childhood experiences in schools may resonate with their students.

Reinvent the School: Developing a Vision for Family and Community Engagement at Young Achievers

Over the years researching family engagement in schools, I have encountered a common refrain from teachers and school administrators. While investing time, effort, and resources into engaging families seems promising, they argue that "there's no extra time in the day for this," "my teachers are already doing so much," or "we can work on this later, but we have some other priorities now." But as many public educators know, time is a constraint, the responsibilities and expectations build and evolve, and "later" never comes. All three of the schools represented in this book—Young Achievers Science and Mathematics Pilot School, Stanton Elementary School, and Dudley Street Neighborhood Charter School—have made firm commitments to and investments in family engagement.

Three of the teachers—Annie, Cinthia, and Julia—teach at Young Achievers. In the early stages of this research project, as I met with teachers and began to form the group of participants for this study, I considered whether teachers who made these significant commitments to families could work alone in schools that were noncommittal to family engagement. I began to understand, however, that to do this work well, teachers need a full system of support and the dedicated resources of a school and district. If engaging students' families is an essential part of successful school improvement efforts, then schools must map out a vision for family engagement that fundamentally alters learning, teaching, and collaboration in the school. Young Achievers Principal Jinny Chalmers explains:[27]

> It is not just that we want everyone to commit to parent conferences or even that you should commit to 100 percent of your families in conferences face to face. What is important is that we have a guiding vision about our work together that is completely integrated with students' families. It is that vision—seeing our work as a partnership with families—that causes us to understand that we should have conferences, that everyone should commit to this, and that we have a responsibility to reach all our families.

It may be tempting to view the five teachers in this book as exceptional—in their craft and in their engagement of families. While I chose to highlight their narratives because they are successful in the relationships they build and sustain with students' families, to call them exceptional diminishes the role that experience, self-examination, critical awareness, and school support play. These teachers were not naturally inclined to be successful in this work, and without sufficient teacher training or education in this area, "if anything, we were set up to be really bad at it," according to Annie. She admits:

I came in here with a good attitude and a belief that families were essential to our success in the school, but I didn't really know what that was supposed to look like and there were times when I was making mistakes, missteps. I needed support—I knew that—and there were people around me who could step in and get me to see things and do things differently. Even though family engagement was the thing I was least prepared to do, it is also the thing that has grown and changed me the most. Being at [Young Achievers] has a lot to do with that.

To view their success as a byproduct of natural abilities, character traits, or exceptionality is to suggest it is unattainable for most. That could not be further from the truth. What may instead be true is that without professional support, teacher training, or the dedicated resources of a school, the best we can expect is for teachers to be mediocre in their interactions with families; in that environment, maybe it is only the exceptional teacher who will succeed.

That three of the five teachers work at Young Achievers is also an important point. The school produced three teachers for this book not because it happened to hire exceptionally talented teachers or teachers that were exceptional in engaging families, but because it has a steadfast commitment and vision for family and community engagement that allows teachers like Annie, Cinthia, and Julia to thrive in their commitment to families.

Partnering with families from the start

When Young Achievers was founded in 1995, family engagement was central to its vision. There was a real opportunity to get parents involved from the get-go, to create a school that both educators and families could get behind. Founding principal Dawn Lewis wanted to create a school that reflected "what I hoped and dreamed for as a parent walking into the school and what I wanted to feel and see, things that should be palpable to me as a parent."

This was rooted in both her professional experience as an educator and her personal experience as a Boston public school parent: "I didn't have a voice, and I just feel like schools wanted parents to speak at certain times for certain things, and that was it. There were very tight boundaries on that voice, and that leaves you feeling very marginalized as a parent, but also for me as an African American parent, as an African American person. That marginalization gets deep, and I said, 'I would never want anyone to feel that way in the school no matter who they were.'" How did educators at Young Achievers seek to engage families and solicit their participation? As Dawn began organizing for the school's opening, she "didn't want to make decisions without families," so she met with parents once a week at the Roxbury Community College (Young Achievers did not yet have a school building) to bring them up-to-date on all that was developing and happening, allowing them to ask questions and provide feedback. She invited parents to participate on all the hiring teams for teachers as well. To ensure that there was agreement about what they were looking for in teachers, they held meetings to discuss the qualities they were seeking, coaching the group to consider how these qualities connected to the mission and vision of the school.

For the first two years, the school was open on Saturdays so that interested parents and caregivers could participate in workshops that provided information and opportunities for discussion on issues that were important to the school, such as how teachers assessed students, how the school understood and enacted the responsive classroom model, and how educators philosophically understood and approached discipline. As Dawn explains, "We were trying to do things nontraditionally and make this an innovative community, so it's very possible that being in this school is going to look and feel different than the schools our families were coming from. We wanted to meet with them, both to provide information and context but also to encourage discussion that would help us get it right."

Parents were also encouraged to spend time in the school building with their children. Because the school started in the early years with a ten-hour day, this often meant that children were in school well before many parents had to be at work. Young Achievers educators took advantage of this, encouraging parents to come into the classroom and read with their child or a couple of children before they headed to work. This early part of the morning became a relaxed time where the room was quiet, children were settling in, and teachers and/or teacher assistants were present to meet and interact with families as well.

Parents and teachers did not always agree about how the school should be run, yet they found ways to work through the disagreement and conflict for the betterment of the school. One point of disagreement was centered on the school's decision not to celebrate holidays. According to Dawn, "families had never been in a school that didn't have hearts, pumpkins, and the Pilgrims," and couldn't understand why the school's policy opposed celebrating those holidays. In order to help parents understand the intentions behind this policy and promote a productive conversation, Dawn invited Enid Lee, an antiracist, multicultural education specialist.[28] Lee ran some workshops for families to give them a sense of how these practices served to dismantle bias, prejudice, and racism in schools and instead create an inclusive, multicultural community.

While parents began to understand educators' intentions behind the policy on holiday celebrations, one issue did not die down—kindergarten graduation. Parents were adamant that the celebration was important, and they envisioned the young students in caps and gowns with a ceremony that included families, extended family, and friends. While they were opposed to this idea for reasons that were similar to those for the holiday policy, Dawn and the teachers understood that the affirmation of children and their accomplishment in school were important to families and, with their collaboration, decided to hold a schoolwide "Step-Up Day." Every child would be celebrated as they concluded the year with their current class and moved on with anticipation to the next. Rather than having students wear the traditional cap and gown, each class submitted a design for a schoolwide T-shirt contest. Students voted for the winning design, and all students wore the shirt to the celebration.

Early-morning time in classrooms, the creation of a Step-Up Day celebration, invitations for parents to serve on hiring teams for teachers, and workshops and meetings to include families in the decision-making and creation of the school—these are just some of the ways Young Achievers carried out a school vision that was centered on engaging families in authentic and meaningful ways.

Recognizing that "families are the heart of what we do":
A school vision for family engagement across all grades and ages

The school's status as a pilot school in the Boston Public Schools allows Young Achievers to have a degree of autonomy and flexibility in key areas such as staffing, school governance, budget, curriculum, and the school calendar. First created in 1994 to encourage models of educational innovation and to serve as research and development sites for effective urban public schools, pilot schools like Young Achievers are public schools that are part of the school district but with added levels of autonomy.[29] This autonomy allowed the school to build an innovative model for family and community engagement.

Across the narratives of Annie, Cinthia, and Julia, it is clear that even decades later, Young Achievers strives to carry out the original vision to engage families and capitalizes on the autonomy afforded them. An important part of this is a school leader's commitment to family and community engagement. Upon Dawn's departure as principal, Jinny Chalmers took over the administrative post. Like Dawn, Jinny had been long committed to the idea that schools should reflect and engage the communities they served. To effectively engage families, Jinny believes the school must make its expectations about family engagement clear to all teachers: "We are just really clear and up front with them about the fact that it's not just one of the standards in their evaluation, but in this school, it's a make-or-break standard. If you can't relate to families in a way that engages them and helps them see their possibilities for their kids, you can't be here. It doesn't work. Families are at the heart of what we do here."

Teachers at Young Achievers have unusual levels of support for their family engagement work. Julia describes the value of having a full day of professional development devoted to family conferences. For middle school teachers, this makes it possible to confer with parents and caregivers as a teacher team. For teachers like Annie who look for opportunities to bring students out into the community as an integrated part of their learning experiences, there is great value in having a staff member at the school who supports community partnerships. All teachers in the early grades are required to conduct home visits before the start of the school year, and they are paid stipends to do so.

This commitment is apparent in how the school recruits and hires teachers as well. When interviewing prospective candidates, the hiring team often presents a vignette of a challenging situation—one that may involve issues of race and culture or that probes a teacher's stance on interactions with families. Jinny insists that they are not looking for candidates who "have it all figured out" but rather for teachers who are not defensive, show an ability to project empathy, and demonstrate a willingness to connect with students' families. Because family engagement is not merely about parent-teacher communication at Young Achievers, Jinny also looks for teachers who have sought "to engage families in a way that enriches the curriculum as well as the learning opportunities for kids."

In myriad ways, large and small, Young Achievers carries out the school's vision for family engagement to ensure that families feel invited, welcome, and engaged. Family conferences are opportunities to listen to and learn about the experiences of parents and caregivers, not for teachers to simply state what they know. These conversations are opportunities for teachers and families to decide together how to support students at home and at school. Parents have a variety of opportunities to be present in the school and become more familiar with their child's experience and the educators who work with them—by attending weekly schoolwide community meetings, one of the four Family Fun Nights that occur throughout the year, or the publishing parties and family presentations that are hosted by each classroom.

Parents can also be central to the teaching and learning within classrooms. Annie, Cinthia, and Julia invite willing and interested parents and family members into the classroom to support students' engagement with the curriculum. When a language barrier might limit any of these opportunities for parents to engage, the school finds ways to provide interpretation because, as Annie explains, "language should never be an excuse to close the door on working with a student's family."

There is a recognition at Young Achievers that families should inform and shape how teachers view their work in the school. As mentioned, kindergarten and first-grade teachers are required to make home visits to their students. For parents of young children, this is an opportunity to start a conversation, build a relationship with a teacher, and become acclimated to the culture of a school, within the comfort and familiarity of their home, if they desire. For teachers, it is a continual reminder that the school is part of a community and the school is not the only place to connect—and likely not the best place to understand students' families.

Family engagement practices, at Young Achievers and in schools across the country, are more pronounced and visible for families of young elementary-age children. Among middle schools and high schools, there is a great need to be clearer about the ways that educators can engage families. The needs of adolescents and how they perceive the presence of parents and caregivers in schools must matter. Given the benefits of family engagement on student outcomes across all ages, schools must find ways to stay connected to the parents of middle and high school students.

While Julia's strategies for engaging families provides a laudable example of how to connect with students' families, what would that look like if she were a science teacher with seventy-five or a hundred students? In reality, the structure of secondary schools runs counter to the development of close and meaningful ties between students' families and the wide assortment of teachers they work with. So, at Young Achievers, middle school teachers find different ways to make this engagement possible—by working in teacher teams that either meet collectively with parents or alternate meetings with parents. Many secondary schools have devised structures to promote more meaningful connections between teachers and students. In some schools, teachers serve as advisors or homeroom teachers to a group of students. These kinds of arrangements may serve the purposes of family engagement well. Still, this is a fruitful area for future research.

Committing resources and staff to support family and community engagement

Clear expectations to engage students' families and communities should go hand in hand with professional support and the dedicated resources of the school. Jinny explains that some of the support comes from skilled leaders in the school building:

> Part of it is that over time, we've got some people now who are very, very skilled at this work, so then the team supports each other in ways that are necessary. It is very likely that there is someone on your team or one of [the administrators] or Abby [the family coordinator] who can get you through a challenge you may be facing, and we try to operate an environment where, yes, we have these high expectations about your work with families, but there is a lot of support around you to help you with it. Everybody gets intimidated or gets hopeless about families or kids in a different way and for different reasons, so it's trying to sort that out as a supervisor and figuring that out. The expectation is that you are working on this with support, not that you are perfect.

While experienced teachers can play a key role in supporting teachers who are newer to the role, at Young Achievers, all three teachers—Annie, Cinthia, and Julia—attest that the support from Abby Rodriguez, the school's family coordinator, is essential. It is quite difficult to describe what Abby does, because her job is, in many ways, all-encompassing. As a parent to a Young Achievers fourth grader, she is connected to the families and the community. She can be seen talking to parents in the hallway and introducing parents to teachers and staff. She supports teachers with family conferences—in scheduling them, reaching out to parents who may not respond, and offering to translate. When Young Achievers went through a transition that brought many new Spanish-speaking families and emergent bilingual students to the school, Abby played a key role in helping teachers connect with and communicate with the new families. In planning schoolwide events for families such as the Family Fun Nights, Abby is a key part of recruiting families to attend, even coordinating child care arrangements so that parents can participate. At the event, she is often seen providing simultaneous interpretation in the back of the room through a headset.

Teachers like Annie find Abby to be a critical resource in building and cultivating the kinds of relationships they desire with families:

> It is so important to have someone like Abby who partners with us. She has a big heart and really knows these families well. Over the years, she has developed really tight relationships with kids and families and can advise me—whether it's with new families that I don't yet know that well or families that are presenting some challenges. I hate to say it, but I think that in some of those instances, without her support, I might not have persevered through that or come out of the situation very well.

And at times, Abby provides the clear truth and sense of direction that novice teachers like Julia might appreciate:

> [Abby's] been doing this work for so long, she's so amazing at those relationships and I think she also brings cultural capital to the table that I don't, in the context of relating to Latino families. I remember when I had my first publishing party, she came right to me afterwards and said, "You and I need to coordinate." She knew that she had to help me set the right tone with families about their presence. So later that year, she really framed it in a way that I needed to hear. She was like, "You just have to be very direct and say, 'I don't care who it is, if it's mom, grandma, your cousin, your neighbor, your auntie, somebody needs to be there. Somebody from your family can come. Who's coming if you can't? What do you need in order to get there? Do you need a ride? We'll get you a ride. Do you need a babysitter? Bring your kids.'" She just stripped away all those barriers and helped me see that getting everyone in the room was not just possible, it was necessary.

Abby's position as family coordinator is not one that every school in Boston has, and over the years, Jinny admits that it has been difficult to continue to fund the position. Abby's role in the school is so critical, however, so teachers and administrators can't imagine the school without it. Currently, 30 of the 125 schools in Boston have a person dedicated to family and community engagement. None of these positions are funded by the district. Instead, as at Young Achievers, schools budget for the position.[30] It will be difficult, if not impossible, for schools to engage families effectively if there is an absence of dedicated staff and resources to support their efforts.

The school finds ways to bring parents and community members into the classroom in more significant ways as well. From the beginning, the school created the position of community teacher—a position similar to a teaching assistant or paraprofessional. Positions were open to parents and community members, and as Dawn explains it, they wanted to encourage any parents who wished to pursue the role and further their training and experience in education to apply. As teachers sat down and met parents during home visits, they found that there were parents, some with experience in their native countries, who were both interested and well suited for the classroom roles. Four of the school's first community teachers were parents and, through the experience, each has gone on to pursue further education and degrees in social work and education. At the time, Dawn believed it was important for schools "to find different ways for parents and community members to be part of the life of the school, not just as visitors but as real contributors."

Julia considered her partnership with Ms. Vides, a community teacher in her classroom, a vital part of the classroom dynamic. As an immigrant from Guatemala who went through the Boston Public Schools and has experience as a parent, community member, and parent liaison for a school, Ms. Vides was an effective partner in the classroom. Students saw her as a community mentor, someone they could look to for support and communicate openly with about issues. Julia felt it was important and powerful that students saw them work together as a team.

■ ■ ■

Across the five teachers' experiences and the three school environments—Young Achievers, Stanton Elementary School, and the Dudley Street Neighborhood Charter School—there are many ideas that can prove useful to educators who want to build effective ties with families. Some ideas may seem more feasible or relevant; some strategies might be easier to start with. And while the establishment of family conferences, home visits, Academic Parent Teacher Team meetings, well-attended publishing parties, and translation at family events will serve any community well, it is important to note that these ideas were born out of conversations between educators and families. This book may prove to be a useful guide to rethink family engagement in schools, but every school's mission to strengthen family-school ties should begin with listening to parents' stories. This is at the heart of what every school must do, as Jinny explains:

> There is something really important in being able to get to these stories and their experience, and listening to the stories and believing they can shape the direction of what you're doing at the school and how you're working with families . . . I think it really has to start with validating a parent's experience and understanding just how traumatic and scary some of this can be for them. In some ways, that means we have to be slow to blame and quick to listen longer. I have had some young teachers who hear this from a parent and their initial response to that is, "It's so disrespectful to me. I would never do that." And I have to tell them that this is not about you; it's about them and their experience in school, and they're sharing a trauma that they had in school, and it's our professional responsibility to have the courage to listen and to take it in, and therefore to understand the fury that they bring to any critique that they hear of their child's experience.

The schools in this book have built a commitment to engaging families into the mission and vision of the school. When schools set a vision for family engagement that is central to school culture and decision-making, it can lead to the reinvention of a school—from one that operates in isolation or apart from families to one that is grounded in the experiences of students' families and communities.

NATURAL ALLIES

Partnership is giving, taking, learning, teaching, offering the greatest possible benefit while doing the least possible harm.

—Octavia Butler, *Parable of the Talents*

Ilene, Megan, Cinthia, Annie, and Julia describe the relationships between parents and teachers as a necessary alliance. As Ilene explains, "you achieve your best outcomes when you mobilize your allies. And in the context of schools, families are the most important allies that we have." This is why the responsibility of building parent-teacher partnerships must begin with teachers. As Ilene explains:

> [Teachers] have to find ways to be the leaders in our efforts to build partnerships with parents. We know what our expectations and goals are for the year, but we also have to recognize that those goals—they are not my goals, they aren't even the state's goals, but our goals together with families. To foster a strong partnership, teachers have to be willing to step out and engage families and invite them to work together. And that begins by getting to know them as individuals.

With few and infrequent interactions between parents and teachers about a child's experience in the classroom, the stakes are high for each interaction, and the expectations veer into the unreasonable. These situations may lead both parties to insist that they are "right" and the other is "wrong."

True partnership requires an acknowledgment that each party is "giving, taking, learning, and teaching."[31] And rather than being right or wrong, parents and teachers identify a shared interest and goal—that of supporting the child. Embedded in the deep devotion of a parent to their child and of a teacher to her craft is a desire to do what is best for the child so they can grow to become their fullest and best version of themselves.

In this discussion of allyship, it is important to note that parents, especially those from marginalized communities, do not need the kind of allies who will speak or enact change on their behalf. Rather, educators must recognize the marginalizing nature and function of schools and take on the problems that are born of systemic racism and oppression as their own. In some ways, parents and teachers will work together to support students; in other ways, they carve out their own narratives and responsibilities to enact justice in schools. For teachers, this should be a responsibility, not a peripheral interest.

Children benefit greatly when families and teachers work together, but as the teachers in this book demonstrate, students must see the proof that their families and communities are welcome and valued allies. From the family migration projects to the family presentations, letters on the classroom wall from parents about their hopes and dreams for their children, weekly trips to the neighborhood library, and summer home visits, the message is clear. Every school and classroom should display how families are central to the life and function of the school.

At the center of this conversation about family engagement is the child. Every teacher I have come to know through this project and through my professional career as a teacher and education researcher has shown me that a commitment to supporting and mentoring children and youth is at the heart of what they do. I have not yet met a parent who does not have high hopes and dreams for their children. Teachers and parents will not always see eye to eye, nor will they agree on all matters, but if the relationship is grounded in trust, ongoing communication, and a belief in the best in each other, much is possible. If we dismantle and remove the marginalizing effects of schools and instead ground schools in the lives and experiences of families, we will be far less likely to see one another as adversaries. If we focus on why teachers and parents come together in the first place—for the development and collective support of a child—it's clear that parents and teachers are indeed natural allies.

NOTES

Introduction

1. Willard Waller, *The Sociology of Teaching* (New York: John Wiley & Sons, Inc., 1932).

2. Sara Lawrence-Lightfoot, *Worlds Apart: Relationships Between Families and Schools* (New York: Basic Books, 1978); Patricia Phelan, Ann Locke Davidson, and Hanh Cao Yu, "Students' Multiple Worlds: Navigating the Borders of Family, Peer, and Culture," in *Renegotiating Cultural Diversity in American Schools*, ed. Patricia Phelan and Ann Locke Davidson (New York: Teachers College Press, 1993); Patricia Phelan, Hanh Cao Yu, and Ann Locke Davidson, "Navigating the Psychosocial Pressures of Adolescence: The Voices and Experiences of High School Youth," *American Educational Research Journal* 31, no. 2 (1994); Fabienne Doucet, "(Re)Constructing Home and School: Immigrant Parents, Agency, and the (Un)Desirability of Bridging Multiple Worlds," *Teachers College Record* 113, no. 12 (2011).

3. Carola Suarez-Orozco and Marcelo M. Suarez-Orozco, *Children of Immigration* (Cambridge, MA: Harvard University Press, 2001).

4. Joel Spring, *The American School 1642–2004* (New York: McGraw Hill, 2001).

5. Barbara Beatty, *Preschool Education in America: The Culture of Young Children from the Colonial Era to the Present* (New Haven: Yale University Press, 1995); David B. Tyack and Larry Cuban, *Tinkering Toward Utopia: A Century of Public School Reform* (Cambridge: Harvard University Press, 1997); Spring, *The American School*.

6. Luis C. Moll et al., "Funds of Knowledge for Teaching: Using a Qualitative Approach to Connect Homes and Classrooms," in *Theory into Practice* 31, no. 2 (1992): 132–41; Leigh Patel, *Youth Held at the Border: Immigration, Education, and the Politics of Inclusion* (New York: Teachers College Press, 2013).

7. Antonia Darder, Marta P. Baltonado, and Rodolfo D. Torres, eds., *The Critical Pedagogy Reader* (New York: Routledge, 2008); Lilia I. Bartolome, "Understanding Policy for Equity in Teaching and Learning: A Critical-Historical Lens," *Language Arts* 85, no. 5 (2008); Paulo Freire, *Pedagogy of the Oppressed* (New York: Herdner and Herdner, 1970).

8. Sara Lawrence-Lightfoot, "Toward Conflict and Resolution: Relationships Between Families and Schools," *Theory into Practice* 20, no. 2 (1981): 97–104.

9. Anne T. Henderson et al., *Beyond the Bake Sale: The Essential Guide to Family-School Partnerships* (New York: New Press, 2007); Anne T. Henderson and

195

Karen L. Mapp, *A New Wave of Evidence: The Impact of School, Family, and Community Connections on Student Achievement* (Austin, TX: National Center for Family and Community Connections with Schools, 2002).

10. Soo Hong, *A Cord of Three Strands: A New Approach to Parent Engagement in Schools* (Cambridge, MA: Harvard Education Press, 2011).

11. Hong, *A Cord of Three Strands*; Karen L. Mapp, Ilene Carver, and Jessica Lander, *Powerful Partnerships: A Teacher's Guide to Engaging Families for Student Success* (New York: Scholastic, 2017).

12. Kathleen V. Hoover-Dempsey et al., "Why Do Parents Become Involved? Research Findings and Implications," *Elementary School Journal* 106, no. 2 (2005).

13. Michelle Fine, "[Ap]parent Involvement: Reflections on Parents, Power, and Urban Public Schools," *Teachers College Record* 94, no. 4 (1993): 684.

14. Concha Delgado-Gaitan, "Involving Parents in the Schools: A Process of Empowerment," *American Journal of Education* 100, no. 1 (1991): 20–46.

15. Sorca O'Connor, "Voices of Parents and Teachers in a Poor White Urban School," *Journal of Education for Students Placed at Risk (JESPAR)* 6, no. 3 (2001).

16. Doris A. Santoro, *Demoralized: Why Teachers Leave the Profession They Love and How They Can Stay* (Cambridge, MA: Harvard Education Press, 2018).

17. Benjamin Michael Superfine and Alea R. Thompson, "Interest Groups, the Courts, and Educational Equality: A Policy Regimes Approach to 'Vergara v. California,'" *American Educational Research Journal* 53, no. 3 (2016); Diane Ravitch, *Reign of Error: The Hoax of the Privatization Movement and the Danger to America's Public Schools*, 1st ed. (New York: Alfred A. Knopf, 2013); Joanne Barkan, "Got Dough?: How Billionaires Rule Our Schools," *Dissent* 58, no. 1 (2011): 49–57, https://www.dissentmagazine.org/article/got-dough-how-billionaires-rule-our-schools.

18. Kyle Stokes, "Vergara v. California: Ruling That Would Have Ended State's Teacher Tenure Rejected on Appeal," Southern California Public Radio, April 14, 2016, https://www.scpr.org/news/2016/04/14/59624/appeals-court-overturns-lower-court-s-ruling-on-ca/; Daniel B. Wood, "Vergara v. California: Do State Laws Protect Teacher Jobs over Students?" *Christian Science Monitor*, January 28, 2014, https://www.csmonitor.com/USA/Education/2014/0128/Vergara-v.-California-Do-state-laws-protect-teacher-jobs-over-students; Todd A. DeMitchell and Joseph J. Onosko, "Vergara v. State of California: The End of Teacher Tenure or a Flawed Ruling?" *Southern California Interdisciplinary Law Journal* 25, no. 3 (2016).

19. Brenda Iasevoli, "Teacher-Tenure Battles Continue After *Vergara*," *Education Week*, August 31, 2016; David Finley, "Teacher Tenure: An Innocent Victim of *Vergara v. California*," *Education Week*, March 3, 2015.

20. Rachel M. Cohen, "New Jersey Teacher Tenure Lawsuit Dismissed," *American*

Prospect, May 5, 2017, https://prospect.org/article/new-jersey-teacher-tenure-lawsuit-dismissed.

21. Beatrice Dupuy, "Judge Rejects Challenge to Minnesota Teacher Tenure Laws," *Star Tribune* (Minneapolis, MN), October 27, 2016.

22. Iasevoli, "Teacher-Tenure Battles."

23. Bill Raden and Gary Cohn, "David Welch: The Man Behind *Vergara v. California*," *Capital and Main* (Los Angeles, CA), February 20, 2014, https://capital andmain.com/david-welch-the-man-behind-vergara-versus-california.

24. Campbell Brown, "Campbell Brown Responds to TIME Cover," *Time*, October 28, 2014, http://time.com/3544600/campbell-brown-rotten-apples-cover/; Eliza Shapiro, "Campbell Brown Tearfully Files Tenure Suit," *Politico*, July 28, 2014, https://www.politico.com/states/new-york/city-hall/story/2014/07/campbell-brown-tearfully-files-tenure-suit-000000; Haley Sweetland Edwards, "Taking on Teacher Tenure," *Time*, October 30, 2014.

25. Abe Feuerstein, "Parental Trigger Laws and the Power of Framing in Educational Politics," *Education Policy Analysis Archives* 23, no. 79 (2015); Josh Cunningham, *Parent Trigger Laws in the States*, National Conference of State Legislatures, October 15, 2013, http://www.ncsl.org/research/education/state-parent-trigger-laws.aspx.

26. Barkan, "Got Dough?"

27. Feuerstein, "Parental Trigger Laws."

28. Barkan, "Got Dough?"; Ravitch, *Reign of Error*.

29. Motoko Rich and Kitty Bennett, "A Walmart Fortune, Spreading Charter Schools," *New York Times*, April 25, 2014, https://www.nytimes.com/2014/04/26/us/a-walmart-fortune-spreading-charter-schools.html; Ravitch, *Reign of Error*; Pauline Lipman, *The New Political Economy of Urban Education: Neoliberalism, Race, and the Right to the City* (New York: Routledge, Taylor & Francis Group, 2011).

30. Mark Warren, ed., *Lift Us Up, Don't Push Us Out!: Voices from the Front Lines of the Educational Justice Movement* (Boston: Beacon Press, 2018).

31. Brandon Johnson, "Fighting for Teachers, Children, and Their Parents: Building a Social Justice Teachers Union," in Warren, *Lift Us Up*.

32. Johnson, "Fighting."

33. Keith Catone, "Teachers Unions as Partners, Not Adversaries," *Voices in Urban Education*, no. 36 (2013), https://files.eric.ed.gov/fulltext/EJ1046363.pdf.

34. Amanda Sims and Stevie Croisant, "Parents, Students Support Striking Chicago Teachers," *Time Out Chicago*, September 11, 2012, https://www.timeout.com/chicago/kids/activities/parents-students-support-striking-chicago-teachers.

35. Sims and Croisant, "Parents, Students."

36. Eve L. Ewing, *Ghosts in the Schoolyard: Racism and School Closings on Chicago's South Side* (Chicago: University of Chicago Press, 2018).

37. Jitu Brown, "#FightForDyett: Fighting Back Against School Closings and the Journey for Justice," in Warren, *Lift Us Up*.

38. Ewing, *Ghosts in the Schoolyard*, 47.

39. Natasha Capers, "The School Is the Heart of the Community: Building Community Schools Across New York City," in Warren, *Lift Us Up*.

40. Henderson and Mapp, "A New Wave"; Joyce L. Epstein and Susan L. Dauber, "School Programs and Teacher Practices of Parent Involvement in Inner-City Elementary and Middle Schools," *Elementary School Journal* 91, no. 3 (1991): 289–305.

41. Henderson and Mapp, "A New Wave"; Epstein and Dauber, "School Programs"; Rhoda McShane Becher, *Parent Involvement: A Review of Research Principles of Successful Practice* (Washington, DC: National Institute of Education, 1984); Margaret Caspe, M. Elena Lopez, and Cassandra Wolos, *Family Involvement in Elementary School Children's Education* (Cambridge, MA: Harvard Family Research Project, 2006/2007); Sandra L. Dika and Kusum Singh, "Applications of Social Capital in Educational Literature: A Critical Synthesis," *Review of Educational Research* 72, no. 1 (2002).

42. Dana Markow and Suzanne Martin, *The MetLife Survey of the American Teacher: Transitions and the Role of Supportive Relationships* (New York: MetLife, Inc., 2005), https://files.eric.ed.gov/fulltext/ED488837.pdf.

43. Dana Markow and Andrea Pieters, *The MetLife Survey of the American Teacher: Teachers, Parents and the Economy* (New York: MetLife, Inc., 2012), https://files.eric.ed.gov/fulltext/ED530021.pdf.

44. Hong, *A Cord of Three Strands*.

45. Markow and Pieters, *The MetLife Survey*.

46. Markow and Pieters, *The MetLife Survey*.

47. Markow and Pieters, *The MetLife Survey*.

48. Emma Beresford and Angus Hardie, "Parents and Secondary Schools: A Different Approach?" in *Home-School Work in Britain: Review, Reflection and Development*, ed. John Bastiani and Sheila Wolfendale (London: David Fulton Publishers, 1996).

49. Jaleel K. Abdul-Adil and Alvin David Farmer, Jr., "Inner-City African American Parental Involvement in Elementary Schools: Getting Beyond Urban Legends of Apathy," *School Psychology Quarterly* 21, no. 1 (2006); Ellen Brantlinger, "Low-Income Parents' Perceptions of Favoritism in the Schools," *Urban Education* 20, no. 1 (1985).

50. Lawrence-Lightfoot, "Toward Conflict and Resolution"; Concha Delgado-Gaitan, "Involving Parents in the Schools: A Process of Empowerment," *American Journal of Education* 100, no. 1 (1991); Fine, "[Ap]parent Involvement."

51. Annette Lareau and Wesley Shumar, "The Problem of Individualism in Family-School Policies," *Sociology of Education* 69 (1996): 24–39.

52. Angela Valenzuela, *Subtractive Schooling: U.S.-Mexican Youth and the Politics of Caring* (Albany: State University of New York Press, 1999).

53. A. M. Ishimaru, "When New Relationships Meet Old Narratives: The Journey Towards Improving Parent-School Relations in a District-Community Organizing Collaboration," *Teachers College Record* 116, no. 2 (2014); Mavis G. Sanders, "Community Involvement in Schools: From Concept to Practice," *Education and Urban Society* 35, no. 2 (2003); Mavis G. Sanders, *Building School-Community Partnerships: Collaboration for Student Success* (Thousand Oaks, CA: Corwin Press, 2005); Mavis G. Sanders, "How Parent Liaisons Can Help Bridge the Home-School Gap," *Educational Research* 101, no. 5 (2008); Mavis G. Sanders, "Collaborating for Change: How an Urban School District and a Community-based Organization Support and Sustain School, Family, and Community Partnerships," *Teachers College Record* 111, no. 7 (2009); Margaret Caspe et al., *Teaching the Teachers: Preparing Educators to Engage Families for Student Achievement* (Cambridge, MA: Harvard Family Research Project, 2011).

54. Ishimaru, "New Relationships."

55. Ishimaru, "New Relationships."

56. Annette Lareau, *Home Advantage: Social Class and Parental Intervention in Elementary Education* (New York: Falmer, 1989); Dan C. Lortie, *Schoolteacher: A Sociological Study* (Chicago: University of Chicago Press, 1975).

57. Ishimaru, "New Relationships"; A. M. Ishimaru, "Rewriting the Rules of Engagement: Elaborating a Model of District-Community Collaboration," *Harvard Educational Review* 84, no. 2 (2014); Ann M. Ishimaru et al., "Reinforcing Deficit, Journeying Toward Equity: Cultural Brokering in Family Engagement Initiatives," *American Educational Research Journal* 53, no. 4 (2016); Jane Van Galen, "Maintaining Control: The Structure of Parent Involvement," in *Schooling in Social Context: Qualitative Studies*, ed. George W. Noblit and William T. Pink (Norwood, NJ: Ablex Publishing Corporation, 1987).

58. Tara J. Yosso, "Whose Culture Has Capital? A Critical Race Theory Discussion of Community Cultural Wealth," *Race, Ethnicity and Education* 8, no. 1 (2005): 1.

59. Lareau, *Home Advantage*; Waller, *The Sociology of Teaching*; Lawrence-Lightfoot, *Worlds Apart*.

60. Danielle Pillet-Shore, "The Problems with Praise in Parent-Teacher Interaction," *Communication Monographs* 79, no. 2 (2012); Danielle Pillet-Shore, "Being a 'Good Parent' in Parent-Teacher Conferences," *Journal of Communication* 65, no. 2 (2015); Danielle Pillet-Shore, "Criticizing Another's Child: How Teachers Evaluate Students During Parent-Teacher Conferences," *Language in Society* 45, no. 1 (2016); Sara Lawrence-Lightfoot, *The Essential Conversa-*

tion: What Parents and Teachers Can Learn from Each Other (New York: Random House, 2003); Joan M. T. Walker and Benjamin H. Dotger, "Because Wisdom Can't Be Told: Using Comparison of Simulated Parent-Teacher Conferences to Assess Teacher Candidates' Readiness for Family-School Partnership," *Journal of Teacher Education* 63, no. 1 (2012); Emily Richmond, "When Students Lead Parent-Teacher Conferences," *The Hechinger Report*, April 6, 2016, https://hechingerreport.org/when-students-lead-parent-teacher-conferences/.

61. Pillet-Shore, "Being a 'Good Parent.'"

62. Anthony Bryk and Barbara Schneider, "Trust in Schools: A Core Resource for School Reform," *Educational Leadership* 60, no. 6 (2003).

63. Karen L. Mapp and Paul J. Kuttner, *Partners in Education: A Dual Capacity-Building Framework for Family-School Partnerships* (Austin, TX: Southwest Educational Development Laboratory, 2013).

64. Karen L. Mapp, Ilene Carver, and Jessica Lander, *Powerful Partnerships: A Teacher's Guide to Engaging Families for Student Success* (New York: Scholastic, 2017); Henderson et al., *Beyond the Bake Sale*.

65. Hong, *A Cord of Three Strands*; Concha Delgado-Gaitan, *The Power of Community: Mobilizing for Family and Schooling* (Lanham, MD: Rowman & Littlefield Publishers, 2001); Edward M. Olivos, *The Power of Parents: A Critical Perspective of Bilcultural Parent Involvement in Public Schools* (New York: Peter Liang, 2007); Mark R. Warren, Karen L. Mapp, and The Community Organizing and School Reform Project, *A Match on Dry Grass: Community Organizing as a Catalyst for School Reform* (New York: Oxford University Press, 2011); Gerardo R. Lopez, "The Value of Hard Work: Lessons on Parent Involvement from an (Im)migrant Household," *Harvard Educational Review* 71, no. 3 (Fall 2001); Gustavo Perez Carreon, Corey Drake, and Angela Calabrese Barton, "The Importance of Presence: Immigrant Parents' School Engagement Experiences," *American Educational Research Journal* 42, no. 3 (2005).

66. Lawrence-Lightfoot, "Toward Conflict and Resolution"; Sara Lawrence-Lightfoot and Jessica Hoffmann Davis, *The Art and Science of Portraiture* (San Francisco: Jossey-Bass, 1997).

67. Doucet, "(Re)Constructing Home and School."

68. Lawrence-Lightfoot, "Toward Conflict and Resolution"; Sara Lawrence-Lightfoot, *The Good High School: Portraits of Character and Culture* (New York: Basic Books, 1983); Keith Catone, *The Pedagogy of Teacher Activism: Portraits of Four Teachers for Justice*, vol. 11 (New York: Peter Lang Publishing, Inc., 2017); Carla Shalaby, *Troublemakers: Lessons in Freedom from Young Children at School* (New York: New Press, 2017); Gloria Ladson-Billings, *The Dreamkeepers: Successful Teachers of African American Children*, vol. 2 (San Francisco: Jossey-Bass, 2009).

69. Lawrence-Lightfoot and Davis, *The Art and Science of Portraiture.*
70. Lawrence-Lightfoot and Davis, *The Art and Science of Portraiture*, 9.
71. Real names are used for the teachers, administrators, and staff who were interviewed for this study. Parents, caregivers, and children were given pseudonyms. It is important to recognize the schools and communities that allow access to researchers, particularly in research settings where goodness is explored. This transparency allows the reader to understand more fully how local context influences school experience. While some of the parents in the study were willing to be named, because they were asked to participate in a study that asked them to explore their interactions with their child's teacher and the interviews would take place during the year of relationship-building, it was important to keep parents unnamed in the study..
72. Norman K. Denzin, *Interpretive Ethnography: Ethnographic Practices for the 21st Century* (Thousand Oaks, CA: Sage Publications, 1997).
73. The conceptualization of culturally sustaining pedagogies was a fundamental source of inspiration for the framework developed in this book. For more about culturally sustaining pedagogy—how it is conceived, defined, and practiced—see Django Paris, "Culturally Sustaining Pedagogy: A Needed Change in Stance, Terminology, and Practice," *Educational Researcher* 41, no. 3 (2012); Django Paris and H. Samy Alim, "What Are We Seeking to Sustain Through Culturally Sustaining Pedagogy? A Loving Critique Forward," *Harvard Educational Review* 84, no. 1 (2014); Django Paris and H. Samy Alim, *Culturally Sustaining Pedagogies: Teaching and Learning for Justice in a Changing World* (New York: Teachers College Press, 2017).

Chapter 1

1. Ilene's innovative practices in engaging families are highly regarded through her work as a published author as well. In 2017, she, along with coauthors Karen L. Mapp and Jessica Lander, published *Powerful Partnerships: A Teacher's Guide to Engaging Families for Student Success* (New York: Scholastic, 2017).
2. Dudley Street Neighborhood Charter School, "2016–17 Family & Scholar Handbook," https://www.dropbox.com/s/0pzec6iem4ore4f/2016-17%20Family%20%26%20Scholar%20Handbook.pdf?dl=0.

Chapter 2

1. Peter Hermann, "Deadly Violence Has Become All Too Common in One D.C. Neighborhood," *Washington Post,* August 6, 2015, https://wapo.st/2YCPmTk.
2. Throughout the book, I refer to the school as Stanton Elementary School. It is the school name that parents, teachers, and community members use, and the one listed on the District of Columbia Public Schools website.

3. Eve L. Ewing, *Ghosts in the Schoolyard: Racism and School Closings on Chicago's South Side* (Chicago: University of Chicago Press, 2018).
4. Steven B. Sheldon and Sol Bee Jung, *The Family Engagement Partnership: Student Outcome Evaluation* (Baltimore: Johns Hopkins University, Center on School, Family, and Community Partnerships, 2015).
5. Robert Balfanz, Liza Herzog, and Douglas J. MacIver, "Preventing Student Disengagement and Keeping Students on the Graduation Path in Urban Middle-Grades Schools: Early Identification and Effective Interventions," *Educational Psychologist* 42, no. 4 (2007); Martha Abele MacIver and Matthew Messel, "The ABCs of Keeping On Track to Graduation: Research Findings from Baltimore," *Journal of Education for Students Placed at Risk* 18, no. 1 (2013); Steven B. Sheldon, "Improving Student Attendance with School, Family, and Community Partnerships," *Journal of Education for Students Placed at Risk* 100, no. 5 (2007).
6. Sheldon and Jung, *Family Engagement Partnership*.

Chapter 3

1. Sara Lawrence-Lightfoot, *Worlds Apart: Relationships Between Families and Schools* (New York: Basic Books, 1978); Kris D. Gutiérrez, "Developing a Sociocritical Literacy in the Third Space," *Reading Research Quarterly* 43, no. 2 (2008); Fabienne Doucet, "(Re)Constructing Home and School: Immigrant Parents, Agency, and the (Un)Desirability of Bridging Multiple Worlds," *Teachers College Record* 113, no. 12 (2011); Kris D. Gutierrez and Marjorie Faulstich Orellana, "The 'Problem' of English Learners: Constructing Genres of Difference," *Research in the Teaching of English* 40, no. 4 (2006); Marjorie Faulstich Orellana and Kris D. Gutiérrez, "What's the Problem? Constructing Different Genres for the Study of English Learners," *Research in the Teaching of English* 41, no. 1 (2006); Patricia Phelan, Ann Locke Davidson, and Hanh Cao Yu, "Students' Multiple Worlds: Navigating the Borders of Family, Peer, and Culture," in *Renegotiating Cultural Diversity in American Schools*, ed. Patricia Phelan and Ann Locke Davidson (New York: Teachers College Press, 1993); Patricia Phelan, Hanh Cao Yu, and Ann Locke Davidson, "Navigating the Psychosocial Pressures of Adolescence: The Voices and Experiences of High School Youth," *American Educational Research Journal* 31, no. 2 (1994).
2. Sara Lawrence-Lightfoot, *The Essential Conversation: What Parents and Teachers Can Learn from Each Other* (New York: Random House, 2003); Doucet, "(Re)Constructing Home and School"; Fabienne Doucet, "Parent Involvement as Ritualized Practice," *Anthropology & Education Quarterly* 42, no. 4 (2011).
3. Jaleel K. Abdul-Adil and Alvin David Farmer Jr., "Inner-City African American Parental Involvement in Elementary Schools: Getting Beyond Urban

Legends of Apathy," *School Psychology Quarterly* 21, no. 1 (2006); Fabienne Doucet, "How African American Parents Understand Their and Teachers' Roles in Children's Schooling and What This Means for Preparing Preservice Teachers," *Journal of Early Childhood Teacher Education* 29, no. 2 (2008); Guadalupe Valdes, "The World Outside and Inside Schools: Language and Immigrant Children," *Educational Researcher* 27, no. 6 (1998); Michael J. Smith, "Right Directions, Wrong Maps: Understanding the Involvement of Low-SES African American Parents to Enlist Them as Partners in College Choice," *Education and Urban Society* 41, no. 2 (2009).

4. Carola Suarez-Orozco, Amy K. Marks, and Mona M. Abo-Zena, eds., *Transitions: The Development of Children of Immigrants* (New York: New York University Press, 2015); Marjorie Faulstich Orellana, "The Work Kids Do: Mexican and Central American Immigrant Children's Contributions to Households and Schools in California," *Harvard Educational Review* 71, no. 3 (2001); Charles R. Martinez Jr., Heather H. McClure, and J. Mark Eddy, "Language Brokering Contexts and Behavioral and Emotional Adjustment Among Latino Parents and Adolescents," *Journal of Early Adolescence* 29, no. 1 (2009); Linda Prieto and Sofia A. Villenas, "Pedagogies from 'Nepantla': 'Testimonio,' Chicana/Latina Feminisms and Teacher Education Classrooms," *Equity & Excellence in Education* 45, no. 3 (2012); Carola Suarez-Orozco and Marcelo M. Suarez-Orozco, *Children of Immigration* (Cambridge, MA: Harvard University Press, 2001).

5. Paulo Freire, *Pedagogy of the Oppressed* (New York: Herder and Herder, 1970).

6. Lisa Delpit, *Other People's Children: Cultural Conflicts in the Classroom* (New York: The New Press, 1995).

7. Vichet Chhuon and Tanner LeBaron Wallace, "Creating Connectedness Through Being Known: Fulfilling the Need to Belong in U.S. High Schools," *Youth & Society* 46, no. 3 (2014).

8. Brian Daly et al., "Promoting School Connectedness Among Urban Youth of Color: Reducing Risk Factors While Promoting Protective Factors," *Prevention Researcher* 17, no. 3 (2010).

9. Mark R. Warren et al., "Beyond the Bake Sale: A Community-Based Relational Approach to Parent Engagement in Schools," *Teachers College Record* 111, no. 9 (2009).

10. Carla Shalaby, *Troublemakers: Lessons in Freedom from Young Children at School* (New York: The New Press, 2017).

11. Lawrence-Lightfoot, *The Essential Conversation*.

12. Anne T. Henderson et al., *Beyond the Bake Sale: The Essential Guide to Family-School Partnerships* (New York: New Press, 2007).

Chapter 4

1. Bella English, "Boston Public Library's Copley Branch Getting a Makeover," *Boston Globe*, December 3, 2013, https://bit.ly/2CUy0s6.

2. James Vaznis, "Boston's Schools Are Becoming Resegregated," *Boston Globe*, August 4, 2018, https://bit.ly/2OgGaOH; John Hilliard and Emily Williams, "Increased Segregation of Boston Schools Could Deepen Racial, Economic Divides, Say Advocates," *Boston Globe*, August 6, 2018, https://bit.ly/2OhHIYz.

3. Gary Orfield and Chungmei Lee, *Why Segregation Matters: Poverty and Educational Inequality* (Cambridge, MA: Civil Rights Project at Harvard University, 2005).

4. Martin J. Walsh, "Op-Ed by Mayor Walsh: A Library for Chinatown," *Sampan* (Boston), January 18, 2017, https://sampan.org/2017/01/op-ed-by-mayor-walsh-a-library-for-chinatown/.

5. Because of the knowledge I gained through my research on Annie's efforts to support the Chinatown library campaign, I was invited to join the board of Friends of the Chinatown Library after concluding my research project. I obtained information about the library announcement and opening after my research in the school had concluded, but it seemed significant to include recent events as well as the presence of Annie and former students at the library opening.

Chapter 5

1. In November 2002, Massachusetts voters approved, by a large majority, Chapter 386 of the Acts of 2002. The law requires Sheltered English Immersion as the method of English language acquisition. At the time of this research project, schools, including Young Achievers, were beholden to Chapter 386. For more information on Chapter 386 and restrictive language policies, see Miren Uriarte et al., "Impact of Restrictive Language Policies on Engagement and Academic Achievement of English Learners in Boston Public Schools," in *Forbidden Language: English Learners and Restrictive Language Policies*, ed. Patricia Gándara and Megan Hopkins (New York: Teachers College Press, 2010). On November 22, 2017, Massachusetts legislators and Governor Charlie Baker signed into law Bill H.4032: An Act relative to language opportunity for our Kids (LOOK). H.4032 allows school districts to establish ELL programs that best meet the needs of students, such as Sheltered English Immersion programs or other alternative programs that meet state and federal requirements including two-way immersion programs and transitional bilingual education.

2. While Massachusetts passed H.4032, which opened new possibilities for bilingual education, at the time of the research for this project Julia was working in a school that was shaped by the Chapter 386 law passed in 2002. All classroom

observations of Julia were conducted in her stand-alone ESL class, where she takes the lead in instructional planning and activities.

3. I use the term *emergent bilingual* to describe students for whom English is a second or other language that is spoken. In contrast to the term *English learner* or *English language learner*, *emergent bilingual* focuses on the development of bilingualism rather than language limits or deficiencies. The term was first coined by Ofelia García, "Emergent Bilinguals and TESOL: What's in a Name?" *TESOL Quarterly* 43, no. 2 (2009).

4. For more on systemic functional linguistics, see Meg Gebhard, "Teacher Education in Changing Times: A Systemic Functional Linguistics (SFL) Perspective," *TESOL Quarterly* 44, no. 4 (2010).

5. Angela Valenzuela, *Subtractive Schooling: U.S.-Mexican Youth and the Politics of Caring* (Albany: State University of New York Press, 1999); Yolanda Padrón, Hersh C. Waxman, and Héctor H. Rivera, "Issues in Educating Hispanic Students," in *Yearbook of the National Society for the Study of Education: Globalization and the Study of Education* 101, no. 2 (2002), 66–88.

6. Fabienne Doucet, "(Re)Constructing Home and School: Immigrant Parents, Agency, and the (Un)Desirability of Bridging Multiple Worlds," *Teachers College Record* 113, no. 12 (2011).

7. For a research study on the experiences of Vietnamese parents and their children in Boston after the implementation of Chapter 386, see Rosann Tung, *English Language Acquisition and Heritage Language Maintenance for English Language Learners: Vietnamese Parent Perspectives* (Boston: Institute for Asian American Studies, University of Massachusetts Boston, 2014). For studies that explore this issue more generally, see Patricia Gandara and Frances Contreras, *The Latino Education Crisis: The Consequences of Failed Social Policies* (Cambridge, MA: Harvard University Press, 2009); Carola Suarez-Orozco and Marcelo M. Suarez-Orozco, *Children of Immigration* (Cambridge, MA: Harvard University Press, 2001); Alejandro Portes, ed., *The New Second Generation* (New York: Russell Sage Foundation, 1996).

8. As noted in an earlier footnote, new legislation in Massachusetts (H.4032) has allowed for the return of bilingual education programs.

9. Valenzuela, *Subtractive Schooling*; Gandara and Hopkins, *Forbidden Language*.

10. Nancy E. Hill and Diane F. Tyson, "Parental Involvement in Middle School: A Meta-Analytic Assessment of the Strategies That Promote Achievement," *Developmental Psychology* 45, no. 3 (2009).

11. Yun Mo and Kusum Singh, "Parents' Relationships and Involvement: Effects on Students' School Engagement and Performance," *Research in Middle Level Education* 31, no. 10 (2008).

12. This is a choice that Young Achievers makes in part due to the autonomy that it is afforded as a pilot school, but as Principal Jinny Chalmers explains, "it

is also a choice we make as a staff to devote the time we have to serve these purposes."

13. Dana Markow and Suzanne Martin, *The MetLife Survey of the American Teacher: Transitions and the Role of Supportive Relationships* (New York: MetLife Inc., 2005).

Chapter 6

1. Willard Waller, *The Sociology of Teaching* (New York: John Wiley & Sons, Inc., 1932).

2. Waller, *The Sociology of Teaching*, 69.

3. Sara Lawrence-Lightfoot, *The Essential Conversation: What Parents and Teachers Can Learn from Each Other* (New York: Random House, 2003).

4. Jessika H. Bottiani, Catherine P. Bradshaw, and Tamar Mendelson, "A Multilevel Examination of Racial Disparities in High School Discipline: Black and White Adolescents' Perceived Equity, School Belonging, and Adjustment Problems," *Journal of Educational Psychology* 109, no. 4 (2017); Shawn Ginwright, "The Future of Healing: Shifting from Trauma Informed Care to Healing Centered Engagement," *Medium*, May 31, 2018, https://bit.ly/2xAonyt.

5. Office of Planning, Evaluation and Policy Development, US Department of Education, Policy and Program Studies Service, *The State of Racial Diversity in the Educator Workforce* (Washington, DC: US Department of Education, 2016), https://www2.ed.gov/rschstat/eval/highered/racial-diversity/state-racial-diversity-workforce.pdf.

6. Carol D. Lee, *Culture, Literacy, and Learning: Taking Bloom in the Midst of the Whirlwind* (New York: Teachers College Press, 2007); Django Paris and Arnetha F. Ball, "Teacher Knowledge in Culturally and Linguistically Complex Classrooms: Lessons from the Golden Age and Beyond," in *Handbook of Research on Literacy and Diversity*, ed. Lesley Mandel Morrow, Robert Rueda, and Diane Lapp (New York: Guilford Press, 2009); Geneva Smitherman, *Talkin and Testifyin: The Language of Black America* (Detroit: Wayne State University Press, 1985); Guadalupe Valdes, *Con Respeto: Bridging the Distances Between Culturally Diverse Families and Schools: An Ethnographic Portrait* (New York: Teachers College Press, 1996).

7. For an excellent account of the structural forces, particularly racism, that shape past and present educational policy and practice, see Eve L. Ewing, *Ghosts in the Schoolyard: Racism and School Closings on Chicago's South Side* (Chicago: University of Chicago Press, 2018).

8. Lisa D. Delpit, "The Silenced Dialogue: Power and Pedagogy in Educating Other People's Children," *Harvard Educational Review* 58, no. 3 (1988).

9. Karen L. Mapp and Soo Hong, "Debunking the Myth of the Hard-to-Reach

Parent," in *The Handbook on School-Family Partnerships for Promoting Student Competence*, ed. Sandra L. Christenson and Amy L. Reschly (New York: Routledge, 2010).

10. Michelle Fine, "[Ap]parent Involvement: Reflections on Parents, Power, and Urban Public Schools," *Teachers College Record* 94, no. 4 (1993).

11. Mark R. Warren et al., "Beyond the Bake Sale: A Community-Based Relational Approach to Parent Engagement in Schools," *Teachers College Record* 111, no. 9 (2009): 2213.

12. Warren et al., "Beyond the Bake Sale."

13. Keith Catone et al., *Agency into Action: Teachers as Leaders and Advocates for Public Education, Communities, and Social Justice* (Providence, RI: Annenberg Institute for School Reform at Brown University, 2017).

14. Geneva Gay, *Culturally Responsive Teaching: Theory, Research, and Practice*, 2nd ed. (New York: Teachers College Press, 2010); Courtney B. Cazden and Ellen L. Leggett, *Culturally Responsive Education: A Response to LAU Remedies II* (Washington, DC: US Department of Health, Education, and Welfare, National Institute of Education, 1976); Gloria Ladson-Billings, "Toward a Theory of Culturally Relevant Pedagogy," *American Educational Research Journal* 32, no. 3 (1995): 465–91.

15. H. Samy Alim and Django Paris, "Whose Language Gap? Critical and Culturally Sustaining Pedagogies as Necessary Challenges to Racializing Hegemony," *Journal of Linguistic Anthropology* 25, no. 1 (2015); Django Paris and H. Samy Alim, "What Are We Seeking to Sustain Through Culturally Sustaining Pedagogy? A Loving Critique Forward," *Harvard Educational Review* 84, no. 1 (2014); Django Paris and H. Samy Alim, *Culturally Sustaining Pedagogies: Teaching and Learning for Justice in a Changing World* (New York: Teachers College Press, 2017); Django Paris, "Culturally Sustaining Pedagogy: A Needed Change in Stance, Terminology, and Practice," *Educational Researcher* 41, no. 3 (2012).

16. Paris, "Culturally Sustaining Pedagogy"; Paris and Alim, "What Are We Seeking"; Ladson-Billings, *Theory of Culturally Relevant Pedagogy*.

17. Dan C. Lortie, *Schoolteacher: A Sociological Study* (Chicago: University of Chicago Press, 1975), 62.

18. Peter Smagorinsky and Meghan E. Barnes, "Revisiting and Revising the Apprenticeship of Observation," *Teacher Education Quarterly* 41, no. 4 (2014).

19. Margaret Buchmann, "Teaching Knowledge: The Lights That Teachers Live By," *Oxford Review of Education* 13, no. 2 (1987): 161.

20. Sharon Feiman-Nemser, *Learning to Teach* (East Lansing: Michigan State University, 1983); Pamela L. Grossman, "Overcoming the Apprenticeship of Observation in Teacher Education Coursework," *Teaching and Teacher Education* 7, no. 4 (1991).

21. Lawrence-Lightfoot, *The Essential Conversation*, 80.

22. Shawn A. Ginwright, *Hope and Healing in Urban Education: How Urban Activists and Teachers Are Reclaiming Matters of the Heart* (New York: Routledge, 2016).

23. Dana Markow and Suzanne Martin, *The MetLife Survey of the American Teacher: Transitions and the Role of Supportive Relationships* (New York: MetLife Inc., 2005).

24. Markow and Martin, *MetLife Survey*; Elizabeth Graue and Christopher P. Brown, "Preservice Teachers' Notions of Families and Schooling," *Teaching and Teacher Education: An International Journal of Research and Studies* 19, no. 7 (2003); Anne C. Broussard, "Preparing Teachers to Work with Families: A National Survey of Teacher Education Programs," *Equity and Excellence in Education* 33, no. 2 (2000).

25. Ken Zeicher et al., "Engaging and Working in Solidarity with Local Communities in Preparing the Teachers of Their Children," *Journal of Teacher Education* 67, no. 4 (2016): 277–90; Robert E. Lee, "Breaking Down Barriers and Building Bridges: Transformative Practices in Community- and School-Based Urban Teacher Preparation," *Journal of Teacher Education* 33, no. 2 (2018): 118–26; Eva Zygmunt et al., "Loving Out Loud: Community Mentors, Teacher Candidates, and Transformational Learning Through a Pedagogy of Care and Connection," *Journal of Teacher Education* 69, no. 2 (2018): 127–39.

26. Peter C. Murrell, *The Community Teacher: A New Framework for Effective Urban Teaching* (New York: Teachers College Press, 2001).

27. After the conclusion of this research project, Principal Jinny Chalmers retired from her position and was replaced by a new administrative leader. With new leadership often comes new directions in school change. This analysis represents the views and perspectives of those teachers and principals who participated in the study and may not reflect current experiences.

28. For an information-rich resource that explores how schools can celebrate all students in respectful and dignified ways and dismantle the marginalization that exists in school celebrations, educators may want to explore Enid Lee et al., *Beyond Heroes and Holidays: A Practical Guide to K–12 Anti-Racist, Multicultural Education and Staff Development* (Washington, DC: Teaching for Change, 1998).

29. Boston Public Schools, "School Types," https://www.bostonpublicschools.org/Page/941.

30. Email communication with Office of Engagement, Boston Public Schools, February 15, 2019.

31. Octavia E. Butler, *Parable of the Talents* (New York: Warner Books, 1998).

ACKNOWLEDGMENTS

This book would not have been possible without the enduring love, support, counsel, and encouragement of many.

To Annie, Cinthia, Ilene, Julia, and Megan—for your unwavering support of this project and your faith and confidence in me as a scribe who could tell a story that needed to be told. I thank you for the countless hours you spent in conversation with me and for the ways you opened up your lives, your classrooms, your struggles, and your accomplishments to me. It is a strange and unfamiliar experience to be the subject of someone's study, and I thank you for the courage you displayed as well as your faith in the unknown when we began this journey.

To the parents, caregivers, and family members who invited me into their lives: to be fully compelling and persuasive, this story demanded your presence and participation. You shared your hopes and dreams for your children and shed light on their beauty, strength, and limitless potential. You shared stories of teachers who listened to you, inspired you, partnered with you, and taught you. But you also shared raw and emotional stories of the teachers who produced fear, insecurity, and harm. You taught me what it means to be a strong, committed advocate for your child, even if it produces conflict and hard feelings. Your children are blessed to have you in their lives. This book would be incomplete without your stories.

To the school administrators who opened their schools to me—for your support of this project and the freedom you gave me to meet with teachers, parents, and school staff, and to be a part of any school function or event I became interested in. Caroline John, Rena Johnson, Christine Landry, and Jinny Chalmers: your invitations to me were no different than the welcome invitations you extended to parents and caregivers every day.

To the students and families over my teaching career—for the ways you shed light on the importance of engaging families. I had neither training nor experience in connecting with families as a teacher, but through our conversations and our relationships, you showed me how critical it was to my humanity as a teacher. I found a renewed sense of joy and optimism in my work as a teacher through the lessons learned from you.

To Sara Lawrence-Lightfoot, for lighting the way with a research methodology that encourages us to seek goodness, to explore fully and with rapt attention, and to create work that reflects the beauty and complexity of human experience in ways that deny simplicity and demand rigor.

To the research assistants at Wellesley College who have supported this project over the years—Brienna Kightlinger, Chelsie Ahn, and Leslie Fuentes—your attention to detail, your creative analysis of the research field, and your insight into early drafts of the teacher chapters were informative and helpful. I look forward to seeing how you shape and contribute to the field in the future.

To the friends and colleagues who provided careful attention and substantive feedback to this manuscript—Sarah Bruhn, Sarah Dryden-Peterson, Joanna Geller, Carolyn Rubin, Noah Rubin, Phitsamay Sychitkokhong Uy, and Rosann Tung—to have your feedback and insight into this work was an honor. Your insight as researchers devoted to youth, families, and communities enhanced the manuscript and pushed me to consider new ideas and frameworks that made this book better.

To my editor at Harvard Education Press, Caroline Chauncey—for your belief in this project from its inception. This journey began at the conclusion of *A Cord of Three Strands* when new questions emerged and I became curious about the role of teachers in building and sustaining family engagement. Your embrace of the messy, complex, and multi-dimensional nature of schools and your encouragement that I roll up my sleeves and take on this multiyear study were pivotal. While you paid close attention to this manuscript as it was developing and it is all the better for it, you also showed grace, patience, and understanding throughout the project. For that I am truly grateful.

To my crew, Irene Mata and Laura Grattan—for your steadfast love and support, both for me and for this project. Your friendship was a much-needed source of light and inspiration in the final stages of this writing project. Your messages of support were a profound reminder that as scholars, we do this work together and in solidarity. Together with Charlene Galarneau, we learned that we need to carve out space to support our development as scholars and writers as well as to stay true to the sources of inspiration in our work. Our writing retreat in Wellfleet was a catalyst in taking this manuscript to the finish line.

To my brother Warren—for the many conversations that lifted my spirits. It's always been my wish that we lived closer together, but our conversations always make the distance irrelevant. Since this project began, you became a parent to two lovely children. I always cherish the time we have with you, Erin, Declan, and Maisie. This is a book about family, and that's what you are to me.

To my first and best teachers, Mom and Dad—because this story starts with you. Throughout my life, you have been my biggest cheer-leaders, my fiercest advocates, and my strongest supporters. Mom, when the intensity of this writing project began to take over my life, you stepped in as you always do, to provide support, cook meals, pray, and have faith that I would do good work. There's a sacrifice that comes with writing sometimes; you need solitude and space to cultivate the ideas that you believe in. You made sure that this sacrifice, which some-times seemed strange and unusual to you, would not impact my family. Throughout my childhood, you and Dad went to every parent-teacher conference, attended every school concert, applauded me at every art festival, and essentially provided Warren and me with everything we needed to be successful in school and in life. This book is about you both, your role in my life, and your deep influence. I wish my teach-ers had appreciated you more and saw you for the invaluable mentors and teachers you were to us. That wish is one of the core motivations of this project.

To Lauren and Christopher—for the love and support you provided to me throughout every step of this project. I'm thankful every day for the light, love, and joy that you bring into my life. You taught me what it means to be a parent—being fully devoted to your well-being, health, and happiness; brimming with love and adoration for the person you are becoming; and fiercely protecting you from any harm. When I sat to listen to the stories of parents in this project, one thing was always true: they had a love and devotion for their children and great hopes and dreams for them, too. As I listened to their stories, I always thought of you. And when this project became all-consuming, I know that, at times, it was hard for you, too. From the late nights of writing to the rushed meals and my tired demeanor, you always understood and supported me. Your notes, your text messages, your hugs—every little thing you did to show me that you had faith in me mattered. It gave me the strength and resolve to finish this project and to make you proud. Writing can be a tiresome and monotonous endeavor, and wow, did you provide me with some excellent moments of escape and restoration. From watching you, Christopher, play on the championship-winning fourth-grade boys' travel basketball team to watching you, Lauren, jump from the freshman team to the JV team with your game-high points and assists, I was truly lucky. You always gave me something to look forward to.

To my partner in love and life, Edwin—for your steadfast belief in me. A central message of this book is that we must recognize the strength and wealth of families, because in doing so, we can fully realize the potential of their partnership. Your belief in me fuels my own ability to take risks, start ambitious projects, and take my message out into the world. I am truly blessed to have your support, your partnership, and your love. You taught me the most important things about being a parent—inspiring curiosity, providing unending and unconditional love, knowing when to provide space for independence, and getting the high arch of a good jump shot. I feel so lucky to have a life partner whom I can share all of my loves with—love of family, love of living life to its fullest, love of supporting communities, and love of basketball.

ABOUT THE AUTHOR

SOO HONG is a sociologist of education whose research interests lie at the intersection of schools, families, and communities. Born in South Korea and raised in Baltimore by a rich, vibrant, loving immigrant family and community, Soo seeks to explore the narratives of young people, their families, and educators in communities that strive to dismantle racism, address social inequality, and build liberatory and transformative school communities. Her research and teaching is deeply influenced by her experiences as an elementary and middle school teacher. She is the author of *A Cord of Three Strands: A New Approach to Parent Engagement in Schools* (Harvard Education Press, 2011). Soo is an associate professor of education at Wellesley College.

INDEX

Academic Parent Teacher Team (APTT), 64–67

adversarial relationships. *see* distrust; power struggle between schools and parents

Alliance to Reclaim Our Schools (AROS), 12

back-to-school events, 61–62, 125–126, 139–140

Boston Teacher Residency (BTR), 148–150

Carver, Ilene. *see also* Dudley Street Neighborhood Charter School (Boston, MA)

background of, 40–42

family conferences, 34–40, 44

family literacy event, 25–27

as family outreach leader, 42–44, 193

home visits, 32–34

relationships with families, 27–34, 168, 170, 171–172, 173

Step Up Day event, 44–46

teaching literacy, 37, 39

training by, 43–44

Chicago Teachers Union (CTU), 10–11

Coalition for Educational Justice (CEJ), 12

coalitions between parents and teachers, 10–12

Colón, Cinthia. *see also* Young Achievers Science and Mathematics Pilot School (Boston, MA)

background of, 78–84, 176

inviting parents into classroom, 87–91

relationships with families, 87, 93–99, 172

sharing her story with parents, 92–93, 137–138

sharing her story with students, 85

teaching students about the world, 77–78, 84–85

teaching students about voice and agency, 85–87

communication

benefits of, 28, 68–69, 94–95, 144–145, 172–174

initiating, as teacher's role, 28–31

methods of, establishing, 29, 67–68, 172

in middle schools, 146–148

mind-set for, 96–97, 99, 143–144, 162–163

two-way conversation with families, 162–163, 171–174

community

activism for, students participating in, 101–104, 121–123

diversity of, not reflected in schools, 159–160

diversity of, reflected and sustained by schools, 160–161, 164–166

partnerships with, 105–107, 185

teaching students about, 101–105, 107–115, 121–123

Comprehensive Family Engagement Partnership Pilot, 52

conferences

family conferences, individual, 34–40, 44, 64–67, 187

family conferences, with teacher team, 144, 147–148, 149–151

family coordinator's role in, 189

immigrants' expectations for, 139

conferences, *continued*
traditional practices of, 5–6, 35, 150,
166–167, 172
CTU (Chicago Teachers Union), 10–11
cultural assimilation, 4–5, 134–136
cultural differences. *see also* equity; race
addressing, 136–140
marginalization and discrimination
based on, 110–111, 134–136
multicultural learning regarding,
113–115, 119–120, 164–166
not reflected in schools, 159–160
power affected by, 4–5, 134–136
reflected and sustained by schools,
160–161, 164–166
teachers' stance regarding, 187
teachers' stories of, 78–87, 89–92,
175–176
culture of power, 85, 161
culture of school. *see* school culture

deficit orientations, 5, 16, 18–19, 96,
160, 170
Dignity in Schools Campaign (DSC), 12
distrust
of schools and teachers, 6, 15, 19,
30–31, 33, 58, 155–156, 173
of teacher unions, 10
diversity. *see* cultural differences
DSC (Dignity in Schools Campaign), 12
Dudley Street Neighborhood Charter
School (Boston, MA). *see also*
Carver, Ilene
background of, 25
family conferences, 34–40, 44
family literacy event, 25–27
mission of family engagement, 43–44
Step Up Day event, 44–46

education reform
parents initiating, 7–9
parent-teacher alliances as part of, 9,
13–16, 24, 44, 193–194
equity. *see also* cultural differences; race

family engagement important to,
161–162, 163
parent-teacher coalitions and, 12
RETELL initiative and, 134–135
society's inequities reflected in school,
157–158
teacher unions and, 10

families. *see also* parents; students
engagement with. *see* relationships
between families and teachers
interactions with, APTT meetings,
64–67
interactions with, back-to-school
events, 61–62, 125–126, 139–140
interactions with, family conferences,
34–40, 44, 64–67, 144, 147–148,
149–151, 187
interactions with, family literacy
event, 25–27
interactions with, Step Up Day event,
44–46, 185
trust development with. *see* trust
development
family coordinator, 189–191
Finkelstein, Julia. *see also* Young
Achievers Science and Mathematics
Pilot School (Boston, MA)
background of, 126–130
connections between parents,
fostering, 140–143
connections to students, 130–131,
136–137
family conferences with teacher team,
144, 147–148, 149–151
family history project, 132–133, 136
as interpreter for school events, 125–
126, 139–140
relationships with families, 137–140,
143–147, 151–153, 174, 177–178
sharing her story with students,
136–137
teaching emergent bilinguals,
131–136

training and support for, 147, 148–
151, 179, 186–187, 190–191
Flamboyan Foundation, 52–54, 56–57,
73

Grassroots Education Movement (GEM)
Alliance, 10–11
grounded institutions, schools as,
160–166

home visits
by Ilene Carver, 32–34
by Megan Lucas, 48–49, 53–57, 59–61,
63–64
support for, 187
training for, 52, 74

institutional mourning, 50
institutional scripts, 15. *see also* traditional
practices of family engagement

libraries
activism for, students participating in,
101–104, 121–123
teaching students about, 102–103,
107–108, 110, 112
literacy event, 25–27
Lucas, Megan. *see also* Stanton
Elementary School (Washington,
DC)
APTT meetings, 64–67
background of, 49–50
back-to-school event, 61–62
first year experiences at Stanton,
50–53, 57–58
home visits by, 48–49, 53–57, 59–60,
63–64, 172
relationships with families, 58–60, 62–
63, 67–75, 156, 172, 173, 177–178
sharing her story with parents, 59–60
training and support for, 52–54,
56–57, 66, 180
training by, 74

marginalizing institutions, schools as,
157–160
mistrust. *see* distrust; trust development

parents. *see also* families
perceptions about teachers, 54–55,
57–58, 63–64, 87–89, 93–95, 98–99,
155–156, 158
presence in the classroom, 87–91,
184–185, 187–188
schools as unwelcoming to,
158–159
teachers' perceptions about, 15–16,
51–52, 55–56, 58, 62–63, 72, 86–87,
95–98, 156, 158
trust development with. *see* trust
development
parents' rights movement, 6–9
parent-teacher alliances, 9, 13–16, 24,
44, 193–194. *see also* relationships
between families and teachers
parent-teacher conferences. *see*
conferences
Parent Teacher Home Visits (PTHV),
52, 53–55
parent trigger laws, 8–9
portraits in this book, 20–22. *see also*
Carver, Ilene; Colón, Cinthia;
Finkelstein, Julia; Lucas, Megan;
Shah, Annie
power, culture of, 85, 161
power struggle between schools and
parents
background of, 3–12, 156–160
cultural assimilation and, 4–5,
134–136
dismantling, 163
examples of, 1–2
in parents' rights movement, 6–9
professional development. *see* training
and support
PTHV (Parent Teacher Home Visits),
52, 53–55

race. *see also* cultural differences; equity
classroom culture and, 3, 136–140
marginalization and discrimination
based on, 110–111, 134–136
multicultural learning regarding,
113–115, 119–120, 164–166
teachers' activism regarding, 40–41,
127–130
teachers' experiences regarding, 78–
84, 115–120, 175–176
white teachers addressing, 29–31,
59–60, 63–64, 136–137
relationships between families and
teachers. *see also* communication
adversarial. *see* distrust; power struggle
between schools and parents
as alliances, 9, 13–16, 24, 44, 193–194
benefits of, 13–16, 28, 68–75, 94–95,
144–145, 151–153, 172–174
building, challenges of, 14–17
building, conditions required for, 16,
17–18, 56–57, 73
building, strategies for, 27–34, 58–60,
62–63, 119–120, 161–162, 168–174,
181–192
building, trust required for. *see* trust
development
collaboration on academics, 64–67
in middle and high schools, 145–147
mind-set for, 96–97, 99, 143–144,
162–163
parents' negative experiences with,
1–2, 30–31, 32–34, 54–55, 156
positive examples of, 9–12, 25–27,
34–40, 44–46, 47–49, 63–64, 73–75,
87–95, 98–99, 109–110, 120–121,
136–140, 145
research regarding, 13–14, 16–17, 69,
82, 146
studied in this book, 19–22
traditional practices of, 5–6, 15, 35,
150, 166–168, 172
research
of family-teacher relationships,

historical, 13–14, 16–17, 69, 82,
146
of family-teacher relationships,
needed, 18–19, 181, 189
of school culture, 15–16
for this book, 19–22. *see also specific
teachers and schools*

school culture
changes in, requirements for, 16
communities' diversity celebrated and
sustained in, 160–161, 164–166
communities' diversity not reflected
in, 159–160
parent-teacher alliances as part of, 9,
13–16, 24, 44, 193–194
past and present trauma, effects of,
158, 169–170
past and present trauma, examples of,
1–2, 30–31, 32–34, 54–55, 156
past and present trauma, healing,
168–174
race and identity, addressing within, 3,
136–140
research regarding, 15–16
society's inequities reflected in,
157–158
as unwelcoming to parents, 158–159
schools. *see also* Dudley Street
Neighborhood Charter School
(Boston, MA); Stanton Elementary
School (Washington, DC); Young
Achievers Science and Mathematics
Pilot School (Boston, MA)
community engagement by, 105–107,
160–161, 163–166, 184, 185, 186,
187
family engagement by, family-
centered, 160–166, 168–192
family engagement by, school-
centered, 5–6, 157, 158–159,
166–168
family engagement by, traditional, 5–6,
15, 35, 150, 166–168, 172

as grounded institutions, 160–166
as marginalizing institutions, 157–160
studied in this book, 23–24
Shah, Annie. *see also* Young Achievers
Science and Mathematics Pilot
School (Boston, MA)
activism for Chinatown library, 101–
104, 121–123
background of, 115–120, 175
community partnerships, 105–107,
187
library trips with students, 107–108,
110–112
public service announcements by
students, 108–109
relationships with families, 109–110,
119–121, 162–163, 178, 187–188
teaching students about community,
101–105, 107–115, 121–123
tour of Chinatown, 105–107,
113–114
training and support for, 178–179,
182, 190
Stanton Elementary School (Washington,
DC). *see also* Lucas, Megan
APTT meetings, 64–67
background of, 50–57
back-to-school event, 61–62
partnership with Flamboyan
Foundation, 52–54, 56–57, 73
Step Up Day event, 44–46, 185
students. *see also* families
connections with teachers, 85, 130–
131, 136–137
cultural differences between. *see*
cultural differences
equity in education for. *see* equity; race
interaction with community, 101–104,
107–112, 121–123
learning about the world, 77–78,
84–85
learning about voice and agency,
85–87
parents' knowledge and care about,

28–29, 31–32, 62, 87, 95–98, 129,
144, 156–157, 170, 172, 194
studies. *see* research
supports for teachers. *see* training and
support

teachers. *see also* Carver, Ilene; Colón,
Cinthia; Finkelstein, Julia; Lucas,
Megan; Shah, Annie
agency of, supporting, 163–164, 167
collaborative leadership by, 18,
163–164
of color, perspectives of, 175–177. *see
also* Colón, Cinthia; Shah, Annie
novice, perspectives of, 177–181. *see
also* Colón, Cinthia; Finkelstein,
Julia; Lucas, Megan; Shah, Annie
parents' perceptions about, 54–55,
57–58, 63–64, 87–89, 93–95, 98–99,
155–156, 158
perceptions about parents, 15–16,
51–52, 55–56, 58, 62–63, 72, 86–87,
95–98, 156, 158
relationships with families. *see*
relationships between families and
teachers
studied in this book, 20–24
training and support for. *see* training
and support
white, addressing race, 29–31, 59–60,
63–64, 136–137
teacher tenure, 7–8
teacher unions, 10–11
Teach For America (TFA), 49–50
traditional practices of family
engagement, 5–6, 15, 35, 150,
166–168, 172
training and support
APTT model for, 66
at Boston Teacher Residency, 148–151
by Flamboyan Foundation, 52–54,
56–57
by Ilene Carver, 43–44
inadequate, 179–181

training and support, *continued*
by Megan Lucas, 74
requirements for, 18, 178–183,
189–191
traditional practices of, 166–168
at Young Achievers, 147, 178–179,
182–183, 186–187, 189–191
trust development. *see also* distrust
conditions required for, 17–18,
161–162
strategies for, from Flamboyan
Foundation, 52–55
strategies for, overview of, 168–174
strategies for, used by Annie Shah,
120–121
strategies for, used by Cinthia Colón,
93–95
strategies for, used by Ilene Carver,
29–34
strategies for, used by Julia Finkelstein,
136–137, 143–145, 147
strategies for, used by Megan Lucas,
57–60

Walter H. Dyett High School, 11, 13, 19

Young Achievers Science and
Mathematics Pilot School (Boston,
MA). *see also* Colón, Cinthia;
Finkelstein, Julia; Shah, Annie
background of, 42, 111–112, 146
back-to-school event, 125–126,
139–140
family conferences with teacher team,
144, 147–148, 149–151
interpretation at school events, 126
inviting parents into classroom, 87–91,
184–185, 187–188
library trips with students, 107–108,
110–112
school and community meetings, 184,
185, 187
Step Up Day event, 185
strategies for family engagement,
161–163, 181–191
training and support by, 147, 178–179,
182–183, 186–187, 189–191